Discipline
and
Practice

Discipline
and
Practice

The (Ir)resistibility of Theory

Edited by
Stefan Herbrechter
and Ivan Callus

Lewisburg
Bucknell University Press

Associated University Presses
2010 Eastpark Boulevard
Cranbury, NJ 0851

The paper used in this publication meets the requirements of the American National Standard for Permanence of Paper for Printed Library Materials Z39.48–1984.

Library of Congress Cataloging-in-Publication Data

Discipline and practice : the (ir)resistibility of theory / edited by Stefan Herbrechter and Ivan Callus.
    p. cm.
Includes bibliographical references and index.
 ISBN 0-8387-5565-8 (alk. paper)
 1. Literature—Philosophy. I. Herbrechter, Stefan. II. Callus, Ivan, 1967-

PN45.D5558 2004
801—dc22

2003017400

Contents

Preface

DISCIPLINE AND PRACTICE OWES AN OBVIOUS DEBT TO THE TITLE OF Alan Sheridan's English translation of Michel Foucault's *Surveiller et punir: naissance de la prison* (1975) [Discipline and Punish: The Birth of the Prison]. Our return upon one of the prominent works in "theory"—this strange combination of literary criticism, linguistics, psychoanalysis, philosophy, cultural, social, and political theory—is undertaken not only in the knowledge that there is now a certain *discipline* about theory (demonstrated by its becoming associated with certain protocols and repertoires of reading and critique, and also by the fact that it has acquired a canon decreeing, for instance, that Foucault's *Discipline and Punish* is an "important" work, just like, though for different reasons and with contrasting foci, Barthes's *Mythologies* [1957], Lacan's *Écrits* [1966], Derrida's *Of Grammatology* [1967], Kristeva's *Séméiotiké* [1969] and *Polylogue* [1977], and Gilles Deleuze and Félix Guattari's *A Thousand Plateaus* [1980]), but also in awareness that theory has accrued what we shall be calling "disciplinarity." Theory is now one of the *disciplines*, with a presence in the university that exerts a disciplining force upon it, houses it in "centers" and "departments," and makes it examinable: another "subject" which one can graduate in, and for which one can get grades and marks. In other words, there is now matter to theory, which has become something of a *métier*. Hence, to quote Foucault in a way that extends the decontextualizing liberties we are taking in our invocations of his book, "the examination [in theory] enable[s] the teacher, while transmitting his knowledge, to transform his pupils into a whole field of knowledge." Many "teachers" of theory—among them, famously, Paul de Man and in a different sense Derrida, and then in turn many of those who were "taught" by them or listened to their seminars or

commented on and/or translated their works—extended the constituency of theory by conferring upon it a profile, in places like Yale
or the École Normale Supérieure and in all the subsequent exchanges between French and Anglo-American institutions, that proved irresistible to many even while others were resisting it mightily.

The "punishment" this success conferred upon theory, amidst all
the rewards accumulating around it in the university as this institu-
tionalizes and disciplines it, concerns the *practice* of theory. This is
not about the paradox of something called "theory" being interested
in practice. It is rather about the fact that what theory has had to
punish itself with as it has become "established" is the thought of having compromised upon its capacity for radical practice. Theory's
claims on a radical practice have in fact always been one of its defining characteristics, as signaled by the title of Catherine Belsey's influential introduction, *Critical Practice* (1980), and at least since the
heady days of the Parisian journal *Tel Quel*, in which Kristeva and others first linked "revolution" to "poetic language."[1] What this book is
therefore interested in is whether, in the process of this institutional
disciplining, the practice of theory in its very diverse forms has become resistible (the institution, having co-opted theory, makes it
somehow less compelling), or whether it has become *ir*resistible as a
result of that disciplining (the institution, having co-opted theory,
surrounds it with a certain ineluctability). Hence our subtitle: *The
(Ir)resistibility of Theory*.

Now we have been told that theory is *passé*, and the reports have
not generally been wistful. Theory is apparently no longer as compelling as it was. The suggestion is that there is growing disenchantment with a discourse that since the 1960s seems to have flowed from
France into an Anglo-American academic scene that never quite
overcame the unease that there might have been a fundamental quality that remained un- or misrecognized in this *arrivant*: something un-
or mistranslated. Indeed, despite the tendency within universities in
English-speaking countries to accommodate theory within departments of *English*, the term *theory* retains irrepressible associations of
"Frenchness" that appear to be most palpable within (post)struc-
turalism and/or deconstruction. It is this specific form of theory that
seems to have exasperated some and "ashamed" others who would
like to be seen as having moved "beyond" it. (French) theory, to that
constituency, has lost its verve, its attraction, its radicality—and this
despite (or even, perhaps, because of) the numerous Anglo-Ameri-

can translations and interpretations of it. And here there might arise the suspicion that talk about "post-theory" has a slightly chauvinistic undertone: no longer does any kind of conceptual lead have to be sought in France, this republic with a universal ambition, which is under siege from all sides. The return to pre-theoretical states, or the progress toward post-theoretical clearings, is therefore arguably readable in terms of a desire for the (re)assertion of a cultural and academic hegemony in which the interplay between the homegrown and the foreign, as well as the transdisciplinary approaches that theory made possible, will no longer be quite so vexing to those who hope that post-theory will turn out to be nothing more than the affirmation of anti-theory.

Perhaps only *more* theory and a renewal of radical critical practice can resist this desire. And yet how can the relation between theory and its practice be reconstituted at a time when the former seems to have lost some if not all of its early "radicality" and productivity? How to inform the "post-theoretical" that perhaps, after all, we have never been theoretical (enough)? The only certainty amidst all these doubts is that theory's claims on a "radical" critical practice are undermined unless as a discipline it keeps practicing critically upon itself. That process would surely have to address also the problematic privileging of *inter*disciplinarity as a favored methodological frame when "reading" texts and culture: a privileging that is today very often seen as synonymous with theory as such. The problems that arise out of this privileging have much to do with a misapprehension of the specificities of different disciplinary knowledges and methodologies. How, indeed, should the student of theory, loyal to the calling of interdisciplinarity but mindful of the enduring importance of those specifities for any rigorous critical practice, "read" textuality and culture? How, in other words, does the call of (inter)disciplinarity both help and hinder the practice of theory, and how is theory to be "done" without "undoing" itself by its increasing institutionalization? In short, the old question resurfaces: "Can and should theory be taught?" And should theory be afraid of its own "disciplining" and its pedagogical vocation?

The contributors to this volume (a significant number of whom can look back on a long career during which they helped to shape the history and disciplining of theory, as well as its repertoires, approaches, and critical practice), share these concerns about the (inter)disciplinary nature of theory and the rethinking of its practice. They believe that there has never been nor will there ever be a time "after" theory: not as long as theory compulsively rethinks its critical practice(s). What the essays in this volume demonstrate very powerfully is that a theoretically informed practice that is radical (in the sense of pointing/stretching toward limits) is one that continues to derive its authority and legitimation out of self-reflexivity. For this reason, it is striking that the essays all advocate a return to and on theory. They constitute renegotiations and rearticulations that seek to provoke or invoke theory's own repressed: the roads not taken, the crossroads revisited. In French (this *incontournable* resource of thinking) one would be tempted to say that what these essays perform is *revenir sur* (going back over, returning to, and revisioning) theory. The overall effect these essays achieve is therefore a demonstration of how, through a careful renegotiation of conceptual translations and (inter)disciplinary orthodoxies, theory can be sustained without misrepresenting any crucial specificities. In the process—and as a result (and also to reecho Foucault) of a punishing *surveillance* upon itself, of a (re)disciplining of itself—theory reads (itself) better. The relations between (inter)disciplinarity and (radical) practice, then, is what this volume seeks to understand, examine, and critique.

As editors, we have attempted to provide a frame for the essays of the contributors. The frame we are proposing here comes in two parts: an "introduction" and an "extroduction." An extroduction, defined as a "drawing," a "leading" (*Oxford English Dictionary*), is something that might, in a context like the present, seek to draw out recurrent concerns in the essays collected here and lead them to some kind of "concerted effort" that could then—in view of the word *practice* in our title—be held up as representative of what the project as a whole is "advising." But we have faith that the essays can reveal shared concerns in a manner unbidden and unforced by us. We shall make no claim on a "recapture" of the various openings each essay provides, as we do not want to restrict or even censor the possible dissent between these contributions, or to lead them anywhere predetermined. Variety has always been in the interest of theory. What we do hope to achieve across the introduction and the extroduction, however, is a pointing out (or a drawing out) of the precarious location and problematic "positioning" of theory at present, but also its capacity for survival. This, too, has to do with the "(ir)resistibility" of theory, a notion that will be taking on different associations in what follows.

It might be helpful to acknowledge, here, that faith in the old de Manian paradox dies hard: the more theory is resisted, the more irresistible it becomes.[2] Although this "reflex" is useful when assisting in a critique of anti-theoretical desire located "outside" the institutions of theory, it risks leaving theory dangerously exposed to certain positionings "inside." In our introduction, therefore, we explore how certain constructions of the "(ir)resistibility of theory" continue to inform the attempts of theory at revisiting (*revenir sur*), while in our "extroduction" we subject a specific pretender to the succession upon theory—"posthumanism"—to a reading that dramatizes the kind of revisiting mindful of the lasting relevance of theory. It is argued that the "irresistibility" of posthumanism—its apparent inevitability, and the notion that the posthuman is what much seems to be currently "drawn" to, or to "lead" to—is best critiqued (and resisted) by a return to a theory that is, reportedly, increasingly resistible. While the introduction is thus a revisiting of notions in Paul de Man (among others) and of contemporary forms of the "resistance of theory," the "extroduction" forces posthumanism to return to and recognize its own beginnings in theory. We think that this "draws" and "leads" in a manner that is fairer and less intrusive on the contributors' essays and hopefully more useful and provocative.

Although, as claimed above, all the essays in some way constitute "revisitings" of the articulations and conceptualities of theory, we have opted to divide the contributions into two main sections: " 'Disciplining Theory'—Revaluations" and "Theory and Critical Practice—Rearticulations." The four essays in the first section attempt to question the disciplinarity of theory. They provide revaluations of that (ongoing) process, and of opportunities both lost and seized. The essays in the second section (including our "extroduction") revisit theory through a questioning of changing critical practice(s), and propose rearticulations that seek enhanced negotiation of the relation between the teachability and radicality of theory.

In many ways Catherine Belsey's essay, "Beyond Literature and Cultural Studies: The Case for Cultural Criticism," is programmatic of the revaluation of theory as discipline and (critical) practice, and it is for this reason that it has been placed at the start of this collection. It is needless to remind the reader of Belsey's formative role in the "disciplining" of theory, her contribution to the understanding of poststructuralism in Britain and elsewhere, and her continued productive use of theory in her critical practice. Her essay reconsiders the history of cultural studies. It argues against both cultural studies and "traditional" English studies by advocating a "Cultural Criticism" that "would take seriously theory's contribution to our understanding of the signifying practice that constitutes the inscription of culture." This is magnificently eclectic, taking in "cultures in the plural, global, and ethnic, past and present; theories in the plural, too, of course, as they develop; and all signifying practice with no a priori exclusions, entailing reading skills appropriate to writing, speech, images, music." It, too, echoes Foucault, who in *Discipline and Punish* (which we here continue to decontextualizingly quote, reassured by the uncanny appositeness to our purposes of all that was inaugurated there), remarked: "This discipline could now abandon its textual character and take its references not so much from the tradition of author-authorities as from a domain of objects perpetually offered for examination."[3] Yet while very clearly endorsing a more ample view of what it is that constitutes culture, Belsey is also very clearly anxious to show how it is through acknowledging the place of the signifier that cultural criticism, with its extended territories of reading, can make a positive and critical contribution to the rethought humanities of the future.

Jean-Jacques Lecercle's "What Is a False Interpretation?" returns to notions of interpretation—a particularly problematic component of theory's "repressed." Lecercle's contribution follows from his recent work in the area.[4] While he rejects the idea of a "true" interpretation, Lecercle argues that rigorous critical practice needs to distinguish between "false" and "just" readings in order to guard against relativism (or "dementia," as he calls it). He proposes a number of "theses" about interpretation; here it suffices to remark that he shows that a "just" interpretation would be one that is loyal to the demands of a practice renegotiated on the basis of the singularity of what is to be read, which is not subservient to the demands of theory's (or any other) orthodoxies and indeed (and perhaps especially) "unorthodoxies," and which is disposed to "intervene" in order to indicate the "negativity of error" but also its "positivity," its "necessity."

What Lawrence Venuti's and Laurent Milesi's contributions share is the idea that theory's progressive "disciplining" has been determined to a large extent by translation and its effects. Venuti's "Translating Derrida on Translation: Relevance and Disciplinary Resistance" should be read in the context of his promotion of a theoretically informed critical translation practice in the United States. In his translations and metatranslational work, Venuti has looked toward theory as an ally, while criticizing it at the same time for its repression of translational effects.[5] In his contribution to this volume, he theorizes his experience of translating an essay by Jacques Derrida that recently appeared in *Critical Inquiry*: "What is a 'Relevant' Translation?"[6] That experience, he claims, put into perspective how the labor of translation can be brought to bear on a renegotiated understanding of the practice of cultural studies. Venuti argues that cultural studies has approached translation with a theoreticism that has stripped it of its material specificity, whereas translation studies, dominated by linguistic and formalist perspectives, has approached translation with an empiricism that has stripped it of the philosophical and political implications so important for the study and practice of translation. Venuti's intention in translating Derrida's essay was therefore strategic or "disciplining," namely to intervene in an existing academic situation where the prevailing relations between (inter)disciplinarity and practice could be instructive for both cultural and translation studies.

Laurent Milesi, in "French Thinking/Thinking French—In Translation," revisits crucial "translational" moments in the evolution of theory's disciplinarity. His claim is that one way of characterizing the rapidly changing panorama of English studies since the end of the 1970s is to recognize how critical attitudes in the discipline have been influenced and reshaped by the import of ideas, concepts, and thinking/writing practices from France. As critical agendas reshaped themselves in the light of these new trends that sometimes acquired the status of new alternative "orthodoxies," scant attention was paid to the various processes of "translation" that such foreign ideas underwent as they were renegotiated and redeployed in a radically different academic environment. This "disciplining" of theory therefore underestimated the impact, both potential and actual, of different national, institutional, and curricular contexts on the practice of criticism. Milesi examines some examples of that negligence in/of translation by first looking at the parallel histories and developments of three basic concepts inherited from French ways of thinking or their labeling (namely "theory" itself, "poststructuralism," and "the death of the author"). He also considers how these conceptual migrations, (re)appropriations, and implementations in turn generated an academic "tradition" fraught with unthought assumptions about its intellectual borrowings and institutional recontextualizations and "nativizations" or naturalizations.

The second section of this volume proposes rearticulations of theory and critical practice. In "Teaching Deconstruction: Giving, Taking, Leaving, Belonging, and the Remains of the University," Simon Morgan Wortham pursues further his work on deconstruction and the university.[7] "Teaching Deconstruction" assesses the teachability of theory in relation to Derrida's own work on teaching. The phrase that gives the essay its title is explored in its semantic ambiguity: should deconstruction (or theory) as a way of reading or thinking simply be assimilated and then applied according to certain academic protocols or disciplinary procedures? Or should deconstruction, in its putative capacity as an errant and mischievous force in the university, itself be taught a lesson? Or, yet again—if one were to imagine restoring an otherwise invisible hyphen so as to understand the title in the sense of "teaching-deconstruction," similar to the grammatical construction "job creation," where both words are deployed as nouns, modifying each respectively—one might now be talking about a deconstruction done to teaching, where deconstruction, far from simply being presented in the title as "teachable" or "taught," perhaps teaches teaching a lesson. Or, through even another reading of the same title, one might now talk of deconstruction as teaching a lesson to that which would teach *it* a lesson or teach it *as* a lesson. The plural and undecidable legibility of the title is therefore at once somewhat disorientating and yet perhaps salutary, perhaps a lesson in itself. In respect of such undecidably plural effects emanating from this title, Wortham's essay weaves together a complex set of questions, addressing: (a) the problematics, as far as deconstruction is concerned, which surround teaching (understood as "giving an account") in the era of the interdisciplinary study of culture; (b) the possibility, thereafter, of accounting (responsibly) for the teaching given by deconstruction; (c) the issues and effects that, for deconstruction, crop up in the vicinity of questions about academic freedom, tradition, teaching, and responsibility; and (d) some issues relating to the performative aspects of teaching, both within and (as it were) beyond deconstruction. The essay is also useful in reviewing and commenting on a number of prominent explorations of culture and the discipline and practice of cultural studies, among them those of J. Hillis Miller and Bill Readings.

"Naïve modernism," or the "unreflective view that a representation, practice, or theory is transparently connected to what is modern," is what exercises Susan Hegeman's contribution, "Naïve Modernism and the Politics of Embarrassment." Hers is a historical view of the question of how theories of culture and the history of ideas and affects relate to critical practice. For Hegeman, postmodern theory in general finds "modern" expressions of progressivist faith too easy. Hegeman, however, returns to this reaction of "embarrassment" and even "shame" to ask, instead, whether there might not after all be a place for a little "naïveté" in theory— doing so on the basis of her reading of the anthropology of Ruth Benedict, Elsie Clews Parsons, and Margaret Mead, but also and more performatively through an attention to the fiction of Sherwood Anderson.

The relationship between contemporary cultural studies and political philosophy, particularly as it involves post-Marxism, is at the center of Suzanne Gearhart's contribution, "Interpellations: From Althusser to Balibar." In the area of the relationship of theory to practice, Gearhart returns to Louis Althusser's thinking of society and, more specifically, ideology, particularly as this develops around his well-known notion of "interpellation." Gearhart rereads Althusser through the recent (and untranslated) work of Etienne Balibar, whose interventions in current social and political debates about immigration need to be understood not only as having a practical political dimension but also as invitations for theory's urgent readdressing of concepts like nationalism, colonialism, race, *citoyenneté*, and— binding all these together in a very *determined* manner—translation and interpellation itself. Gearhart in the process gives a very compelling demonstration of how the practice of a post-theory, of theory taking to heart the ethic of *revenir sur*, could involve theory's revisiting and rethinking of its most canonical concepts.

Arkady Plotnitsky's "Essentially Ambiguous: On the Nature of Language, the Epistemology of Modern Science, and the Relationship Between the 'Two Cultures' " focuses on the negotiations of theory with science. Plotnitsky takes further his ongoing exploration of the relationships between the humanities, the disciplines of modern mathematics and science, and what he calls "nonclassical thinking" and the theories to which this thinking gives rise.[8] He argues that "nonclassical" thinking (as exemplified most accurately by quantum physics but also by certain analogical orientations within some areas of theory) radically redefines epistemology by making the unknowable the irreducible part of knowledge (insofar as the ultimate objects under investigation are seen as being beyond any knowledge and even conception, both in practice and in principle). It is the acceptance of unknowability in principle that defines the standpoint of "nonclassical" theory. Conceived in broader conceptual and epistemological terms, Plotnitsky's contribution is also indirectly a response to both long-standing and more recent debates concerning the "two cultures," and seeks to establish a more productive approach to understanding the relationships among the various disciplines involved in these debates.[9]

The essays in this volume demonstrate the effectiveness of theory's surveillance upon its own disciplinarity. Some return critically and renewingly to established conceptualities within theory, others assess theory's place in the institution, and all in their different ways consider how theory's disciplinarity impinges upon its practice. As editors we have been struck by the recurrence of certain motifs: the issue of translation, for instance, or the interest in interdisciplinarity, or the attention to relations between textuality and "culture." Above all it has been instructive to witness a reaffirmation of the relevance of theoretical approaches that in the main have a commitment to a focus upon the operations of the signifier as a paradigm for theory. For, as is too well known and too uncritically accepted, it sometimes looks as if "the deconstructive phase of critical thought . . . has lost its effectiveness."[10] While many of the essays in this volume attest to the continuing tenacity and pertinence of that thought, it is perhaps true that the capacity of theory for resisting binary (and more complex) oppositions, and for "living on borderlines," has become resistible at a time when the rhetoric of globalization has itself undone many polarities. Possibly the assertion of "culture" as a privileged and even preeminent field for the practice of theory should be read also in the light of this historical juncture, when there occurs a general awareness of the opportunities but also resentments occasioned by a globalized and capital-savvy culture. The irresistibility of theory would therefore need to entrench itself in an engagement with the consequences of that culture. Our "extroduction" attempts an experiment in how this might be done by trying to work through an awareness of how theory will be defeated by its own mannerisms if it becomes (and here we are lifting words, again, from Foucault), too comfortable in its disciplinarity, too identified with an institution or an apparatus, too much a type of power and a modality comprising a whole set of instruments, techniques, procedures, levels of application, and targets.[11] For this reason we have looked at theory's problematic understanding of digital technology, the latter being arguably the product that emerges most irrepressibly and most irresistibly from the age of globalization. Can theory's irresistibility face down this other irresistibility? We therefore read recent developments that seek to reposition theory before what has been called "posthumanism."

Constructions of the posthuman have, broadly, based themselves on two formulations. The first perceives posthumanism in the sense of an endgame, as that which definitively signals the passing of humanism; the second regards the posthuman as that which manifests, in the words of N. Katherine Hayles, "no essential differences or absolute demarcations between bodily existence and computer simulation, cybernetic mechanism and biological organism, robot teleology and human goals."[12] Both formulations carry crucial implications for the theory and practice of disciplines within the humanities. The "extroduction" focuses on some of those implications for the academic study of culture. It reviews how the posthuman, in its current configurations, has tended to ally itself to glib pronouncements on eclipsed paradigms and emerging *epistemes*, even though such talk has become wearisome in an age which has made it a habit to sound the last post for everything. We try to explain why any temptation on the part of theory to contemptuously dismiss the posthuman and its investment in apocalyptic discourse would be unwise—especially in view of certain perspectives that position posthumanism as coextensive with what has been termed "new cultural theory." The "extroduction" examines attempts to institute posthuman*ism* as a "knowledge" and a discipline by, among other means, deflecting the kind of problematization of "*post-*" that critical and cultural theory have made possible. It also assesses whether posthumanism can live up to claims that it can found a "new cultural theory" that would renegotiate the stakes for critical practice. Consequently it asks whether it is true that theory will have to rethink its role in the age of the posthuman, and also whether it might be more correct to say that theory is an instantiation of the discourse that is most capable of approaching the posthuman critically. For at the end, if theory is not equally mindful of how *ends* can spell both destination and termination, objectives and obsolescence, how can it commit itself to the *revenir sur*, to its almost spectral revisiting upon itself?

These essays, in their different ways, attempt that haunting.

NOTES

1. For an indication of the kind of radical attitudes (envisaging a correspondence between poetic language and politics) struck by Kristeva in the early, *Tel Quel* phase of her writing, see her 1967 essay, "Towards a Semiology of Paragrams," trans. François Lack, in *The Tel Quel Reader*, ed. Patrick ffrench and Roland-François Lack (London and New York: Routledge, 1998), 25–49. See also Julia Kristeva, *Revolution in Poetic Language*, trans. Margaret Waller (1974; New York: Columbia University Press, 1984).

2. See Paul de Man, "The Resistance to Theory," in *The Resistance to Theory* (Minneapolis: University of Minnesota Press, 1986), 3–20.

3. Michel Foucault, *Discipline and Punish: The Birth of the Prison*, trans. Alan Sheridan (London: Penguin, 1979), 186.

4. See Jean-Jacques Lecercle, *Interpretation as Pragmatics* (Basingstoke: Macmillan, 1999).

5. See, for instance, Lawrence Venuti, *The Scandals of Translation: Towards an Ethics of Difference* (London: Routledge, 1998).

6. Jacques Derrida, "What is a 'Relevant' Translation?," trans. Lawrence Venuti, *Critical Inquiry* 27 (2001): 174-200.

7. See Simon Wortham, *Rethinking the University: Leverage and Deconstruction* (Manchester: Manchester University Press, 1999).

8. See Arkady Plotnitsky, *Complementarity: Anti-Epistemology after Bohr and Derrida* (Durham: Duke University Press, 1994) and *The Knowable and the Unknowable: Modern Science, Nonclassical Thought, and the Two Cultures* (Ann Arbor: University of Michigan Press, 2002).

9. For an insight into the issues and debates involved in "the culture wars," see Paul R. Gross and Norman Levitt, *Higher Superstition: The Academic Left and Its Quarrels with Science* (Baltimore: Johns Hopkins University Press, 1994); Alan Sokal, "Transgressing the Boundaries: Toward a Transformative Hermeneutics of Quantum Gravity," *Social Text* 46–47 (1996): 217–52; Alan Sokal and Jean Bricmont, *Impostures intellectulles* (Paris: Odile Jacob, 1997); Alan Sokal and Jean Bricmont, *Fashionable Nonsense: Postmodern Intellectuals' Abuse of Science* (New York: Picador, 1998). See also the special number of *Yale French Studies* 100 (2001), edited by Ralph Sarkonak and entitled *France/USA: The Cultural Wars*, dedicated to this issue.

10. Michael Hardt and Antonio Negri, *Empire* (Cambridge: Harvard University Press, 2000), 217.

11. See Foucault, *Discipline and Punish*, 215.

12. N. Katherine Hayles, *How We Became Posthuman: Virtual Bodies in Cybernetics, Literature, and Informatics* (Chicago: University of Chicago Press, 1999), 3.

Acknowledgments

WE WOULD LIKE TO THANK THE CONTRIBUTORS TO THIS VOLUME, FOR showing faith in the project and sharing our concerns about theory's disciplinarity, practice, and (ir)resistibility.

Lawrence Venuti's contribution previously appeared as "Translating Derrida on Translation: Relevance and Disciplinary Resistance" in the *Yale Journal of Criticism* 16, no. 2 (2003), © Yale University and The Johns Hopkins University Press. Reprinted with permission of The Johns Hopkins University Press.

We would like to thank Raphael Vella, for providing the image of *Study Table* and for his generous interest in our volume.

We would also like to express our gratitude to the editorial staff at Associated University Presses and Bucknell University Press (especially Julian Yoseloff, Laura Rogers, Christine Retz, Kathleen Cioffi, and Greg Clingham) for their generous support and advice.

And finally, a big thank you also to Nawel and Anne-Marie, for putting up with hearing so much about theory and post-theory.

Discipline
and
Practice

Introduction
The Resistibility of Theory: Repositioning, Returning, Reclaiming Critical Practice

Stefan Herbrechter and Ivan Callus

THEORY'S POSITIONS ON/IN DISCIPLINARITY

IT IS SAID THAT ARCHIMEDES WOULD HAVE LEVERED THE WORLD. IT IS certain that Bruno Latour has spoken of science's raising of the world from a laboratory.[1] It is doubtful whether either of the two tasks is easier than positioning theory. The doubts arise not only because of debate over the nature of theory (in other words, over what it is precisely that is to be positioned), but also because of perplexity over who, or what, the positioning of the theory could possibly be down to, and the not unreasonable suspicion that it might not actually be down to anybody or anything at all. In other words, nobody and nothing is responsible for theory, in much the same way that nobody and nothing can be responsible for mathematics, or philosophy, or English. Martin Heidegger, who was remarkably pragmatic when conceding that "we simply have to acknowledge the fact that a philosophy is the way it is," would have understood this.[2] Theory "just is." Weightily, it resists (re)positioning.

Of course, it was not always so. There was a time when theory was not. That is to say that there was a time when theory was not in the university, and there was then a time when it very incontrovertibly was. Any account of this development would need to recall how theory "took on" disciplinarity by making itself subject to institutional apparata that called it into being with identifications of genealogies and repertoires that were particularized enough to make up the matter of a "new" discipline. This encounter with disciplinarity, however, was something that theory also experienced according to the connotation of confrontation that can be conveyed by the phrase *take on.* In other words, theory took on disciplinarity by attempting to contest the process of its own transformation into a distinct object of pedagogy.

It could be argued that theory cannot but engage in that contestation. This obligation arises from curricular presence within the university being consequent upon participation in an academic infrastructure that busies itself with all kinds of practicalities. Such participation is necessary to the operations of disciplinarity, but just as it is to be supposed that few radicals will appear very insurrectional if seen going about their chores, so theory must work to resist any suggestion of being too domesticated by the structures which host it. It would not do, for a discipline like theory that believes itself singularly appointed to radical critical practice, to appear too restricted by the practicalities binding it to the university. Like nations, disciplines must tell themselves and the world at large narratives concerning their own engendering and uniqueness—and theory has often responded to this call by regularly reasserting its commitment to radical critical practice, which thereby (this, at least, is the suggestion) renders it resistant to any denaturing that might derive from collusion with disciplinarity.

The twist to this story is that theory has so often offered itself up as the object of its own radical practice. As our preface showed and indeed itself reaffirmed, theory repeatedly undertakes a commitment to critically return upon itself. This task grows particularly urgent if, as argued by Mas'ud Zavarzadeh and Donald Morton in *Theory as Resistance* (1994), the principal menace facing theory becomes lodged within the very disciplinarity of theory in a manner which compromises its practice.[3] In such circumstances it is theorists themselves, and they alone, who can mount the counter that might sustain theory's irresistibility, acting against the institutionality of theory from within. And in a dramatic gesture exemplifying this ethic, Zavarzadeh and Morton sounded a call to "daily hand-to-hand combat with the liberal pluralism that underlies today's resistance to theory," doing so in the wake of their profound disaffection with the results of what they regarded as the increasingly stultifying disciplinarity of theory in universities in the United States. Their disenchantment arose from resistance within the discipline to their campaigning in favor of a form of radical practice which they called "critical cultural studies." This would have entailed "a study that implicates knowledge and subjects in the political economy of knowing and working," with theory understood in the sense of "a grasping of the world historically for the sake of transforming it in a collective fashion."[4] In the fallout, Zavarzadeh and Morton were cast as proponents of ideas that were "extremist" and "dogmatic"; they responded by arguing that theory's disciplinarity was a variation on the motif of "bourgeois institutions . . . constantly absorbing the elements of culture that oppose them." Through that process, "tenured radical," far from being seen as integral to theory and to an ethos committed to a certain kind of critical practice, ends up shunned.[5]

The bitterness of the struggle is brought home, in a remarkable demonstration of theory at odds with itself, in Zavarazadeh and Morton's taking to task of some of the very figures represented most prominently in the "curriculum" of theory:

> The resistance to theory is being promoted today in dominant academic and intellectual circles by a large number of writers: (post)-structuralists like de Man, Derrida, Lyotard; pragmatists like Fish and Rorty; performativists like Jardine and Butler; old liberals like Graff and Henry Louis Gates; advocates of the cult of experience like bell hooks, Lawrence Grossberg, Constance Penley, Andrew Ross, and other cultural studies critics; and those post-Marxists like Spivak, Aronowitz, Mouffe, and Laclau, who have in fact legitimated most of the dominant theories.[6]

This indictment suggests that, contrary to what might conventionally be thought, it is in being seen to try to put its house in order that theory's credentials as a firebrand are most effectively sustained. Theory moves to safeguard its own radicality and to prevent the domestication that arises from institutionalization by going about the chore of laundering its linen publicly, by coming clean about itself.[7] To this view, theory is most irresistible when it counters "outside" attempts to test its irresistibility with preemptive moves ensuring that it does not become resistible to itself or to its most radical instantiations. Only thus will it be able to return to the fray, purged, revitalized, and steeled against those who resist it.

Accordingly, and at some length, here are Zavarzadeh and Morton, preparing to sweep clean:

For quite some time now . . . contemporary theory (antitheory theory) has been the captive of professionals of ideology. These are persons who have made careers out of watching over theory's "purity" and promoting what they regard to be its "strict" and "proper" uses within the confines of bourgeois academic and intellectual institutions. . . . In their hands theory has lost its radical, transformative power and become just one more institutional discourse among many others. . . . In other words, although at one time, theory constituted a stubborn and resistant "outside" to the academy, it has become an insider.[8]

This is a contestation of what is proper *to* theory that proceeds by questioning what is proper *in* theory. The English ambiguity over *proper* as "belonging or relating to the person or thing in question, distinctively" and as "in conformity with rule" (*Oxford English Dictionary*) is overlaid with the French denotation of cleanliness through the word *propre*. Zavarzadeh and Morton speak of how theory can be made to claim back what is proper to it, of how cleaning up its act must paradoxically involve ensuring that theory gets itself dirty, so that it reclaims what is proper to it by not being too proper, too prim, too correct. Theory, then, must "clean up" by getting "stuck in." The chore of this particular radical within the academy, then, involves not being too much within the academy. Theory puts its house in order by not being too happily within it, by reasserting a radicality that it believes is at the origin of its being and upholding it. This, in a reworking of Freudian returns, is the uncanniness of theory. It is at home, it is engaged in putting its house in order, it is *heimlich*, when it is not too much inside because it is about, busying itself with the *unheimlich* quality of getting round returning to itself, and thence being radical. And it is this uncanniness, this return, this revisiting [*revenir sur*] anticipated in the preface, that secures the irresistibility of theory.

This goes some way toward explaining the compulsiveness with which theory thinks its own nature, and its disciplinarity. There surely cannot ever have been a discipline with quite such an abiding interest in itself. *Resistance to Theory, Theory as Resistance, The Limits of Theory, In the Wake of Theory, The Theory Mess, Post-Theory, The Future of Theory, Disciplinarity at the Fin-de-Siècle*: titles like these, in books either contesting or championing the probity and longevity of theory, assert the fact of theory's disciplinarity by investigating that disciplinarity as such, in all its implications.[9] The essays in this volume, which in their different ways all attempt a renegotiation of theory's disciplinarity and practice, themselves exemplify this trend. Their containment within these covers is a demonstration that theory, in probing yet again the conditions of its own positioning within the university, goes on to affirm its presence there. Indeed, if there is anything that is a constant in the essays that follow it is that the *fact* of the disciplinarity of theory is not resented. Indeed many of the essays (like those by Venuti, Milesi, or Wortham), dwell on how it might be more cogently readdressed.

That kind of position appears to be opposed to that of Zavarzadeh and Morton. This is not to say that the latter position is not justified in hoping that the irresistibility of theory rests on something that not only goes beyond the practicalities that have made it possible to graduate in theory and indeed to make a career in theory, but also on something unswayed by theory's almost pathological indulgence of the autotelic (which some might prefer to regard as the egotistical) and its instinct to regard this as security against its own imperishability. This something would need to resist theory's self-consciousness about its own disciplinarity and practice with the call from and of an "outside" that theory cannot but apprehend and attempt to answer. In fact Zavarzadeh and Morton argue that theory should maintain the notion of an "outside" to the existing system's "inside," urging what they refer to as "disparticipation," that is, pointing to "the *possible* which is suppressed in the pragmatic *is*" (authors' emphasis).[10] This recalls a point made at the beginning of this essay. If theory as a discipline, now, "just is," it surely cannot be fulfilling the ethic of radicality that it believes itself singularly called to. That radicality is not easily reducible to a teachable content; nor should it be amenable to a pragmatic and established disciplinarity that "just is" there, rather like a challenging mountain for intrepid undergraduates and postgraduates to climb. Nor is it necessarily safeguarded by the notion that the singularity of theory is bound up with an experience of the "aporetic" and the "living on borderlines"—in other words with what escapes pedagogic capture and makes inapprehensibility to disciplinarity *the* matter of theory.[11]

A difficulty consequently arises from differences over what precisely it is that constitutes the singularity of theory, its radicality, and hence its "outside." Particularly relevant here is a view—one contrary to Zavarzadeh and Morton's—that regards the best practice of theory as one that plants, at the base of theory's disciplinarity, a radix that does not necessarily equate radicality with growth toward a politicized outside but is happy to remain rooted in itself. The consequence of this view is the belief that theory is singular because it can constitute its own outside, so that it suffices that theory return upon itself for it to be radical, with resistance being construed as self-resistance. At stake, then, is an even more powerful articulation of the view of the autotelic impulse within theory, such that the disparticipation of theory would then not only not require cooperation with the "pragmatic *is*," but would involve theory being impossible, in all senses of that word. The nature of this (im)possibility demands closer scrutiny.

THE IMPOSSIBLE IRRESISTIBILITY OF THEORY

The best known expression of the impossibility contemplated above is to be found in the conclusion of Paul de Man's essay "The Resistance to Theory":

> Nothing can overcome the resistance to theory since theory *is* itself this resistance. The loftier the aims and the better the methods of literary theory, the less possible it becomes. Yet literary theory is not in danger of going under; it cannot help but flourish, and the more it is resisted, the more it flourishes, since the language it speaks is the language of self-resistance. What remains impossible to decide is whether this flourishing is a triumph or a fall.[12]

An (un)cannier policy underwriting the survival of theory could scarcely have been devised. The best resistance to theory, de Man suggests, is the challenge that originates from within theory's own discourse, which fortifies it against challenges proceeding from without. Despite a superficial similarity between positions that both seem to charge theory with the responsibility of looking within itself in order to "look out" better, this challenge is not analogous to that mounted by Zavarzadeh and Morton upon theory's disciplinarity and curricula. This is because the challenge foreseen by de Man is entrenched in rhetoricity and in the elusiveness of the signifier. It stands aloof from any practice or agitation undertaken in allegiance to an achievable signified. Theory, as a discourse, ensures its own survival by questioning itself, by binding itself to the ethic of self-vigilance which in other contexts—for instance, in Jacques Derrida's references to the call for "interminable self-critique"—it enjoins upon others.[13]

It is tempting to invoke here a clichéd motif from T. S. Eliot's "Little Gidding." Might it not be true that the compulsion of theory to repeat returning upon itself occurs because only thus can it know itself for the first time, whence comes the capacity for its own renewal and its rediscovery of its radical potential, but also the dangers of complacency? Yet de Man's words are not to be so easily glossed, nor so easily glossed over. Surely it is significant that theory is pointedly represented throughout his essay as *literary* theory. Here, in fact, lies the particularity of de Man's understanding of the return of theory upon itself. It is from this that the impossibility proceeds: from his investment in the *literary* signifier. He shuns using the word *theory* in generalized reference to what goes on under designations like *critical theory, cultural theory*, or what Zavarzadeh and Morton have called "critical cultural studies." What this lexical choice asserts is that only theory that takes literature as its object can discover resources for mounting the kind of resistance he speaks of. That supposition is probed in greater detail below; for the moment it is enough to note that to this view the implications of theory taking as its object, for instance, "culture" (as it has done, and very cogently too, in certain essays in this volume, to take just one example) are that it then finds its capacity for self-resistance diminished. Similarly, if it sets itself up specifically to be *critical*—thereby taking to heart its presumed vocation for a radical and determining intervening—it is debarred from the special capacity for resistance and self-resistance accorded to *literary* theory.

There is more. "Literary theory" becomes less possible, in de Man's opinion, if its aims become "loftier" and its "methods" better. Aims and methods are the stuff of pedagogy; indeed, of disciplinarity. In other words, disciplinarity is liable to impair what is best about theory. This, at least, provides a point of convergence between de Man's text and the position staked out by Zavarzadeh and Morton. The latter's suspicion of the institutionalization of theory comes from their mistrust of a professionalized theory.[14] In tone, if not in perspective, this is not too far away from de Man's well-known ambivalence about the inescapability of pedagogy. This ambivalence may seem surprising, particularly in view of de Man's sponsorship of "Yale" criticism (which could be very professional), and also in the light of Wlad Godzich having pointed out de Man's abiding interest in "questions of pedagogy and institutional determination."[15] But de Man, it must be remembered, could be scornful of the obligations and compromises necessitated by disciplinarity and pedagogy: "The only teaching worthy of the name is scholarly, not personal; analogies between teaching and various aspects of show business or guidance counselling are more often than not excuses for having abdicated the task. . . . For a method that cannot be made to suit the 'truth' of its object can only teach delusion."[16] This invocation of truth is perhaps incongruous or at any rate disingenuous coming from a poststructuralist, but it serves to stress the strength of feeling at work here about the propriety of theory. Most of all, it frets at the aggravating distance from the best instantiations of theory that is opened up by processes of disciplinarity that reduce theory to a teachable content, to a "pragmatic *is.*"

The fear is that once those processes dole theory into discrete curricular packages that make it amenable to the operations of transmissibility, assessment, and accreditation, what results can be only a delusion of theory. What theory could be, at its best, becomes denatured, so that what is instituted in its name becomes subject to the processuality of an enveloping disciplinarity and a misting of the vision of what could have been achieved by having theory enter the university. A number of essays in this volume understand that all too well, remarking with wistfulness and sensitivity upon what our preface referred to as crossroads revisited and roads not taken. Other commentators, too, feel it is ever more urgent that certain ill-trod paths be abandoned, and (inter)disciplinary distortions resisted: Herman Rapaport, for instance, has written excellently about how deconstruction has often been violently misapprehended within the university.[17] It is all part of an ongoing revisiting, a *revenir sur*, on theory, and what proceeds thus is at its best not merely a chronicling or an archivization but a revisioning.

Analogously, both Zavarzadeh and Morton on the one hand and de Man on the other converge again to hold that the disciplinarity of theory equates to a deplorable "theory now, theory as it has betrayedly become," whereas when they speak about theory, in their two separate and very different visions, it is to hold forth about what it could envisionedly be. Of course, theirs are two very different visions, at one only in demonstrating that the letter of theory is peculiarly averse to certain disciplinary processes that propagate its dissemination within the academy, and that this aversion cuts across the denominations of theory. It might seem, however, that essentially what this consensus amounts to is nothing more than the platitude that to teach something is to kill it. Reworked, this platitude is being made to say that to have anything enter the university is necessarily to invite the delusion of those who have the highest hopes for that entrance. Whereupon it becomes ever more urgent to consider whether the irresistibility of theory, at this time when it becomes opportune for theory to reconcile itself to the inescapability of its disciplinarity, can still most effectively proceed from within (according to the logic of self-resistance propounded by de Man), or from answering to an "outside" (according to the *engagé* ethic favored by Zavarzadeh and Morton).

How, in other words, might the (ir)resistibility of (post-)theory emerge, and how could it be radical? To start to answer this, and to move toward the response anticipated in the last section of this introduction and then developed more fully in our extroduction, we would first like to return to de Man's contention that theory, if it is to be itself by taking the literary as its subject, "speaks the language of self-resistance," whereupon it must flourish, even if "what remains impossible to decide is whether this flourishing is a triumph or a fall."[18] If we are intrigued by the uncertainty de Man affects over that flourishing, it is because of the suspicion that there might have been there an intuition that certain practiced assumptions about the nature of the literary would eventually wear thin—especially as they embody a certain kind of poststructuralist orthodoxy. Central to that orthodoxy is the Derridean notion that "this strange institution called literature" lends fiction "*in principle* the power to say anything, to break free of the rules, to displace them, and thereby to institute, to invent and even to suspect the traditional difference between nature and institution, nature and conventional law, nature and history" (Derrida's emphasis).[19] In these constructions, literature becomes a discourse apart, and literariness its indefinable essence, such that de Man can claim that "the definition of . . . literariness, has become the object of literary theory.[20] It would thereby follow that theory is most rewarding, most pressed, most challenged, most resisted, when it configures itself as *literary* theory, concerned above all with the impossible pursuit of a very elusive literariness and exhilarated by a radicality defined by the rootlessness of literature and its resistance to any anchoring in the programmatic or protocol bound. Beside that, a concern with culture or practice is a distraction, as *cultural* theory must presumably concern itself with artifacts that fall short of such adequacy or radicality, while *critical* theory, which must take on an ethic of a radicality differently defined, cannot avoid being ulterior.

In other words, theory is most worth doing when it is about literature. Cultural theory and critical theory are alibis for that, even excuses for not doing theory "properly." Not surprisingly, Zavarzadeh and Morton have little patience with this view, perceiving in it a loyalty to "*literaturnost,*" a displaced form of "class politics." However, they themselves are concerned by certain aspects of cultural theory, by the passage of "literary to cultural studies" spoken of by Antony Easthope.[21] For what sometimes appears to be forgotten in this passage from the literary to the cultural is the critical. How, then, is one to renegotiate critical theory, and how to renegotiate its relation with literary and cultural theory? What *is* the critical in theory, and how might it be reclaimed in post-theory?

THE OPTIONS FOR THEORY

Theory's reclaiming of critical practice might contemplate a number of options. In this volume, for instance, Catherine Belsey affirms faith in the "cultural" option, as long as it maintains an understanding of the place of the signifier, while in her reinterpretation (through Balibar) of Althusser Suzanne Gearhart provides a practical demonstration of how theory can "read" its own most cherished notions more closely and profoundly. Jean-Jacques Lecercle argues for a reclaiming of notions which theory had perhaps somewhat marginalized, like interpretation; others stress the importance of an intensified attention to issues like translation or interdisciplinarity, while a few *embrace* the "disciplinarity" of theory as they ponder the implications of its curricular presence. On our own part, there are two options that we believe should be reemphasized here, as they appear to define two poles of a continuum along which theory's different denominations position themselves. The first involves what we call "the letteral-mindedness of theory," while the second implicates theory's radicality.

The Letteral-Mindedness of Theory

The first option, which would not endear itself to the pole of opinion occupied by Zavarzadeh and Morton, concerns itself with what Derrida has called, in *Demeure*, "the *literality of literarity*" (Derrida's emphasis).[22] In keeping with this, it is significant that a renewed focus on the signifier was urged by Catherine Belsey in her contribution to the volume on *Post-Theory*. Belsey's adumbration over twenty years ago of what a critical practice might be is revisited with a renewed awareness of the importance of not overlooking the dimension of textuality and the place of the signifier.[23] Considerations of the cultural construction of meaning—which pervade a cultural theory predicated on a position, outlined in a different essay by Belsey, that holds that "no genre and no form of signifying practice would be excluded a priori from the field of enquiry," as "signifying practice is not exclusively nor even primarily verbal"[24]—should not then be allowed to overlook the materiality of language, or the specificity of the particular instantiations of the signifier that produce effects explicable only by reference to a letteredness of meaning: "If I have an anxiety about English studies in the postmodern condition, it is that we may have neglected the signifier. . . . How ironic if poststructuralism, which draws attention to the opacity of language, should be invoked in support of a new assumption of its transparency."[25]

In other words, and whatever the stakes, theory cannot forget its capacity to be language about language. The moment that is accepted, however, is the moment when theory's metalinguistic propensities may appear coextensive with the metaliterary, and indeed likely to find their most fulfilling manifestation there. This is best understood through reference to de Man's ideas on the capacity of language for "freedom for referential restraint," when "[language's] use can no longer be determined by considerations of truth or falsehood, good and evil, beauty and ugliness, or pleasure and pain." An "autonomous potential of language" is thereby discernible, and whenever it can be "revealed by analysis" it sanctions the conclusion that "we are dealing with literariness and, in fact, with literature as the place where this negative knowledge about the reliability of linguistic utterance is made available."[26] This negative knowledge occurs as it is not "*a priori* certain that literature is a reliable source of information about anything but its own language."[27] Literarity, therefore, is about its own intrinsicality. Extrinsicality distorts it. Any disposition to oppose that idea is regarded by de Man as an example of how "the resistance to theory is a resistance to the use of language about language"[28]—and, it might be added, to literature and the metaliterary as well.

De Man's statement suggests that there can be nothing to leave theory behind, nothing to displace it, not as long as theory—which is *itself* "the resistance to the use of language about language," and therefore co-reflective of the very impulses which resist it—continues to inscribe, performatively but also analytically, the residues of inde-termination which language (particularly *literary* language) itself compels. Indeed, theory *must* do this: it has no option. This is what it does and has always done. And as the residues are always already within language, theory's work of facilitating their "coming into dis-course, as such,"[29] can neither be consummated nor exceeded. No post-theory then, not now—and definitely not in any simplistic sense of supersedence, which necessarily appears almost crass when com-pared with de Man's sophisticated strategies of making the rhetorical and the counterintuitive so cogent.

De Man's is a powerful position. Perhaps it is even invulnerable, as the residues de Man speaks of can never not be in language. The work of theory can therefore never be complete, and the defense of theory that is implicit in language is therefore always apt. But the doubts over whether the irresistible flourishing is a triumph or a fall linger. And it is at least arguable that they do so because de Man's is a position that has now become so much part of the poststructuralist perspective on the necessary symbiosis between language and liter-ariness and literary theory that it has become "correct." *Correct* is not ordinarily a positive term in English, and de Man himself famously disliked approaches which are "generalizable and highly responsive to systematization," which are "technically correct."[30] It would be a rich irony if the idea he himself was propounding were to become imbued with such characteristics. And there can be little doubt (as will be clarified below, in the last section of this essay) that de Man's has become a very proper poststructuralist argument, even part of the "curriculum" of poststructuralism. Hence it has become teach-able, solid, "correct." It has become too easy and too comforting for theorists to say that theory cannot help its own flourishing, that lan-guage and rhetoricity can always potentially undo the logical and the referential, and that theory undertakes this better than any other dis-cipline. It was with this in mind that we said, above, that we were in-trigued by de Man's indecision over whether the flourishing of theory is a triumph or a fall, and by the possibility of his having intu-ited that his ideas on the nature of that flourishing would become to seem too practiced.

In that context, is it really arguable that a "return to literature" is advisable, on the grounds that theory finds its optimally and most mutually defining object there? Is it by having, through the process of disciplinarity that led it to negotiate different fields of analysis, "abandoned" literature that theory compromised its capacity to be critical? And is the nature of that manner of being critical—indeed, of being *radical*—ineluctably bound up with the Derridean notion that literature remains "an unstable function," that "it depends on a precarious juridical status," so that even "when it harbors the unconditional right to say anything, including the most savage antinomies, disobedience itself, its *status* is never assured or guaranteed permanently [*à demeure*], at home, in the inside of an "at home" (Derrida's emphasis)?[31]

To take this line of questioning further: does not the unsettledness of literature, which, true radical that it is, is never "at home," remind us of our remarks on theory's own chafing at domesticity? Here, in case the identification is not yet clear, is Derrida again, speaking about literature which will not demurely stay at home, *à demeure*:

> This at least is the hypothesis I would like to test and submit to your discussion. There is no essence or substance of literature: literature is not. It does not exist. It does not remain at home, *abidingly* [*à demeure*] in the identity of a nature or even a historical being identical with itself. It does not maintain itself abidingly [*à demeure*], at least if "abode [*demeure*]" designates the essential stability of a place; it only remains [*demeure*] *where* and *if* "to be abiding [*être à demeure*]" in some "abiding order [*mise en demeure*]" means something else.[32]

Theory might wish, with this in the background, to take literature as a model. To be unstable (like literature), to be "precarious" in its "juridical status" (like literature), to be "disobedient" (like literature), to never have its status guaranteed permanently by never being "at home" (like literature), to have no "essence" or "substance" and "not exist" (like literature), it would appear that it needs to act like literature. It needs, then, to take a leaf out of literature's book. But this can only happen if theory remembers how to be about books, how to be book-ish. To be like literature it must be lettered, it must be (as de Man never doubted), primarily *literary* (not eclectically *cultural*), and then it might (re)learn how to be critical, again. To act like literature, theory has to be an act of literature. Things thereupon become difficult, for theory, realistically, cannot now shed its disciplinarity, cannot help being "at home" in the university sometimes, even as it pines and aspires to the condition of literature.

"To aspire to the condition of literature": is an identification between theory and literature possible? Might theory *be* literary? There is a certain history that speaks of the possibility of an "articulation" of these two orders of discourse, and chronicles efforts to effect it. For instance, Derrida discovers in the poetry of Francis Ponge a singularity that destabilizes the foundations of criticism, and demands from the critic or theorist the capacity to be Pongean about what is irreducibly and singularly Pongean.[33] With singular texts, in other words, an ethic of "limit-criticism" is called forth, uniquely and unrepeatably, by the "limit-text," obliging criticism to take after the literary, and to order its signifier accordingly, *literarily*. This has sometimes been taken to justify attempts to write theoretical fiction, or to try to produce theory that aspires to the order of the literary. It is an aspiration that arguably plays itself out in the most inventive of Derrida's texts, underpinned as they are by the techniques of "autography," hieroglyphs, the signature, homonymy, anasemia, and others that are variously and inventively used in Derrida's writing in a manner cognizant of the age of the end of the book but one not forgetful of the resources of literality/literarity.[34]

That said, Derrida himself has consistently been aware of the impossibility of coincidence between literature and other discourses. This is demonstrated by the fact that his "dream of a new institution without precedent, without pre-institution" that might arise from the "dream of a writing that would be neither philosophy nor literature, nor even contaminated by one or the other, while still keeping . . . the memory of literature or philosophy" must remain, precisely, a dream.[35] There needs to be a certain distance whenever two discourses contrive to be "very close; but also too close," leading to "avoid[ance] . . . *because* of . . . identification."[36]

Theory cannot itself be literary, and should not. But it can be an act of literature by remembering to be about literature, perhaps even to be about it above everything else. The disciplinarity of theory will not enable it to be about literature exclusively, nor should it. In this respect it is telling that most of the essays in this volume are not primarily about literature, though they are all, in one way or another, at least as much about language, or the (linguistic) signifier, as they are about culture, for instance, or politics. But it may be no bad thing for

theory to believe that it can contrive to be most radical, most resistant to recuperation, most "unseizable," when it is about literature. It
can thereby be a *critical* theory by learning to critique what is most
radical, by addressing what happens at "the limits of literature." Theory would then act in the belief that de Man and Derrida are ultimately right when they suggest that literature, as a discourse, is
peculiarly radical, and would seek to engage with it in the conviction
that this character would rub off on any other discourse focused on
the letter-ality of literarity. But there remains, irresistibly, some scep-
ticism.

The Radicality of Theory

The problem—and this raises the second point about the reclaiming
of critical practice—is that in being letter-al minded theory cannot
but make a virtue of detachedness. Its credentials as an agent for
practice would then appear tenuous. How can one be *engagé* unless
one is ready to get "stuck in," and how is that reconcilable with the
bookish? The argument that theory can be radical by being about literature might be ingenious, but what emerges is not the radical—or,
indeed, the theory—that is envisaged by Zavarzadeh and Morton,
who instead take "theory to be a critique of material intelligibilities."
Their distance from de Man's position is made clear in that for them
"labor, not language . . . is the frame of intelligibility that determines
the regime of signification,"[37] hence their insistence that "theory
should always be a "*criti(que)al* theory, that is to say, it should provide
critical (not simply affirmative) knowledges of social totality for the
student so that he or she sees his or her positionality in social collectivity" (our emphasis).[38] That requires a disciplinarity of theory that
breaks free from "a curriculum that professionalizes theory, robbing
it of its political edge" in the name of " 'reform-ism'—changing some
insignificant features in order to relegitimate the dominant structure." The answer, then, does not lie in interdisciplinarity, but in
transdisciplinarity, which is not "the peaceful, interactive coexistence
of fields of knowledge but a transgressive form of redrawing the map
of learning in a fashion that opens up new space for rising radical
and revolutionary subjectivities."[39]

Zavarzadeh and Morton's attempt to reclaim the critical as
"criti(que)al" is fundamentally removed from de Man's vision for
theory. Indeed, they engage directly with de Man's argument, which

they regard as a "structure of understanding" built on "a transhistorical general 'literariness' that resists theory." De Man's idea of a *literary* theory that resists itself is thereby overturned to suggest that it
produces only a resistance to the theory *they* endorse. This is because
they view de Man's position as one that allows "poetry [literature]" to
be "a transdiscursive act that is autointelligible, . . . meaningful in
and of itself outside all cultural mediations and without being entan-
gled in the materiality of the signifying practices of society": a mode
of investigation culminating in theory becoming "a purely cognitive
matter."[40] Theirs is therefore a radicality that can be summed up in
the view that critical practice must depend not on literary criticism
or a faith in literariness, but on "critique," an "investigation of the enabling conditions of production of meaning in culture."[41]

The two positions outlined above both attempt to reclaim the critical. Both are driven by a vision for theory that is committed and well
intentioned. The problem is that the road to a stultifying disciplinarity, which amounts to theory's hell, is full of precisely such good intentions. The vexing thing about this is not so much the difficulty of
any adjudication of the two positions' respective merits. It is rather
that they have each critiqued the other so well as to impair the credibility of either in its efforts to mount a critique of culture (however
critique or culture are to be defined, for that, of course, is also and
above all what is in question). One could indeed shuttle between a
position and another and discover that these two contrary movements within theory (which, between them, define the continuum
along which the different denominations of theory's broad church
are strung out) have read each other (and themselves) much more
rigorously than other attacks mounted from "anti-theory" (which lies
outside the broad church of theory). For instance, Zavarzadeh and
Morton complain that poststructuralism is committed to a "self-re-
flexiveness" defined textually rather than politically[42]—something
which Derrida, who for his part has admitted to having doubts about
the "vibrating in unison" necessary to most forms of concerted ac-
tivism, might be ready to concede.[43] Meanwhile, Zavarzadeh and
Morton's view that de Man's perspective proposes "the 'literary' as
the mark of the impossibility of the connection between language
and the social"[44] opens itself to the counter ready-built into de Man's
argument, namely that such positions exemplify the "resistance to
language about language." For those who would resist these theoretical positions from "outside" theory, therefore, there is little pur-

chase that theory's own inside has not already sought to gain. Meanwhile, differences of the positions are probably not resolvable. How, then, can theory move beyond this impasse, given that it is an impasse that is at the heart of its very disciplinarity and one that divides its constituency?

"FROM THEORY, POST-THEORY"—BUT HOW?

Any response to the impasse must surely lie in a factor that emerges as an unexpected point of convergence between these opposed modes of envisaging theory. Both visions ascribe theory, albeit differently, with the capacity to resist the positioning that inevitably follows upon theory's taking on of disciplinarity. This brings us back to where we started, with Archimedes and Latour, and the difficulty of anyone or anything positioning theory. To "position" theory implies, grammatically, transitiveness: something will be made to happen to theory. Theory would therefore be "levered." Levers would, in all senses, be applied to it—for is not this, also, an aspect of disciplinarity? We know that Derrida has written about the relevance of levers to discussions of the university, and we know also that one of the contributors to this volume, Simon Morgan Wortham, has written penetratingly about that area of Derrida's work.[45] Certainly the positioning of theory will not be down to an Archimedes-like superman, nor is it plausible that there might be some kind of concerted effort, mounted within or without the law of theory (or, indeed, its "laboratory," the university) to shape theory in any given way. That effort would find itself up against the difference between deliberateness and chance, between self-positioning and being positioned, between the willed event and the prospect that something (probably not very sublime) "is happening" to theory. Most crucial of all is the fact that it must be acknowledged that theory, having been interpellated as such within the university and having acquired disciplinarity under this name, *theory*, has now acquired a life of its own. Indeed, we were tempted to spell *theory* throughout with the first letter in uppercase, disregarding the convention that prefers the lowercase alternative and willing to ride the accusation of an indulgence in anthropomorphization—and that in recognition of the fact that theory, in acquiring a life of its own in the university, has acquired a *will* of its own. If theory, now, truly "just is," and if it is secure in its accommodation

within the university, then it may no longer be sensible to be so up-
tight about the resistance *of* theory (after Zavarzadeh and Morton)
or the resistance *to* theory (after de Man). This would be because
theory, endowed with this will through the acquisition of its immove-
able disciplinarity, may in one sense at least have become irresistible.
It will shift only when it wants to—or needs to.

And yet, naggingly, there remains the fact that talk of post-theory,
in terms of theory's passing, remains persistent. The assertion by the
editors of the volume *Post-Theory* that "nothing stimulates the production of Theory like the proclamation of its own death"[46] is reassuring. But it is also too much like the reflex of those who have learnt
their de Man, and may not convince those for whom the resistibility
of theory is a straightforward matter of seeing it superseded. It is, of
course, very difficult for theory to resist this reflex, and very typical of
it to dismiss as incredibly facile the idea that post-theory might turn
out to be something that could supplant it. For theory, it is not a matter of chronology. Rome may have been followed by darkness, and
counterrevolution may follow on from revolution, but just as
rhetoric is "from" philosophy in a Derridean relation of supplementarity,[47] post-theory is surely "from" theory complexly, for instance in
the context of a Lyotardian problematization of relations of supersedence. Post-theory would therefore need to be comprehended in
the context of "a procedure in *ana-*" and "the paradox of the future
(post) anterior *(modo)*.[48] That comprehending repeats the tendency of
theory to condemn attempts that think its "post" in terms of straightforward decline. "It will come as no surprise," the editors of *Post-The-*
ory acknowledge in their introduction, "to learn that the 'post' in
'post-theory' is not to be taken unequivocally," whereupon "the question of how it *is* to be taken" becomes urgent (authors' emphasis).[49]
To that view—one sanctioned also by Derridean suspicions of "seismisms and newisms"[50]—suppositions of theory's passing are delusively built on acceptance of the categories of successiveness, which
theory has critiqued. In an essay in *Post-Theory* that typifies this critique, Geoffrey Bennington brings to bear one of the most "correct"
notions of poststructuralism to allay fears about a supplanting form
of *Post-Theory*: "The post- has always already been at work in theory,
and . . . we will never reach a post-theoretical state."[51] As already sus-
pected, no post-theory then, not now.

We believe, however, that if theory's (self-) (re)positioning as post-
theory is really to be irresistible, it must depend on something more

than this reflex whereby talk of its supersedence is dismissed. It is a reflex that risks becoming a mannerism. Revisioning theory's radicality *à la* de Man, on the assumption that theory flourishes irresistibly because it cannot help resisting itself, is mannered, and revisioning theory *à la* Zavarzadeh and Morton, on the presumption that it can be an agent of transformation, is mannered as well. Perhaps theory needs to learn that it cannot take the de Man line, or the Zavarzadeh and Morton line, so manneredly any more. Its revisiting should not focus solely on the roads it has most productively traversed, but on the roads not taken, the crossroads revisited—this point, already made in the preface, bears repeating. For theory to argue that it is singularly appointed to radical practice, and then to debate with itself whether this practice is best derived from a preoccupation with literariness or with praxis, is a position struck too often by its pasts. Such arguments are now too firmly within the repertoire of theory, too much part of theory's disciplinarity and perhaps also of a certain disciplining of its doubts about itself, even when what they do is rail against that very disciplinarity. In other words, they are positions that theory strikes if it is returning upon itself with a sterile repeatedness rather than renewingly. This aggravates what the editors of *Post-Theory* call "the sclerosis of theoretical writing, the hardening of Theory's lexical and syntactical arteries." Such writing risks its own credibility, because it is so practiced at what it does that it can lead to "a self-satisfied and hypostasized 'Theory.' "[52]

In that case, it would be useless to try to position theory "after" de Man or, contrastingly, "after" Zavarzadeh and Morton, with this *after* understood in the twin senses of successiveness and "in the manner of." Theory now "just is" by being interdenominational and disciplined, even if very unharmoniously so. Yet to say that theory "just is" amounts to being complacent about its existence: to believing, precisely, in its irresistibility. This might be a mistake, and the mistake might arise because the irresistibility of theory might, conceivably, be put in question by the appeal of something yet more irresistible that theory itself, endowed with a will of its own though it now undoubtedly is, might be unable to resist. It is for this reason that in the extroduction we shall speak of the posthuman: one of the most direct and uncomplicated manifestations of the view that the days of theory (and of much else besides) are numbered, and what supersedes it is a time when perhaps what becomes more relevant is an attention to the digital rather than to the signifier and the letter-al and the political. The binarism between de Man's letter-al and Zavarazadeh and Morton's political has arguably been undone not by any poststructuralist deconstruction, but by the disciplinarity of theory now engaging with "other" disciplinarities arising from the encroachment of this digitality and the "new" order from which it emerges. Theory, we therefore argue, *must* resist the idea of its own superseding—by posthumanism or anything else—but it must do so by undertaking a revisiting of itself, a *revenir sur,* that is not too practiced in the orthodoxies of the kind of polarized returns (exemplified by the radicality differently envisaged by de Man and Zavarzadeh and Morton) in which it has shown so much faith. Post-theory would find that very resistible. Instead, the revisiting should not be too correct, too much part of the disciplinarity and teachability of theory, to prevent it from reclaiming practice. An engagement with the posthuman therefore becomes important because it can serve as a figure, an allegory, of the way in which theory might go about this reclaiming in its encounter with post-theory.

These, then—our introduction and the extroduction—are the two parts of the frame which, as editors, we are proposing for this volume's exploration of the (ir)resistibility of theory's disciplinarity and practice in a time of post-theory. But a frame can only border, just as disciplinary partitionings do, and it is time to leave it to the contributors to this volume to illustrate how theory might return upon itself, renewingly.

NOTES

1. See Bruno Latour, "Give Me a Laboratory and I Will Raise the World," in *Science Observed* ed. Karen Knorr-Cetina and Michael Mulkay (London: Sage, 1983), 141–70.

2. Martin Heidegger, "The End of Philosophy and the Task of Thinking," in *Basic Writings,* ed. David Farrell Krell, rev. ed. (1966; London: Routledge, 1993), 433.

3. See Mas'ud Zavarzadeh and Donald Morton, *Theory as Resistance: Politics and Culture after (Post)structuralism* (New York: Guilford, 1994).

4. Ibid., 146, 160.

5. Ibid., 149, 151.

6. Ibid., 3–4.

7. Ibid., 157.

8. Ibid., 6.

9. The full bibliographic references for those texts mentioned here that are as yet uncited in these notes are: Paul de Man, *The Resistance to Theory* (Minneapolis:

University of Minnesota Press, 1986)—especially the essay "The Resistance to The-ory," 3–20; Thomas M. Kavanagh, ed., *The Limits of Theory* (Stanford: Stanford Uni-versity Press, 1989); Paul Bové, *In the Wake of Theory* (Middleton, Conn.: Wesleyan University Press, 1992); Herman Rapaport, *The Theory Mess: Deconstruction in Eclipse* (New York: Columbia University Press, 2001); Martin McQuillan and others, eds., *Post-Theory: New Directions in Criticism* (Edinburgh: Edinburgh University Press, 1999); Jean-Michel Rabaté, *The Future of Theory* (Oxford: Blackwell, 2002).

10. Zavarzadeh and Morton, *Theory as Resistance*, 150.

11. See Jacques Derrida, *Aporias*, trans. Thomas Dutoit (Stanford: Stanford Uni-versity Press, 1993) and "Living On: Borderlines," trans. James Hulbert, in Harold Bloom and others, *Deconstruction and Criticism* (London: Routledge and Kegan Paul, 1979), 75–176. The inapprehensibility to disciplinarity of deconstruction's contem-plations of the aporetic, the undecidable, and the impassable is usefully read in the contrastingly pragmatic context of its contemplations of the university. For a good guide to this context, see Simon Morgan Wortham's essay in this volume.

12. Paul de Man, "The Resistance to Theory," 19–20.

13. See Jacques Derrida, *Specters of Marx: The State of the Debt, the Work of Mourning, and the New International*, trans. Peggy Kamuf (New York: Routledge, 1994), 89.

14. Zavarzadeh and Morton, *Theory as Resistance*, 15–17.

15. Wlad Godzich, foreword to *The Resistance to Theory*, by Paul de Man (Min-neapolis: University of Minnesota Press, 1986), xii.

16. de Man, "The Resistance to Theory," 4.

17. See Rapaport, *The Theory Mess*.

18. de Man, "The Resistance to Theory," 19–20.

19. Jacques Derrida, "This Strange Institution Called Literature: An Interview with Jacques Derrida," in Jacques Derrida, *Acts of Literature*, ed. Derek Attridge (New York: Routledge, 1992), 37.

20. de Man, "The Resistance to Theory," 9.

21. See Antony Easthope, *Literary into Cultural Studies* (New York: Routledge, 1991).

22. Maurice Blanchot/Jacques Derrida, *The Instant of My Death/Demeure: Fiction and Testimony*, trans. Elizabeth Rottenberg (Stanford: Stanford University Press, 2000), 23.

23. See Catherine Belsey's *Critical Practice* (London: Methuen, 1980) and her essay "English Studies in the Postmodern Condition: Towards a Place for the Signi-fier," in *Post-Theory: New Directions in Criticism*, ed. Martin McQuillan and others (Ed-inburgh: Edinburgh University Press, 1999), 123–38.

24. Catherine Belsey, "Towards Cultural History—in Theory and Practice," *Tex-tual Practice* 3 (1989): 160–61.

25. Belsey, "English Studies in the Postmodern Condition," 130–31.

26. de Man, "The Resistance to Theory," 10.

27. Ibid., 11.

28. Ibid., 12.

29. Ibid., 19.

30. Ibid., 19.

31. Derrida, "Demeure," 28.

32. Derrida, "Demeure," 28. The parentheses in the quotation are in the text of the English translation of *Demeure*.

33. Jacques Derrida, *Signsponge/Signéponge,* trans. Richard Rand (New York: Columbia University Press, 1993), ix and 70–72.

34. See Gregory L. Ulmer, *Applied Grammatology: Post(e)-Pedagogy from Jacques Derrida to Joseph Beuys* (Baltimore: Johns Hopkins University Press, 1985).

35. Derrida, "This Strange Institution Called Literature," 73.

36. Ibid., 60.

37. Zavarzadeh and Morton, *Theory as Resistance,* 8.

38. Ibid., 12.

39. Ibid., 19-22, 17.

40. Ibid., 31–32, 79.

41. Ibid., 30.

42. Ibid., 29.

43. Jacques Derrida, "A Madness Must Watch over Thinking," *Points . . . : Interviews 1974–1994,* ed. Elisabeth Weber, trans. Peggy Kamuf and others (Stanford: Stanford University Press, 1995), 348.

44. Zavarzadeh and Morton, *Theory as Resistance,* 174.

45. See Jacques Derrida, "Mochlos," in *Logomachia: The Conflict of the Faculties,* ed. Richard Rand (Lincoln: University of Nebraska Press, 1992), 1–34, and Simon [Morgan] Wortham, *Rethinking the University: Leverage and Deconstruction* (Manchester: Manchester University Press, 1999).

46. Martin McQuillan, Graeme McDonald, Robin Purves, and Stephen Thomson, "The Joy of Theory," in *Post-Theory: New Directions in Criticism,* ed. Martin McQuillan and others (Edinburgh: Edinburgh University Press, 1999), ix.

47. Jacques Derrida, "White Mythology: Metaphor in the Text of Philosophy," in *Margins of Philosophy,* trans. Alan Bass (New York: Harvester Wheatsheaf, 1982), 209.

48. See Jean-François Lyotard, "Note on the Meaning of 'post' " *The Postmodern Explained to Children: Correspondence 1982–1985,* ed. Julian Pefanis and Morgan Thomas (London: Turnaround, 1992), 93 and 24.

49. McQuillan and others, "The Joy of Theory," ix.

50. Jacques Derrida, "Some Statements and Truisms about Neologisms, Newisms, Postisms, Parasitisms, and other small Seismisms," in *The States of Theory,* ed. David Carroll (New York: Columbia University Press, 1989), 63–94.

51. Geoffrey Bennington, "Inter," in *Post-Theory: New Directions in Criticism,* ed. Martin McQuillan and others (Edinburgh: Edinburgh University Press, 1999), 119.

52. McQuillan, McDonald, Purves, and Thomson, "The Joy of Theory," xi–xii.

I
"DISCIPLINING" THEORY— REVALUATIONS

Beyond Literature and Cultural Studies: The Case for Cultural Criticism

Catherine Belsey

1

TWO EVENTS HAVE TAKEN PLACE, ONE LONG-TERM, GRADUAL, AND international, the other sudden, specific, and local but, I believe, symptomatic, and thus broader in its implications than might at first appear. These two events, in my view, propel English departments beyond English literature and cultural studies, toward Cultural Criticism.[1] The first is the advent of "theory" and the unprecedented expansion of the terrain of English studies since the 1960s; the second is the closure in 2002 of the British Centre for Contemporary Cultural Studies at Birmingham University, on the grounds of its poor performance in the government's Research Assessment Exercise. In the 1960s the Centre virtually invented the discipline of cultural studies, and its closure symbolically marks a moment we might see as the end of an era.

What happens next will depend to some degree on our understanding of how and why we came to partition the terrain of culture between distinct institutional powers. History has given us no reason to trust apartheid. Doesn't separate development usually throw up as many problems as it solves? Is it possible that we can now reunite the territory, combining some of the radical energy generated in the appropriation of theory and the construction of cultural studies in the formation of a new discipline that I want to call Cultural Criticism? If this paper offers a contribution to the process of truth and reconciliation, it also constitutes a polemical proposal for a utopian future.

47

I begin with the early days of the story. As luck would have it, 1961 was in some ways a watershed for the British understanding of culture. In October of that year T. S. Eliot, by then an elder statesman of English letters, signed the preface to a new edition of *Notes Towards the Definition of Culture*. The text was now to be issued in "'paper back' form"—and Eliot gives the term in quotation marks, as if to register a distrust of this not-so-new but distinctly popularizing mode. Reading through the original, first published thirteen years before, he saw, he now declared, that he had no desire to change anything substantial.[2]

The *Notes*, which began to take shape in the course of the Second World War, registered an anxiety above all about the effect of egalitarianism on culture as Eliot understood the term. Before the War most serious intellectuals in Britain were on the left in politics. Wartime conditions, mixing the classes both in the armed forces and at home, went on to intensify the fears of the few who were not on the left that the culture they had known was about to disappear for ever. They were probably right: the 1944 Education Act made secondary education at a grammar school free to anyone thought capable of benefiting from it, and was to change the intellectual shape of a whole generation. Immediately after the War, the British population elected a Labour government with a radical commitment to welfare provision for all. The legislation that followed had the effect of transforming social relations.

T. S. Eliot feared for the cultural implications of these changes, and regarded with deep hostility the idea that education alone could be responsible for passing on traditional culture from one generation to the next. Instead, he believed, the central institution for the transmission of culture was the family, understood in the dynastic sense of that term, with its piety toward the dead, and its solicitude for the as yet unborn. The high quality of the culture of the minority depended, he argued, precisely on its minority status, and its continued existence ought to be the responsibility of a cultural elite. This would comprise not the producers of works of art, but rather their consumers or patrons, who preserved and communicated *good manners* in the deepest and most literal meaning of the phrase. Civilized values necessitated the persistence of class difference, Eliot insisted. Socialism and culture were fundamentally incompatible:

> Here are what I believe to be essential conditions for the growth and for the survival of culture. If they conflict with any passionate faith of

the reader—if, for instance, he finds it shocking that culture and equalitarianism should conflict, if it seems monstrous to him that anyone should have "advantages of birth"—I do not ask him to change his faith, I merely ask him to stop paying lip-service to culture.[3]

Despite the defiant phrases, Eliot's text everywhere acknowledges, however unwillingly, that the cause is already very nearly lost. Somewhat eccentrically, the title page of *Notes Towards the Definition of Culture* includes its own footnote, explaining the meaning of the title itself. The footnote cites the first definition of *definition* in *Oxford English Dictionary*: "The setting of bounds; limitation (rare)—1483." As a modernist poet, who was persuaded to equip *The Waste Land* with explanatory notes, Eliot here exploited the plurality of the signifier to complicate what might appear at first glance to be a transparent term. The *Notes* will indeed reflect, they say, on the meaning of "culture," the use and misuse of "a word which nobody bothers to examine"; they will discuss "how much is . . . embraced by the term"; and they will also set out to defend it against abuses by discouraging its misappropriation, since, Eliot adds, "to rescue this word is the extreme of my ambition."[4] That "rescue" process, however, involves imposing sharp limits on a signifier that threatens to slide away from its proper significance, its association with the values and tastes of a minority. To define, according to Eliot's footnote, is also to demarcate, to impose bounds, to restrict.

Aptly enough, the definition of *definition* the footnote invokes is "rare." Eliot's strange, supplementary gloss retrieves etymologically for an everyday word a meaning that is now lost in ordinary, quotidian exchanges. His unusual practice, the provision of an explanatory note to a title, and its inclusion on the title page, reenacts the "rareness" of culture itself, its divorce from the ordinary and the everyday, and in the process pays tribute to the unusual character of culture. This plea for the preservation of minority culture explicitly alludes on its own title page to an unusual meaning. In its rarity, culture too is unusual. Indeed, Eliot announces bleakly, it threatens to become so unusual as to face extinction:

We can assert with some confidence that our own period is one of decline; that the standards of culture are lower than they were fifty years ago; and that the evidences of this decline are visible in every department of human activity. I see no reason why the decay of culture should not proceed much further, and why we may not even anticipate a period, of some duration, of which it is possible to say that it will have *no* culture.[5]

(The poet of *The Waste Land* had in practice been announcing the end of civilization, of course, since at least the 1920s.)

The footnote thus embodies in miniature the issue that concerns the text in its entirety. That the gloss is necessary reveals, like the dangerous supplement it is, an inadequacy in the current ability to grasp the entire significance of Eliot's title. A change of meaning has already, in effect, taken place. Eliot can no longer count on his readers to recognize the "full" definition of *definition*. Instead, he is obliged to provide an explanation because, just as in the case of culture itself, a meaning of the term inherited from the past is now "rare," and becoming rarer. The supplementary meaning he invokes is old, historic, in the process of vanishing.

Moreover, as the footnote demonstrates, meaning, like culture, is the location of a contest. To "define" culture is to reaffirm an increasingly "rare" meaning of the word, and thus to take up a position in a struggle to delimit it, however rare that position may now be. In the context of the empiricist account of language prevalent in 1961, definitions might seem to be innocent, academic affairs, and a definition of culture primarily an abstract question, a discussion at the level of the name that would leave the referent itself untouched. These *Notes*, however, the footnote proclaims, are embattled. If they prophesy disaster, they also propose an alternative, a rescue, and this is seen to consist in the recovery of an old and vanishing meaning.

Much of the text, accordingly, is devoted to discussion of the various possible meanings of "culture." There is, for instance, the anthropological sense, but the inclusion of all of the beliefs and practices of a society under one heading strikes Eliot as inadequate to a developed society like our own. Alternatively, culture may be seen as "that which makes life worth living,"[6] and in this sense Eliot's own culture, he concedes, would embrace a wide range of interests and activities:

> Derby Day, Henley Regatta, Cowes, the twelfth of August, a cup final, the dog races, the pin table, the dart board, Wensleydale cheese, boiled cabbage cut into sections, beetroot in vinegar, nineteenth-century Gothic churches and the music of Elgar.[7]

(The impenetrability of much of that list to many British citizens half a century later would offer proof, if proof were needed, of the cultural relativity of forms of pleasure.)

But Eliot's preferred meaning for culture, the one that resurfaces throughout his text, is more or less synonymous with cultivation, the usage that occurs in biology or, indeed, agri-*culture*. Culture, he maintains, develops the raw material, *improves* on what is given. It is as improvement that culture is in danger of disappearing. And it is that meaning of the term, culture as an object of aspiration, an ideal, and "culture" as the inscription of *that* value, which needs, Eliot believes, to be rescued. The definition of *definition* is thus not incidental: indeed, it deserves its place on the title page. *Notes Towards the Definition of Culture* is about meaning as much as it is about culture. It concerns the rescue of a value inscribed in a meaning. As befits a poet, Eliot conducts the struggle at the level of the signifier.

2

Ironically, a kind of rescue of this view of meaning, though not of culture as Eliot defined it, was at hand in 1961, if from a quarter Eliot himself would surely not have predicted, and with an effect he would almost certainly have deplored. In Paris at this time the reaction to the events of the Second World War took an entirely different turn. The issue in this instance was not the threat to standards represented by a euphoric postwar egalitarianism, but the problem of wartime collaboration with the Vichy government. How was it possible that so many people had so readily succumbed to the values of the German occupation? How, now that France was herself again, to account for her aberration? And how, more broadly still, to explain the takeover of civilized Germany in the 1930s by views that had led, willy-nilly, to the death camps?

These questions, barely speakable at the time, would become explicit only gradually in French theory, in Michel Foucault's emphasis on "resistance," for example, and again in Jean-François Lyotard's repeated return to the issue of the Holocaust. But they were no less pressing, and perhaps at a deeper because unconscious level, in what became known as structuralism. Running through the structural anthropology of Claude Lévi-Strauss was an account of human nature which saw the rules of cultural exchange as so many attempts to establish reciprocity in order to overcome natural hostility. At the level of narrative, A.-J. Greimas would go on to find a universal pattern for all stories, centering on the quest for individual freedom in the teeth of an oppressive order. In each case the implication was that at any time the "balance" might be upset, and a culture could topple into either antagonism or full-scale repression.

Out of this climate sprang the work of Roland Barthes, the title of his 1957 collection of witty journalistic analyses of postwar French culture, *Mythologies*, a silent tribute to Lévi-Strauss, the great mythographer of the day, just as his "Introduction to the Structural Analysis of Narratives" (1966) would acknowledge the work of Greimas. But Barthes was deeply suspicious of "human nature" and universal structures. Instead, his commitment was to unmasking the cultural and historical differences that invoked human nature and the universal as their alibi. The project was still to explain what had happened without ever mentioning it as such, but this time to locate it in the specific circumstances of the moment, rather than an eternal and unalterable human condition. For Barthes culture was comprehensive. It embraced wrestling and advertising, steak and striptease, criticism and cookery, and literature itself. Culture was not just the traditional pleasures of a nation at play, but everything Eliot feared it might become, including the ephemera that appealed to the vulgar majority. In so far as it led people to subscribe to values against their better judgment, it was also profoundly suspect, and it was not divisible between the improving culture of the minority and the improvident tastes of the rest. Instead, culture was shared.

French theory would help to put an end, in due course, to the concept of culture as privileged, a precious tradition to be transmitted to the next generation, in piety toward the dead and solicitude for the future. The influence of theory on the Anglo-American academy would eventually contribute to the demise of the English department as the place of preservation for the minority of an elite, written culture, and it would foster the introduction of cultural studies as a distinct discipline. But it would do so, Eliot might have been pleased to know, on the basis of a close attention to the definition of *definition*. Roland Barthes drew on the much earlier work of Ferdinand de Saussure, putting it for the first time at the heart of cultural analysis. Signification, Saussure's *Course in General Linguistics* (1916) made clear, both depends on and generates differences. Meaning is the effect of the signifier, not its origin, and meaning resides in difference. Definitions do indeed demarcate; they inevitably impose bounds; they specify limits. Culture, in the everyday sense of the term, is perceptible in the form of meanings, those understandings and values that are shared by a group or society; meanings are produced by signifying practice; and these meanings have no guarantees in the world outside signification itself. As a result, definitions are the location of contests. If the contests in culture take place at the level of meaning, the contest *for* culture is appropriately a matter of definitions. In the struggle over the definition of culture, the delimitation of the area the word identifies and the location of its boundaries are precisely what is at stake. T. S. Eliot's strange, supplementary footnote identifies him, paradoxically, as a kind of "theorist" *avant la lettre*, and thus as an inadvertent ally of an intellectual position that could not choose but align itself against the particular meaning of "culture" he held dear.

3

T. S. Eliot's perceived opponents at this time, however, were more likely to have been closer to what had now become his home. In 1961 Raymond Williams published *The Long Revolution*. Where Eliot favored conservatism and elitism, Williams supported reform and egalitarianism. *The Long Revolution* was planned and written, he explains, as a continuation of his *Culture and Society*, which had appeared three years earlier, provoking wide controversy. *Culture and Society* argued against the division of culture between the preferences of a privileged minority on the one hand, and the activities favored by the working class on the other. The reference of the term "culture," Williams insisted, was wider than creative production and recreational activity, but included habits of thought, institutions, the organization of labor, and social relations in their entirety. Thus "a culture is not only a body of intellectual and imaginative work; it is also and essentially a whole way of life."[8] Inequality, class distinction, privilege itself were the real dangers to social well-being. In their place, he urged, "We need a common culture, not for the sake of an abstraction, but because we shall not survive without it."[9]

In more detail, however, the argument paradoxically risks reinstating the very distinction it was designed to overcome. The bourgeois individualist idea of society is currently contested, Williams claims, by two ideas of community. One, the property of the middle class, puts forward the ideal of service as the remedy for division; the other, developed by the working class, relies on solidarity, a commitment to shared interests, "genuine mutual responsibility,"[10] as they

have come to exist in the trade unions, friendly societies and cooper-
atives set up to resist exploitation. This ideal represents the "common culture" that will enable us to survive; this is the "whole"
(meaning entire) way of life that will also make society "whole"
(meaning complete, undivided and, in consequence, healthy).

By thus treating one part of culture as having the capacity to cure
social ills, Williams left open the possibility that his argument could
be seen as no more than partially reversing the terms of Eliot's. Both
regarded culture as remedial, redemptive, but where Eliot favored
the minority, Williams privileged the majority. *The Long Revolution* offers to define culture in three separate ways: first, as a universal ideal,
the record of values which concern the human condition; second, as
a body of intellectual and imaginative work; and third, as a way of life
evident in ordinary behaviour. We should, Williams argues, retain all
three meanings. While it seems improbable that there are "absolute"
standards, he declares, there remain constant ideals that culture can
preserve and transmit:

> For it seems to me to be true that meanings and values, discovered in
> particular societies and by particular individuals, and kept alive by so-
> cial inheritance and by embodiment in particular kinds of work,
> have proved to be universal in the sense that when they are learned,
> in any particular situation, they can contribute radically to the
> growth of man's powers to enrich his life, to regulate his society, and
> to control his environment.[11]

Meanwhile, in the spring of the same key year, 1961, Richard Hoggart was offered a second professorship in English at the University
of Birmingham. He accepted the post on the condition that it included the establishment of a research centre for contemporary cultural studies. Additional resources were secured from the publisher,
Allen Lane of Penguin Books, with further support from the left-of-
centre Sunday paper, the *Observer*, and from Chatto & Windus, who
had also published Raymond Williams. This funded the appointment of Stuart Hall to a senior research post. The Centre for Contemporary Cultural Studies opened early in 1964, and took in its first
Ph.D. students that October.

Cultural studies was now an independent discipline. Other universities were not slow to set up undergraduate degrees, and the rest
is history. In America the development of cultural studies came later
and followed a somewhat different trajectory. There the cultures in

question were more likely to be ethnic than working-class, but once again the discipline defined itself primarily in opposition to the view of culture-as-improvement, and the imposition of the inherited values of a minority on a population whose own values were thereby marginalized or repressed. (If in this essay I concentrate on the story as it occurred in Britain, other contributions to this volume will determine the degree to which it illuminates events elsewhere.)

4

Cultural studies was of necessity interdisciplinary. In the first instance, because its field included aural and visual texts, as well as writings, it rapidly developed new methodologies for reading brass bands and trade-union banners, and then radio and popular music, advertising, film, and television. Second, its most obvious existing academic ally was sociology, which was already considering some of the same material from its own perspective. But there remained, nevertheless, a special institutional and theoretical relationship with English, the discipline cultural studies had broken with in the first instance.

This interrelationship was clearly evident in the early days. Raymond Williams, who must be seen as one of the main founders of cultural studies, had taught English literature in adult education, and went on to become a professor of English at Cambridge, where he remained for the rest of his life. Richard Hoggart's appointment at Birmingham was to a chair of English, and he records in his autobiography that he went on teaching literature in that department, leaving much of the day-to-day work of the Centre for Contemporary Cultural Studies to Stuart Hall.[12] Some of the first products of the Centre were appointed to posts in English departments.[13]

Moreover, Hoggart's own contribution to the work of the Centre at that time was derived from his background in English literature. Hoggart's only quarrel with English was that its field was too narrow. His adult education students had questioned the relevance of the literary canon to their own lives. The Centre for Contemporary Cultural Studies was housed in the English department, and in his inaugural lecture at Birmingham Hoggart set out to make a case for widening the boundaries of English as they were then specified. The sociology of literature and art, he maintained, however informative, had not developed the mode of reading that characterized literary criticism at its best. His own project was to read all texts as astutely as possible, on the basis of "a belief in the power of language itself as the most important indicator of a hold on values."[14]

Furthermore, if they disagreed with T. S. Eliot politically, if they deplored his commitment to privilege and the minority, both Raymond Williams and Richard Hoggart shared an intellectual framework with him, nonetheless. Culture for them too was inscribed in language; certainly, it was everyday, but it was also—and perhaps in consequence—a positive value, and it was to a degree continuous. In Hoggart's account,

> The meanings, the weights, of . . . words and the sense of common assumptions would vary in different periods. Some tones would be available, some not, in each period, and so their meanings would differ from period to period. But all was not historically relative: some words, some weights, would echo down the years and speak to several generations in much the same way.[15]

Raymond Williams had read *Notes Towards the Definition of Culture,* and clearly profited from it. He criticizes Eliot's list of the cultural practices that make life worth living because it leaves out steelmaking, farming, and the stock exchange, but he shares Eliot's hostility to centralized planning, insisting that culture must grow organically. Culture benefits, moreover, Williams argues, from "tending," even while he insists that the project of this tending must be the erasure of division.[16] Meanwhile, T. S. Eliot and his second wife, Valerie, read Richard Hoggart's *The Uses of Literacy* (1957), it appears, in bed.[17] There was evidently a community there, however differentiated.

But if cultural studies was to justify its existence as an independent discipline, these overt connections with English, and with the corresponding problematic in which culture was potentially redemptive, would have in due course to be severed. Since English departments could still be perceived as bearers of the cultural heritage, cultural studies would distinguish itself by concentrating on the present. Hoggart had stressed the "contemporary" at Birmingham because, he says, both he and Stuart Hall found it interesting, because of its relevance to his students in adult education, and because it was neglected in English departments.[18] It is ironic, in view of the stature of Raymond Williams as a cultural historian, that cultural studies in Britain went on to place a more and more exclusive emphasis on the present.

In addition, retaining the populist impulse of the founding figures, but without their specific range of reference in the English classics, cultural studies largely excluded art and literature, and thus reinstated in reverse the division Williams and Hoggart had wanted ultimately to erase. In this way cultural studies retained its autonomy as a field of inquiry, but at the cost of relinquishing in practice the aim of treating culture as a "whole way of life." If cultural studies concerned a whole way of life, it was the way of life attributed, with whatever accuracy, to a segment of society. When in 1961 Raymond Williams offered a case study that would demonstrate the implications of the form of cultural analysis he was proposing, he chose the 1840s, and included among the materials for research *The Times* newspaper, the popular press, Dickens, Thackeray, and the Brontës, popular fiction, pornography, Carlyle, Ruskin, and Arnold, music halls, public libraries, museums, and parks, the repeal of the Corn Laws, the Young England Movement, Chartism, and W. H. Smith's station bookstalls.[19] It would be interesting to see how many more recent cultural studies courses would want to match the range and variety, as well as the historicity, of that list.

Insofar, however, as the new discipline looked to French theory to provide legitimation and a methodology for a new kind of textual analysis, its isolation of contemporary popular culture made very little sense. Roland Barthes was interested in what he identified as bourgeois mythology in its entirety. No Marxist himself, Barthes knew, nevertheless, as Marx and Engels had known, that the ruling ideology is the ideology of the ruling class. When Louis Althusser came to reread Marx, he included both literature and the trade unions among the ideological apparatuses as places where cultural values are shaped.

In practice, moreover, a radical distinction between elite and popular culture does not hold. It is not clear now that the working class is indifferent to artistic practice, for example. Indeed, the tabloid press in Britain proves remarkably vociferous in its evaluation of prize-winning installations at Tate Modern. Baz Luhrmann presented his film of *Romeo and Juliet* (1996) to a majority audience with no necessary literary training. Meanwhile, the middle class do not perceive themselves as slumming when they watch films directed by Martin Scorsese or Quentin Tarantino. The primary motive for the isolation of popular culture in the academy, therefore, would seem to be the preservation of an institutional distinction or, in other words, the integrity of cultural studies as a separate academic discipline.

But that integrity comes into question the moment English departments (and to a lesser degree Art History departments) let go of the corresponding integrity of the canon. Once T. S. Eliot's definition of culture as confined to what is rare, old, and vanishing no longer restricts the content of the English curriculum, the independence of a discipline that emphasizes the popular, new, and everyday is revealed as contingent, derived from the structure of universities rather than the shape of culture itself or, indeed, the motives that prompted its analysis.

And ironically, the energy that informed cultural studies began almost at once to invade the English department itself, with the effect precisely of undermining the idea of the literary canon. English (like Art History) now addresses a much wider range of texts, and embraces signifying practices way outside the narrow canon that existed in 1961. If the theory that cultural studies had drawn on played a part in this development by refusing to recognize any role for the canonical heritage, except as itself a cultural construct and thus an object of knowledge, protagonists of new forms of politics, as committed and as radical as Raymond Williams and Richard Hoggart, came to identify the heritage of privileged minority culture as contributing to the oppression they contested. Within a decade of 1961, feminism had denounced the canon for its masculinity. In due course, its whiteness and its heterosexual bias would also be unmasked. Forgotten writings by women, slaves, homosexuals, would take their place in the English curriculum. In America anthropology exerted a major influence on the "cultural poetics" of New Historicism, bringing hitherto obscure texts to the fore. Moreover, the isolation of written material itself began to seem arbitrary. But ultimately, if English invaded virtually every area of the humanities, including the terrain of cultural studies, it was on the model of cultural studies itself that it did so. The movement that Williams, Hoggart, and others inaugurated, and French theory facilitated, was unstoppable.

5

English has swelled above its own banks. No longer purely English if, indeed, it ever was, it is no longer purely literary either. Recent developments have done much to erase the line between English and its surrounding disciplines. Literary scholars are now required to be not only historians, but also interpreters of materials other than written texts: paintings, portraits, monuments, rituals, dramatic performances, cityscapes, and all the materials of everyday life. Meanwhile, cultural studies, driven by this expansion ever closer to sociology in order to affirm its own distinctive character, has progressively shifted its attention away from close reading of culture's inscription at the level of the signifier. And both disciplines have tended to neglect the French theory that initially facilitated their expansion.

After opening up whole new worlds of possibility in the 1970s, at Birmingham, in the pages of *Screen*, at the Essex conferences, and elsewhere, theory elicited a predictable backlash. E. P. Thompson, one of the heroes of cultural studies in its early days, famously denounced Althusser; *Screen*, which had so brilliantly drawn out the implications of French theory for English-speaking readers in the 1970s, reasserted a populist distrust of high theory after 1980; Terry Eagleton went on to repudiate the theory that had made his reputation.

Meanwhile, paradoxically, a version of "theory" was in the process of becoming institutionalized. In English departments, theory courses were suddenly de rigueur, but for that very reason, they were often taught by people who had very little interest in the subject. Introductions proliferated, but they were often written by people who were not in sympathy with French theory. Initially of interest in both disciplines because of its attention to the signifier, as well as to the project, glimpsed as an option in the *Course in General Linguistics*, of studying the signs of a whole society,[20] theory gradually morphed into a succession of "isms," the recitation of a list of assorted "approaches." In this incarnation, "theory" now meant no more than the relentless forward march of formalism, structuralism, Marxism, feminism, poststructuralism, postmodernism, all treated as objects of knowledge. True, there were welcome new fields of study—feminist, postcolonial, queer. But these did not of themselves entail any necessary alteration in the perception of the relationship between the reader and the signifier. They were indeed "approaches," but quite distinct from theory as an account of the relation between human beings and the signifying practice that constitutes them as human. In other cases, "theory" became a form of philosophy for nonphilosophers, and English specialists began to pronounce knowingly on topics like ethics and aesthetics.

In such a climate, cultural studies was propelled even more firmly toward the methodology of the social sciences with a view to preserving its own difference. Indeed, in 1988 the Birmingham Centre for Contemporary Cultural Studies moved out of English and into the Faculty of Social Science. A handful of stalwarts in each discipline continued to pursue the opportunities French theory had made available, and some, indeed, crossed the demarcation line that had divided them from each other. We might think in this context of Edward Said, Gayatri Spivak, Marjorie Garber, and Slavoj Žižek, among others. Elsewhere, however, theory simply failed to deliver what it had promised, not in consequence of its own inadequacies, nor, ironically, of reactionary opposition, but thanks to repressive tolerance instead.

6

What is to be done? Not, I think, a "rescue" of one or other discipline, or theory, in the manner of T. S. Eliot. And not, though I should prefer to take them as role models, a halfhearted disciplinary breakaway in the manner of Raymond Williams and Richard Hoggart, whose altogether honorable desire to expand the narrow limits of their subject was formulated in terms that left open the possibility of institutionalizing the very division they had wanted to erase. But a new discipline, just the same, which would go beyond both literature and cultural studies, would treat all culture as its province, and would take full advantage of the attention French theory pays to the signifier. Let us call it Cultural Criticism.

Cultural Criticism would have no place for the residual definition of culture as improvement. When an anthropologist studies the way of life of a tribe in the rainforest, he or she does not make value judgments about the quality or lasting worth of the beads or face-painting techniques. What is at issue is an understanding of their meaning and place in that society. In practice, the old definition is unlikely to detain us now. Even in 1976 Raymond Williams pointed out that the use of the term *culture* to identify an object of aspiration tended to elicit hostility, whereas the anthropological use of the word caused no embarrassment.[21]

Cultural Criticism, then, would treat "culture" as genuinely synonymous with "the whole way of life," without attributing any residual properties of healing to that word, "whole." It would regard as outmoded the view that culture was usefully subjected to a single, binary dividing line separating "high" and popular tastes, and it would not exclude a priori either opera or Disneyland, poetry, or pushpin. But it would not in consequence regard culture as all one, or homogeneous. On the contrary, if Cultural Criticism directed its gaze in the first instance to the critic's own cultural context, in order to leave ethnology to the ethnologists, it would not make the mistake of supposing that we can any longer justify confining "culture" to the singular form of the word. In the light of globalization on the one hand, and multiculturalism on the other, very few of us can be said to belong to one sole culture, or to possess a single, unified "identity." Instead, we mostly occupy a range of positions as subjects in and to a variety of cultural practices. We speak, in other words, more than one "language" or, at least, more than one dialect, and it follows that we share more than one allegiance. Diversity would replace division.

This new discipline would not privilege either present or past. The centrality of the contemporary for analysts of culture surely goes without saying. But history too is important, not for the transmission of inherited values, but because without it we cannot have a due sense of the relativity of our own moment. A knowledge of the past throws into relief the difference of the present. It also demonstrates that change is inevitable, and in the process makes clear that things do not have to be as they currently are. History therefore gives grounds for hope to those groups whose contribution to the direction of change has been marginalized or repressed; it shows the importance of intervention to bring about the changes we want.

Above all, Cultural Criticism would take seriously the contribution of theory to our understanding of the signifying practice that constitutes the inscription of culture. An account of the signified, meaning, thematic content, is not enough, if we are to understand the dangerous convictions and commitments that will certainly play a part in the power struggles of the twenty-first century, just as National Socialism and collaboration did in the twentieth. The signifier itself enlists, seduces, excludes, represses, betrays, and reinscribes people's hopes, dreams, and desires.

This, in my view, is what distinguishes theory from traditional philosophy: theory concerns the signifier; we might see it as theory of and for Cultural Criticism. Lacanian psychoanalysis has given us access to the duplicity of signification, its elusiveness and difficulty. Psychoanalysis illuminates culture not so much as a content, a story of behavior and its motives, but more as a way of attending to what is apparently not stated, and yet made clear in spite of that, to an astute listener or spectator. It is probably the most highly developed mode of close reading we have. Moreover, psychoanalysis has developed the study of the position offered to a reader or audience by the mode of address of the text itself. Cultural Criticism would attend to the seductive capabilities of what the signifier *does*, as well as what it says, but it would also take account in the process of the proposition that no text can determine in advance its own interpretation. What we are able to find in it may not be what it set out to say. Deconstruction, meanwhile, points to the trace of the excluded other that necessarily returns to disrupt the homogeneity of the selfsame. No position, however apparently fixed and resolute, can fully negate the alternative it so remorselessly repudiates. Textuality as the inscription of culture is opaque, unruly, wayward, elusive. We shall read better, and to better effect, if we draw on the instruments French theory has made available for teasing out the nuances, the subtleties, and the evasions of the signifying practices that make us the cultural subjects we are.

The project is absurdly ambitious, it is true: cultures in the plural, global, and ethnic, past and present; theories in the plural, too, of course, as they develop; and all signifying practice with no a priori exclusions, entailing reading skills appropriate to writing, speech, images, music . . . . No individual could possibly do it.

Exactly! At last knowledge would become explicitly collective. There are a good many of us and, assuming the planet survives, we have a fair amount of time ahead. A number of people are already doing work of the kind I have sketched, but under a range of headings. We have only to call it Cultural Criticism, and carry on. If theory is right in asserting the primacy of the signifier, the new name will also initiate a new beginning.

NOTES

1. *Editors' Note:* The term *Cultural Criticism* is here being spelled with the first letters of its respective words in uppercase, in order to signal more clearly the disciplinary entity to which it refers and thereby avoid any ambiguity involving its alternative sense as an adjectival phrase. Terms designating other disciplines in this essay, as in this volume generally, are mostly spelled with their first letter in lowercase.

2. T. S. Eliot, *Notes Towards the Definition of Culture* (London: Faber and Faber, 1962), 7.

3. Ibid., 16.

4. Ibid., 14, 31, 17.

5. Ibid., 19.

6. Ibid., 27.

7. Ibid., 31.

8. Raymond Williams, *Culture and Society 1780–1950* (Harmondsworth: Penguin, 1958), 311.

9. Ibid., 304.

10. Ibid., 319.

11. Raymond Williams, *The Long Revolution* (Harmondsworth: Penguin, 1965), 59.

12. Richard Hoggart, *An Imagined Life, Life and Times, Volume III: 1959–91* (London: Chatto & Windus, 1992), 97–98.

13. Ibid., 91–92.

14. Ibid., 93.

15. Ibid, 93–94.

16. Williams, *Culture and Society*, 224–38.

17. Hoggart, *An Imagined Life*, 73

18. Ibid., 94.

19. Williams, *The Long Revolution*, 70–88.

20. Ferdinand de Saussure, *Course in General Linguistics*, ed. Charles Bally and Albert Sechehaye in collaboration with Albert Riedlinger, trans. Wade Baskin, rev. ed. (London: Fontana, 1974), 16.

21. Raymond Williams, *Keywords: A Vocabulary of Culture and Society* (London: Fontana, 1976), 82.

What is a False Interpretation?

Jean-Jacques Lecercle

INTRODUCTION

IN THE COURSE OF ITS DEVELOPMENT, "THEORY," IN ORDER TO MAP out its territory, has not only produced whole arrays of new concepts, but also discarded old and venerable ones. Such is the case of interpretation. In several instances, theory can be said to have conceived its strategies in opposition to interpretation. One remembers, for instance, Deleuze and Guattari's notorious hostility to interpretation, and their slogan "never interpret, always experiment": the butt of their critique is of course psychoanalytical interpretation.[1] But the same attitude can be found in Pierre Macherey, who in his *Theory of Literary Production* (1966) contrasts "interpretation" with "explication" and chooses the latter: the sin of interpretation, in this case, is that it is looking for a fullness of meaning, and therefore always states less than the interpreted text (since its product is, hopefully, shorter than the original text), but also more (since it is able to say what the text conceals).[2]

This attitude, which smacks of the tactics of forcible separation, has a cost: it takes the word "interpretation" in a restricted acceptation, and therefore erects a scarecrow, the better to tilt at it. Yet it obviously has a certain rationale: it seeks to avoid a number of philosophical traps into which the tradition of hermeneutics falls, not least the facility of too wide and too liberal a concept of interpretation.

The aim of this paper is not to abandon the constructions of theory, but to test them. I shall look again at the central problem—or paradox—that theory, in the twin fields of culture and literature, seeks to address: how can we block the wild multiplication of readings which philosophical anarchism, of the "anything goes" type, allows us to produce, without returning to the authoritarianism of transcendent truth (that is, there is only one reading, or interpretation, the true one, however such truth is defined)? My thesis, stated tentatively at this point, is that no interpretation is true, but some are false.

Which means that I shall unashamedly keep the old term. I like the fact that it belongs to common parlance; I also like the width of its semantic range, and in particular its systematic ambiguity between result (*an* interpretation is the product of our reading of a text) and process (interpretation is dynamic: an ongoing process). But since I do not wish to fall back into the traps of providing the answers before questions have been asked (this is the gist of Deleuze and Guattari's attack on psychoanalysis), or of aiming at full meaning (in other words, my "interpretation" may well include Macherey's "explication"), I need to make my position explicit through seven philosophical theses, which may amount to a theory of interpretation.[3]

Thesis 1 is pragmatist. It states that interpretation is not concerned with truth (since this is my main thesis, it will be developed later). I seek to do without the transcendence, or guarantee of truth, by which theorists of interpretation usually seek to block the anarchism of "anything goes."

Thesis 2 is an anti-Platonist thesis, inspired by Deleuze: it states that interpretation is not a form of representation. Following Deleuze, it seeks to escape the "dominant image of thought," characterized by the centrality of representation. What exactly does this mean in the field of interpretation? The *process* of interpretation can denote four different types of activity:

> *glossing* (explicating the text in the sense of understanding its language and adding footnotes to clarify the encyclopedia it draws upon);
>
> *guessing* (here the text is treated as a riddle, whose meaning, the *true* meaning, is disclosed by a clever interpreter—I call this practice the "tin opener": when the layer of metal is peeled off, I can tuck into the luscious sardines);
>
> *translation* (the translation of a text into a theoretical language that gives purchase on it and allows me to construct an interpretation);

intervention, where interpretation is a *coup de force*, provoked by the text, which exerts its force upon the interpreter, but the final goal of which is the text, which is modified by the interpretation.

It is clear that the two intermediate stages, "tin opening" and translation, belong to the realm of representation: whether interpretation is true and unique, or constructed and multiple, riddle solving and translation provide images of the text. Only the last stage, intervention, takes us away from representation, following the Deleuzean slogan: "no metaphors, only metamorphoses."

Thesis 3 goes back to the doxic concept of interpretation as a truth-seeking and truth-finding process. The *doxa*, as exemplified by E. D. Hirsch,[4] is that the true interpretation yields the meaning of the text, and that the source of this meaning is the author's intention of meaning. Against this, thesis 3 is anti-intentionalist. It states that the original author's meaning is, in most cases, lost and therefore unknowable, but also constitutively irrelevant, because of the constitutive gap between intention and expression. Misunderstanding is not an accident, but a constitutive possibility of human communication. What this thesis owes to Derrida is clear.

Thesis 4 takes me into the field of the philosophy of language. It states that there is an analogy, or an extended metaphor, between face-to-face interlocution, as captured in the usual diagrams of communication (for instance, Jakobson's celebrated diagram)[5] and literary communication between author and reader through the medium of the text. Interpretation is a form of interlocution: it is one of the family of language games of interlocution, involving the same participants. This thesis is pragmatic in the linguistic sense: it is inspired by the work of Austin, Searle, and Grice, which is not the case with the next one.

Thesis 5 states that communication is not dialogue, that it does not consist in the emission, transmission, and recovery of meaning. My main intuition is that, in what we call dialogue, as in textual interpretation, we do not address the addressee but the representation we construct of her. Since such representations are mental, the addressee has no access to them, except through their inscription in the text as images.[6] Understanding somebody in dialogue is always interpreting a text. Hence the direction of my analogy, which is unusual in that it is the literary situation that provides a model for everyday dialogue.

Thesis 6 draws consequences from thesis 5. It operates a reversal in the usual model of communication. The centre is no longer the two interacting subjects, the sender and the receiver, the author and the reader, but the text, the only element in the situation that does not only exist, but persists. And it no longer deals with the subjects as persons, but as personae, roles, *actants* (to speak like Greimas),[7] or places (to speak like Flahault)[8]—the speech acts are no longer the products of individual subjects, but of collective assemblages of enunciation, of the text or of language itself (in *The Violence of Language*, I have attempted, through the concept of "the remainder," to develop the Heideggerian idea that it is language that speaks).[9]

Thesis 7 considers the distance taken from analytic speech-act theory or theories of communication and dialogue. It operates a Nietzschean or Marxist displacement by reinterpreting the transmission of information in terms of the impulsion of forces. In a way this is being faithful to Austin's concept of the performative, but it goes further. If communication is impulsion of force rather than exchange of information, then it is the site for the Althusserian interpellation of individuals into subjects.

My seven theses may be summed up by a passage from Foucault, which neatly anticipates them:

> We might have reached the moment when we ought to consider discourse not under its linguistic aspect, but—here I draw my inspiration from Anglo-Saxon philosophers—as a series of *games*, strategic games of action and reaction, question and answer, domination and avoidance, in short of struggle. A discourse is at one level a regular set of linguistic data, at another of polemical and strategic elements. Such an analysis of discourse as strategic and polemical games, constitutes my second direction of research.[10]

ILLUSTRATION

Since this is a little too abstract, let us consider a concrete case of interpretation. In 1990, one Richard Wallace published a book called *The Agony of Lewis Carroll*.[11] His thesis is simple: Charles Dodgson was secretly gay, repressed by the moral and legal climate of Victorian Britain, and forced to express his sexuality in Aesopic language, in the shape of nonsense. He then proceeds, in order to prove his thesis, to give an interpretation of Carroll's work.

A number of things must be noted about this:

1. Lewis Carroll must have been *very* repressed: there is no hint in his works, correspondence, or his contemporaries' account of him that suggests that he was gay. Such an argument, however, has no validity for me: Lewis Carroll is what the text allows us to construct.

2. The interpretation is not improbable in our conjuncture (indeed, one has the feeling that it would inevitably have been attempted some day): the development of gay and queer studies is part of our critical *doxa*.

3. The historical hypothesis is not lacking in verisimilitude: think of what happened to Wilde. No wonder Dodgson's sexual orientation remained strictly secret.

4. Nonsense is a good candidate for the Aesopic expression of a repressed sexuality. There is a passage in Freud,[12] where he claims that nonsense words are fragments of repressed sexual words. That there is an undercurrent of sexual energy in the *Alice* books is clear.

5. However, what the text induces us to construct for the figure of its author is not a homosexual position: it is the position of a heterosexual adult hopelessly in love with a little girl. A terrible ghost is raised here: that of the pedophile, the contemporary version of the devil. This is why this interpretation, which is traditional and authoritative, is more difficult to sustain at present—even though it is strongly present in the text, as in all sorts of peritexts (for instance Lewis Carroll's letters to his child friends). I shall be content with quoting one passage in the text to support my argument. At the very end of the first tale, Alice's sister is thinking about Alice, who has run away: "She could hear the very tones of her voice, and see that queer little toss of her head to keep back the wandering hair that *would* always get into her eyes."[13] Am I wrong to read this as an instance of amorous crystallization? The automatic gesture of the beloved is infinitely charming to the lover, who may well be the only one to have noticed it, and is certainly the only one to be enthralled by it.

6. It is, however, when we get to the detail of Wallace's interpretation that things go radically wrong. He is an enthusiastic tin opener, and the tool he uses to open the tin is the same as Saussure's: anagrams.[14] I shall only give two examples.

(a) The exact title of the second *Alice* tale is: *Through the Looking-Glass, and What Alice Found There.* This, you would hardly have guessed, is the anagram for: *Look with a lens through the cute darling, he's a fag don.*

(b) In *The Hunting of the Snark*, there is a famous line in Fit the Second that describes the method of navigation of the boat on which the heroes have embarked: "Then the bowsprit got mixed with the rudder sometimes." This is an anagram of (again: would you have guessed?): *To Mother: Disturbed, I themed the worst pig-sex with men.* Wallace adds that *theme* is a valid Victorian verb. Two conclusions may be risked on this. Wallace's interpretation is more than bizarre: it is the product of a typical *fou littéraire*. But his "demented" interpretation is also, in a way, faithful to Carroll's own practice, since Carroll's works contain innumerable games played with language, including mirror-image readings, acrostics, and indeed anagrams.

7. In *Interpretation as Pragmatics* (1999), I deal with another *fou littéraire*. Abraham Ettleson, a Jewish surgeon and member of the Hasidic sect, who sought to demonstrate, by a similar method, that Carroll was a secret Jew. Take the name *Jabberwocky* for instance, and read it in the mirror, as Alice herself does: the result is *Rebbaj Ickow* (Rabbi Jacob, the founder of Hasidism).

My argument is that such bizarre, even "demented" readings are (a) readings of the text (they actually engage with it); (b) readings up to a point faithful to the text (Ettleson is no worse than Humpty-Dumpty, in his close reading of the poem "Jabberwocky"); (c) readings that betray the text by forcing its language (anagrams are always indefinitely possible—that is how language works—but historically constrained) or forcing its encyclopedia (which is clearly what both Wallace and Ettleson are doing). But encyclopedias change, and language is indefinitely equivocal. In order to account for this complex situation, I suggest the following four theses about interpretation as result, loosely inspired by the philosophy of Nelson Goodman:

Four theses on interpretation:

Thesis 1: No interpretation is true.

Thesis 2: All interpretations are possible.

Thesis 3: Some interpretations are false.

Thesis 4: And some are just.

The terms used, and the order in which the theses appear, are deliberate. The whole set of theses, of course, revolves round the distinction between the true and the just, which comes from Althusser.[15] And it is no chance if the first thesis is a negative proposition. I shall take them in order.

Thesis 1: No interpretation is true. This thesis derives from my pragmatist stand. The problem with truth in the field of interpretation is that the concept has unwelcome characteristics. Truth has a natural tendency to be unique, stable if not eternal, and universal. And I want to defend a concept of *valid* interpretations that are multiple, bound to a historical conjuncture and bound to specific language games. Please note that this is not a relativist position: I deny the existence of truth for the language game of interpretation, which does not mean that other language games (I am thinking, of course, of the hard sciences) do not have a crucial need of a concept of truth.

And, as I have already hinted, this thesis will also mark an anti-intentionalist position, since the doxic account of truth in interpretation makes truth a function of the author's intention of meaning: there is only one true interpretation of a text (one that is unique, definitive, and universal), the interpretation that recovers the author's intention of meaning. We understand why the *doxa* naturally speaks in terms of creator, creation, and creativity in aesthetic matters: the natural ultimate source of truth is God, and the author is a smaller version of God.

Thesis 2: All interpretations are possible. On the face of it, this looks singularly like the "anything goes" of philosophical anarchism (derived from Feyerabend). It appears to provide a definition of interpretation that is far too wide. This is indeed a liberal thesis (we do not want to constrain the free play of interpretations), but not as liberal as it sounds. Since "interpretation" is a relational concept, the thesis excludes all so-called interpretations that are not interpretations of a specific text, that do not engage with it, but merely use it as a pretext for just one more exposition of a theoretical dogma. This, in the profession of literary and cultural criticism as it is practiced nowadays, excludes many attempts at so-called interpretation.

Thesis 3: Some interpretations are false. This is meant to provide the protection from anarchism we need (this is also the subject of this essay). So, some interpretations are possible not only in that they have empirical existence, but also in that they are *about* the text. Nevertheless, they must be rejected: not because they fail to conform with the author's intention of meaning, or because the author would not have understood them (think, for instance, of a Lacanian reading of a play by Shakespeare), but for two reasons.

The first is that some interpretations, as we have seen, betray the text, because they betray its language (I include in this the obsessive search for anagrams, as well as instances of gross anachronism). They are simply *erroneous*: the interpreter has not done his homework, he has not acquired the relevant philological or historical culture. There are limits to this: I am not at all certain that all anachronistic interpretations are devoid of interest, or false (in a sense, a Lacanian interpretation of Shakespeare is necessarily anachronistic).

The second reason is that some interpretations are simply *delirious*, or *absurd*, in that they ignore the constraints of the encyclopedia (the encyclopedia of the conjuncture of interpretation, but also the encyclopedia of the conjuncture of writing). Thus, our current encyclopedia tells me that Lewis Carroll (for I care little for Charles Lutwidge Dodgson) was a lover of little girls, who did not write *Alex in Wonderland*, with all the difficulties this may cause in these our morally correct times (except of course that authors, being constructions of interpretations, can hardly be practicing pedophiles). The limitations of this analysis are only too obvious: encyclopedias change with the historical conjuncture. Today, Ettleson's Jewish reading of Carroll is plainly delirious. The *Alice* text could only be a cryptogram of the Talmud by a special dispensation of God, a miracle of grace accomplished by the God of the Jews. Nothing guarantees that in two generations a religiously correct encyclopedia will not accept this possibility as a matter of course. In fact, my real criticism of the interpretations of Wallace and Ettleson is not so much that they are delirious (I have a fondness for such straying away from the well-plowed furrow), but that they are doxic: Wallace and Ettleson are too predictable in their interpretation, in that they seek to impose upon us what their chosen section of the encyclopedia impels them to look for in the text (and as we all know, the greatest danger to interpretation is that if we look hard enough for what we want to find, we shall always find it: I have no doubt I could construct an interpretation of Carroll as a secret Leninist or a Corsican nationalist).

Thesis 4: Some interpretations are just. It is important that the negative thesis should come first. Once we have weeded out erroneous and delirious, but possible interpretations, all the interpretations that remain are just. Justice in interpretation is a matter of subtraction, not a positive essence, like truth. Just interpretations are interpretations that accept the constraints of the text, of its language and encyclopedia, as well as the constraints of the language and encyclopedia of the interpreter. Such interpretations are not only multiple, they are indefinitely so. There is always a new and just interpretation of a text round the corner.

Assessment of the Illustration

Wallace's and Ettleson's are *possible* interpretations, insofar as they actually engage with the text, as we saw. The test of this is that they do to the text no more than it does to itself (for instance through the character of Humpty-Dumpty): their reading techniques are often explicitly evoked in the text itself. As we say in French: *il y a provocation.* And Lewis Carroll is on record as saying that he was not responsible for the meaning of his text, being merely the author.

But their interpretations, pleasant as they are (certainly more so than the common run of academic readings), must be said to be false, being either erroneous (Wallace takes anagrams to unacceptable extremes), or delirious (Ettleson goes against the grain of the encyclopedia; Wallace somewhat distorts it, even if he leans on it).

Let us take a closer look at Wallace's interpretation, and what is wrong with it. It is false because it has a twofold relation to truth. Wallace believes in his hypothesis, and this belief imposes itself upon him as an incontrovertible truth (I leave aside the possibility that Wallace is in fact a hoaxer). He also believes in the truth of his results, of what he found because he was looking for it. This redoubling of the truth of interpretation (truth of the theory, or hypothesis that inspires the interpretation; truth of the result that it yields) smacks of Freudian denial: so an interpretation is false because of its excessive appeal to truth, whereby it betrays the text and/or its encyclopedia. In the case of Wallace, this is only too obvious. Not content with his extraordinary interpretation of Carroll, he published a second book (*fous littéraires* are usually afflicted with a compulsion of repetition), in which he "demonstrated," through the usual means that Lewis Carroll was . . . Jack the Ripper.[16] I shall only quote the end of the blurb: " 'Off with their heads!' cried the hateful Queen of Hearts. Would this become the finally explosive means of retribution for an early life of emotional and sexual abuse by a man never able to escape childhood?" The blurb ends on this description of the author, upon which I do not think I need comment: "The author provides psychotherapy to help children overcome the damaging and potentially explosive effects of physical, emotional, and sexual abuse." Having dismissed Wallace's and Ettleson's interpretations as false, I must go on to state that no interpretation of Lewis Carroll is true, not even mine (it costs me a lot to have to confess this).

And what, then, is a just interpretation? Here I shall take the famous example of William Empson's essay, "The Child as Swain."[17] And I do not want to argue that this interpretation, coming from a reputed academic who at the end of his career was Professor of English at the University of Sheffield, is just because it is authorized (although it certainly helps: I leave you to devise cynical, Bourdieu-like developments of this argument for yourselves). I want to argue that the *text* of Empson's interpretation is just.

At first sight, however, his text is as delirious as Wallace's or Ettleson's: it is full of pleasing but outrageous suggestions. Here is Empson on the Gnat, who in *Through the Looking-Glass* (1871) bothers Alice with his feeble jokes and melancholy: "A certain ghoulishness in the atmosphere of this, of which tight-lacing may have been a produce or a potential cause, comes out very strongly in Henry James."[18] The mind boggles (and I love the modal auxiliary). But it may well be jogged into thought (we remember what Deleuze said: people hardly ever think, and they only do so when violently jogged into it— thought is the result of violence). Let us take, therefore, another passage, where Empson claims that the feeling about children evinced in the *Alice* books is linked to the end of dueling:

> The child has not yet been put wrong by civilization, and all grown-ups have been. It may well be true that Dodgson envied the child because it was sexless, and Wordsworth because he knew that he was destroying his native poetry by the smugness of his life, but neither theory explains why this feeling about children arose when it did and became so general. There is much of it in Vaughan after the Civil War, but as a general tendency it appeared when the eighteenth century settlement had come to seem narrow and unescapable; one might connect it with the end of duelling.[19]

What on earth has dueling to do with *Alice in Wonderland?* But, come to think of it, it does. Once jogged into thought, the interpreter's mind establishes connections, *in* the text, *with* the encyclopedia:

(a) There are a number of fights in the *Alice* books: between Tweedledum and Tweedledee, the White and the Red Knights, the Lion and the Unicorn: a schoolyard fight, a tournament and a fight

74   DISCIPLINE AND PRACTICE

to the death so ritualized that it allows "ten minutes for refresh-
ments" and looks like a boxing bout.

(b) Those fights are very close to duels: they have that thoroughly
conventionalized, even ritualized character. This is what Tweedledum says to Tweedledee: "Of course you agree to have a battle?" And
this is Tweedledee's doubtful answer: "I suppose so."[20]

(c) Those fights have not only the ritualized aspect, but also the
pointlessness of duels, together with the feelings such pointlessness
encourages: a feeling of inevitability ("We *must* have a bit of a fight,
but I don't care about going on long"— this is Tweedledum),[21] and
the sad passion of cowardice (Tweedledee is like the hero of a Mau-
passant short story, who commits suicide rather than appear in the
field). In short, all these fights, like duels, are governed by the law of
honor, which must be satisfied—whatever the participants' lack of
enthusiasm, or worse.

(d) Duels play a large part in George Mosse's book on the image
of masculinity and its construction in nineteenth- and twentieth-century Europe.[22] He claims that if duels vanished in Great Britain at the
beginning of the nineteenth century, in striking contrast with what
happened in Germany or France, it is because the values of honor
and chivalry embodied in the duel were integrated into a more hu-
mane and more moral behavior (this is in essence Empson's claim),
in the guise of fair play and respectability. Two institutions inherited
the humanized ritual violence of the duel: sport (as the playing fields
of Eton, where the battle of Waterloo famously was won) and the ritualized agon of the debate (as, for instance, in trials).

(e) We note that, in the *Alice* books, duels involve male characters,
and that those characters are objects of ridicule: they are cowardly
and ineffectual, their encounters always end in stalemate. And sport
and trials are treated no better than duels. The Caucus race, the
game of croquet, the trial of the Knave of Hearts are all caricatures:
they are not governed by fixed rules, the proceedings are unjust or il-
logical, they founder in a state of generalized chaos, pregnant with
potential violence.

(f) In fact, in the *Alice* books, the world of masculinity is mocked
and belittled. Men, or male creatures, are at best ineffectual, at worst
cowardly. We all know who, in the royal couple, wears the trousers:
Wonderland is a matriarchy. We can compare this to *Tom Brown's
Schooldays* (1857) by Thomas Hughes, with its character-strengthen-
ing roasting of the hero's toes.

(g) The *Alice* books, therefore, have indeed something to do with dueling, and Empson's apparently outrageous pronouncement *can* be justified: the books are sites for the deconstruction of the nineteeth-century image of masculinity. Such interpretation (for this entails a reading of the whole text, and not just fragments) is vastly different from Wallace's (who insists on Dodgson's repressed homosexuality and the explosive rage that it provoked in his mind, to the point of turning him into a serial killer), but it covers a similar ground. The difference, however, is that Empson does not betray the text, or its language: he brings together in an easy and unforced manner a host of passages. In doing so, he casts new light on their meaning—he illuminates the text, provokes in the reader (and, in the view of the remarkable survival of Empson's essay, in generations of readers) the exhilaration of the riddle solved, the joke understood, the rule of grammar grasped. The most important point is that such interpretation respects both Carroll's encyclopedia (there is historical corroboration, as appears in the results of Mosse's research) and our encyclopedia: it is, for instance, entirely compatible with our current reading of the text as an Aesopic love letter to a little girl. None of this, of course, depends on the academic position of the critic, or the respectability of his publisher.

This is, therefore, what a just interpretation is. In the immortal words of Heineken, it reaches parts of the text other interpretations do not reach: it recontextualizes the text, gives it a new lease of life. And yet it is a servant of the text: it is constrained by it—it is the text that allows its own recontextualization. In plain terms, there is a certain quality in the text. I am prepared to defend the old-fashioned practice of critical judgment, albeit in relativist and agonistic terms, not in essentialist terms of adequacy of the interpretation to the truth of full meaning. And I think we also understand why certain interpretations, which are obviously false (in that they betray the text) are nevertheless enjoyable: for Wallace's interpretation, too, reaches unheard-of parts of the text, albeit in an illicit and indiscriminate manner. But, demented as they undoubtedly are, *fous littéraires* always have intuitions on the workings of the text: the unrestrained practice of anagrams, for instance, draws our attention to the philosophy of language implicit in Carroll's text, a philosophy of language that both anticipates Chomsky and refutes him in advance.[23]

Conclusion

In conclusion, I would like to make the philosophical underpinnings of my notion of interpretive "justice" more explicit, and go back to the question of theory, which was my starting point.

There are two philosophical origins for the distinction between the true and the just, beyond Althusser's text, which I mentioned earlier. The first is the replacement, in pragmatist philosophers from Goodman to Rorty, of truth with justification. The vestigial presence of the word *truth* in my theses, where it appears under negation, is my contribution to the general anti-Platonism of pragmatist philosophers, my way of invoking the celebrated dichotomies in order to discard them. This is why my theses are constructed around the apparent contradiction of "some interpretations are false" versus "none is true."

The second source is an intuition to be found in Hobbes's *Leviathan*, in chapter 14, which deals with natural laws and contracts:

> So that *Injury*, or *Injustice*, in the controversies of the world, is somewhat like to that, which in the disputations of scholars is called *Absurdity*. For as it is there called an Absurdity, to contradict what one maintained in the Beginning: so in the world, it is called Injustice, and Injury, voluntarily to undo that, which from the beginning he had voluntarily done.[24]

I like the tropic movement from the organization of society, in terms of Justice and Injustice, to the structure of discourse, in terms of Sense and Absurdity. What the trope allows me to do is to think of discourse in terms of contract, with oneself (as the end of the passage suggests) and with others. So that, if we think in those terms, interpretations occur within the terms of a contract (I call this, after Wittgenstein, a language-game), and a false interpretation is in breach of contract. But a contract is a reflection of social practice, not of the laws of nature: it can be adapted, modified, renegotiated, as the text is recontextualized. This yields a definition of justice in interpretation: justice is the equivalent of what philosophers have always called truth, but deprived of its main characteristics (uniqueness, stability, universality): truths-in-a-conjuncture if you like, or truths-within-a-language-game. You understand why interpretation qua process can never be content with glossing, guessing, and translating, why it must involve intervention.

And we also understand, I think, the specific responsibility of theory, in the period of its institutionalization. For theory is, in a sense, responsible for Wallace's false interpretation, which is inconceivable without the existence of a body of psychoanalytic criticism and the development of gay and queer theory. But it is also theory which, by allowing us to construct a concept of interpretation that avoids the usual pitfalls, enables us to discard Wallace's interpretation, but also to understand why it has appeared and how it works. Theory (this is an argument that has its origin in Spinoza) is not content with denouncing the negativity of error, it also seeks to account for its positivity, that is its necessity.

NOTES

1. The most explicit site of this critique is a little-known pamphlet where Deleuze and Guattari read Freud's "Little Hans" case: Gilles Deleuze and Félix Guattari, *Politique et psychanalyse* (Paris: Des mots perdus, 1977).

2. Pierre Macherey, *A Theory of Literary Production*, trans. Geoffrey Wall (London: Routledge and Kegan Paul, 1978), 75–81.

3. I have developed such a theory of interpretation in my *Interpretation as Pragmatics* (New York: St. Martin's Press, 1999).

4. E. D. Hirsch, *Validity in Interpretation* (New Haven: Yale University Press, 1967).

5. Roman Jakobson, "Closing Statement: Linguistics and Poetics," in *Style in Language,* ed. Thomas A. Sebeok, (Cambridge: MIT Press, 1960), 353–58.

6. I am using the vocabulary of the Swiss logician J.-B. Grize: see his *Logique naturelle et communication* (Paris: Presses Universitaires de France, 1996).

7. A.-J. Greimas, *Sémantique structurale* (Paris: Larousse, 1966).

8. François Flahault, *La Parole intermédiaire* (Paris: Seuil, 1978).

9. Jean-Jacques Lecercle, *The Violence of Language* (London: Routledge, 1990).

10. Michel Foucault, *Dits et écrits*, 4 vols. (Paris: Gallimard, 1994), 2:539 (my translation).

11. Richard Wallace, *The Agony of Lewis Carroll* (Melrose, Mass.: Gemini Press, 1990).

12. Sigmund Freud, *The Standard Edition of the Complete Psychological Work of Sigmund Freud*, vols. 4 and 5 (*The Interpretaton of Dreams*, Pts. 1 and 2), trans. James Strachey (London: Hogarth Press, 1953–74), 4:296–300, 302–4; 5:356, 441–3.

13. Lewis Carroll, *The Annotated Alice*, definitive ed., with an introduction and notes by Michael Gardner (London: Penguin, 2001), 131.

14. See Jean Starobinski, *Words upon Words: The Anagrams of Ferdinand Saussure*, trans. Olivia Emmet (New Haven: Yale University Press, 1979).

15.   See Louis Althusser, *Philosophie et philosophie spontanée des savants* (1967; Paris: Maspero, 1974), 50–59. [Louis Althusser, *Philosophy and the Spontaneous Philosophy of Scientists and Other Essays*, ed. Gregory Elliott, trans. Ben Brewster and others (London: Verso, 1990)]

16.   Richard Wallace, *Jack the Ripper, "Light-hearted friend"* (Melrose, Mass.: Gemini Press, 1997).

17.   William Empson, "The Child as Swain," in *Some Versions of Pastoral: A Study of the Pastoral Form in Literature* (1935; Harmondsworth, Penguin, 1966), 201–33.

18.   Ibid., 223.

19.   Ibid., 208.

20.   Carroll, *The Annotated Alice*, 200.

21.   Ibid., 201.

22.   George Mosse, *Images of Man: The Creation of Modern Masculinity* (New York: Oxford University Press, 1996).

23.   On this, see my *The Violence of Language*, and *Philosophy of Nonsense: The Intuitions of Victorian Nonsense Literature* (New York: Routledge, 1994).

24.   Thomas Hobbes, *Leviathan. Authoritative Texts, Backgrounds, Interpretations*, ed. Richard E. Flathman and David Johnston (New York: W. W. Norton, 1997), 73.

Translating Derrida on Translation: Relevance and Disciplinary Resistance

Lawrence Venuti

THE UNIQUE AND THE EXEMPLARY

THIS IS THE STORY OF MY STRUGGLE AS AN ENGLISH-LANGUAGE translator and student of translation who questions its current marginality in the United States. Yet this can also be read as the story of your struggle, you who have an interest in translation, who wish to study and perhaps practice it and who therefore can be affected adversely by the cultural and institutional marginality that limits the opportunities to do both in this country, as well as elsewhere. For since American economic and political dominance sustains the global hegemony of English, ensuring that it is the most translated language worldwide but relatively little translated into, the marginality of translation in the United States inevitably produces adverse effects abroad, notably by continuing unequal patterns of cultural exchange.[1] Thus, in the particular instance of translation, the "you" for whom I claim to speak—and hence the "I" who speaks—may be taken as universal.

Nevertheless, my shift from "I" to "you" must not be so rapid, must not appear so seamless, because my story is fairly unique, occasioned by a recent translation project. I want to discuss the circumstances surrounding my translation of a lecture by Jacques Derrida on the theme of translation. To be sure, translating the work of this contemporary French philosopher requires that one be a specialist in a certain sense, possessing a knowledge not only of the French language, but of continental philosophical traditions, and not only of translation practices between French and English, but of the discursive strategies that have been used to translate Derrida's writing over the past thirty years. Yet these different kinds of specialized knowledge are not sufficient for the task: one must also *desire* to translate Derrida. Indeed, scholars who admire his work, who teach, research, and edit it may decline to translate it, both because his playful, allusive writing poses numerous difficulties to the translator and because translation continues to rank low in the scale of scholarly rewards. Of course, if the hand is willing, it may still be tied by the legal factors that always constrain translation.[2] Derrida's work has accrued such cultural and economic capital that academic presses tend to purchase exclusive world rights from the publisher of the French text and from the author himself. This means that a translator must not only receive Derrida's permission to translate his work, but must negotiate with presses to avoid copyright infringement. The many complicated factors that play into translating Derrida seem to make such a project so special as to undermine any effort to treat it as exemplary. How, then, can I presume to do so?

Derrida can help to answer this question. He has called attention to the "interbreeding and accumulating [*croisant et accumulant*] [of] two logics" that occur in any testimony seeking to be representative, the simultaneous coexistence of empirical individuality—in this case, a marginalized individuality—and universal exemplarity.[3] What happens, he asks, "when someone resorts to describing an allegedly uncommon 'situation,' mine, for example, by testifying to it in terms that go beyond it, in a language whose generality takes on a value that is in some way structural, universal, transcendental, or ontological? When anybody who happens by infers the following: 'What holds for me, irreplaceably, also applies to all. Substitution is in progress; it has already taken effect. Everyone can say the same thing for themselves and of themselves. It suffices to hear me; I am the universal hostage.'"[4]

Derrida's answer to the question of exemplarity hinges on the critique of the linguistic sign embodied in his concept of *différance*. If meaning is an effect of relations and differences along a potentially endless chain of signifiers—polysemous, intertextual, subject to infinite linkages—then meaning is always differential and deferred, never present as an original unity, always already a site of proliferating possibilities which can be activated in diverse ways by the receivers of an utterance, and which therefore exceed the control of individual users.[5] Language use, despite biological metaphors embedded in expressions like "native language" and "mother tongue," is not natural in its origins, but cultural; not only is it acquired from immersion and education in a culture, but that acquisition so infiltrates individual uses as to make them fundamentally, usually unwittingly, collective. And the relation between the individual and the collective in language is never an equality, but always weighted toward the "other," from which or whom one learns a language. As Derrida remarks,

> We only ever speak one language—and, since it returns to the other, it exists asymmetrically, always for *the other*, from the other, kept by the other. Coming from the other, remaining with the other, and returning to the other.[6]

We only ever speak one language, but it is never our own and never simply one language. The point can be rephrased in more specifically social terms: a language is imposed by the exigencies of a social situation that is structured hierarchically, whether that situation be cultural or political, whether it be a matter of addressing a specialized audience from the margins of an institution or a matter of submitting to the limitations and exclusions of a colonial project.

This resemblance between the cultural and political situations of language can be pursued only so far before it effaces the brutality of a project like colonialism. Still, it is worth pursuing a bit further here for the light it can shed on the marginality of a cultural practice like translation as well as the exemplary status of my own translation of Derrida. Taking his comments as a point of departure, then, we can recognize that the "other" that is a cultural institution or political authority may involve the imposition of a monolingualism, an academic or colonial discourse, that seeks to homogenize and limit language use. By the same token, the monolingualism imposed by the other may endow the specificity of individual use with a collective force and hence a transindividual and possibly universal exemplarity. An individual testimony can incorporate a double structure, "that of exemplarity and that of the host as hostage," because "the structure appears in the experience of the injury, the offense," here a restrictive monolingualism imposed on the group of which the individual is a member.[7]

This line of thinking can be illustrated, first, by Derrida's lecture on translation. Entitled "Qu'est-ce qu'une traduction 'relevante'?"

(or, in my English version, "What Is a 'Relevant' Translation?"), the lecture was delivered in 1998 at the annual seminar of the Assises de la Traduction Littéraire à Arles (ATLAS). A French organization with approximately eight hundred members, ATLAS is dedicated to promoting literary translation and to protecting the status of the literary translator. The prospect of addressing an audience that consisted of professional translators, interested primarily in translation practices rather than theoretical concepts, imposed a certain language and mode of address on Derrida's lecture. Not only does he open with an elaborate apology for speaking about translation to experienced translators, but he avoids a purely philosophical presentation of his ideas. Instead of resorting to a speculative commentary on a key text, as he has done elsewhere, he addresses one of the most practical themes in the history of translation theory, notably the antithesis between "word-for-word" and "sense-for-sense" translation that occupied such writers as Cicero and Jerome. He also grounds his remarks on an incisive interpretation of the role of translation in Shakespeare's *The Merchant of Venice*. Derrida's effort to give specificity to his ideas, to locate suggestive applications, is most striking in his exploration of particular translation problems, especially those in which we glimpse him as translator. He proposes a French version for a line in Portia's speech on "mercy" and recalls his own French rendering of a central concept in Hegel's dialectics.

These individual cases, furthermore, come to assume an exemplary status in his exposition—exemplary of a universal concept of "relevant" translation and of the cultural and institutional impact that any translation may have. The relevant translation, Derrida writes, is mystifying: it "presents itself as the transfer of an intact signified through the inconsequential vehicle of any signifier whatsoever."[8] Although he questions this mystification, he sees it as inevitable insofar as every translation participates in an "economy of in-betweenness," positioned somewhere between "absolute relevance, the most appropriate, adequate, univocal transparency, and the most aberrant and opaque irrelevance."[9] He then applies this concept to his use of the French word *relève* to render Hegel's term *Aufhebung*, a translation that was at first "empirically personal," serving his own interpretive interests, but that ultimately underwent "institutional accreditation and canonization in the public sphere," achieving widespread use as the accepted rendering, becoming "known as the most relevant translation possible."[10]

It is remarkable that Derrida's lecture also *resists* the monolingualism imposed by addressing an audience of French translators. Although written in French, although cultivating a translatorly practicality by discussing specific cases, the text is in fact polylingual, incorporating English and German as well, and the argument takes a philosophical turn at points. Thus, Derrida apologizes for choosing a title that is "untranslatable" because the provenance of the word *relevant* remains uncertain: it may be French and therefore translatable into English, or English yet undergoing assimilation into French and therefore resistant to translation. As a result, Derrida argues, the word sheds light on the nature of translation today: because the unity of *relevant* is questionable, because the signifier potentially contains more than one word insofar as it produces a homophonic or homonymic effect, it derails the translation process and makes clear that the so-called relevant translation rests on a particular conception of language, one that assumes "the indivisible unity of an acoustic form that incorporates or signifies the indivisible unity of a meaning or concept."[11] Although Derrida tells his audience that he will forego any discussion "on the level of generality, in theoretical or more obviously philosophical or speculative reflections which I have elsewhere ventured on various universal problems of Translation," his specific cases give rise to philosophical reflections and point to universal problems.[12] In fact, his lecture answers to a second, more philosophical context: the commentary on Shakespeare's play derives from a seminar on forgiveness and perjury that he taught earlier in 1998.

My translation project is likewise situated in two different, even conflicting contexts, straddling two disciplines, addressing two academic audiences, each of whom imposes a particular conceptual discourse on my work, each of whom demands a translation that is relevant in their terms. On the one hand is the field known as "cultural studies," a loose amalgam of approaches that is nonetheless dominated by a theoretical orientation, a synthesis of poststructuralism with varieties of Marxism, feminism, and psychoanalysis. This synthesis has enabled scholars to range across different historical periods and cultural forms, both elite and mass, and to delimit such new areas of research as colonialism, sexual identity, and globalization.[13] On the other hand is the field known as "translation studies," an equally loose amalgam of approaches that is nonetheless dominated by an empirical orientation, a synthesis of such branches of linguistics as text linguistics, discourse analysis, and pragmatics with "polysystem" theory, wherein culture is viewed as a complicated network of interrelations among diverse forms and practices.[14] This synthesis has enabled scholars to study the language of translated texts as well as the norms that constrain translation in particular cultural polysystems, resulting in research that at its most productive combines linguistic and systemic approaches.[15]

Cultural studies and translation studies are not necessarily opposed. My own translation research and practice have consistently drawn on work in both fields. Yet these fields as they currently stand tend to reveal deep conceptual divisions that complicate any project with the goal of addressing scholars in both. The theoretical orientation of cultural studies has marginalized research into specific translations and translation practices, whereas the empirical orientation of translation studies has marginalized research into issues of philosophy and cultural politics. Because both fields are now firmly institutionalized—even if they occupy different institutional sites in different countries—and because they both involve international scholarly communities, they endow my translation project with a universal significance that exceeds the individual case. If I take my own work as exemplary, if I dare to speak for you who share my interest in translation, the reason is that we also share a basic set of institutional conditions, a double academic marginality: on the one hand, the neglect in cultural studies of the materiality of translation; on the other hand, the neglect in translation studies of the philosophical implications and social effects that accompany every translation practice.

Translation in Cultural Studies

To understand the peculiar marginality of translation, I want to turn to Pierre Bourdieu's work on academic institutions, where he has located a "special form of anti-intellectualism."[16] For Bourdieu, academic anti-intellectualism, however oxymoronic the term may seem, consists of a "secret resistance to innovation and to intellectual creativity, [an] aversion to ideas and to a free and critical spirit," which he has linked to "the effect of the recognition granted to an institutionalized thought only on those who implicitly accept the limits assigned by the institution."[17] To work in a field is to accept such institutional limits by maintaining an investment in the materials and practices that define the field, even when a social agent aims to change it in a radical way. As Bourdieu observes, "wanting to undertake a revolution in a field is to accord the essential of what the field tacitly demands, namely that it is important, that the game played is sufficiently important for one to want to undertake a revolution in it."[18] Hence, attempts to introduce different materials and practices are likely to encounter resistance if they represent a fundamental challenge to the value of institutionalized thought, if they seek to shift the importance invested in it to another kind of thinking. The resistance can take the form of sheer exclusion, such as the refusal of publication by academic journals and presses, the rejection of applications for academic appointments, and the denial of tenure and promotion. The resistance can also take forms that are less drastic (such as negative book reviews), or more revisionary (such as the transformation of marginal materials and practices so that they can be assimilated to the current state of the field). The institutional fate of translation studies in the United States has involved many of these forms of disciplinary resistance.

For the fact is that translation has yet to gain a firm foothold in the American academy. Whereas European countries such as the United Kingdom, Germany, Spain, and Italy have recently witnessed a substantial growth of translator training faculties as well as graduate degrees in translation research, the United States has lagged far behind, so that the translation program, even the odd course or dissertation in translation studies remains a rare exception.[19] Translation has encountered the disciplinary resistance that Bourdieu describes, first of all, because it runs counter to institutionalized practices in foreign-language instruction. Since the late 1960s, the most prevalent form of foreign-language pedagogy has been "direct communication" or "total immersion," in which the goal of native proficiency leads to the suppression of any teaching methods that might require the student to rely on the mediation of English. Consequently, translation has been stigmatized and excluded as a method of foreign-language instruction, even though it served precisely this purpose for centuries. Translation has tended to enter the American academy by establishing institutional sites that are relatively autonomous from universities, like the Monterey Institute of International Studies, or crossdisciplinary, like the collaboration between modern foreign languages and applied linguistics that underlies the translation program at Kent State University.

The sheer practicality of translation—the fact that innovative research can shape practice while innovative practices can stimulate research—has played a part in preventing it from gaining wide acceptance within cultural studies. Here the disciplinary resistance seems to be due to the theoretical orientation that has dominated this field since the 1980s. Because much cultural commentary has taken a highly speculative turn, some of the most distinguished academic journals tend to reject articles that, in the editors' eyes, lack theoretical sophistication or that focus on particular works and historical periods without raising theoretical issues that are currently under debate. Translation studies can engage with such issues, but as a linguistic practice it will inevitably raise them in specific textual and social terms that qualify theoretical speculation and ultimately question its value. Theories of translation need an empirical grounding if they are to affect both translation practices as well as research into translation history and criticism. Yet this practical dimension has not been welcomed by journals. *Critical Inquiry*, for example, which has acquired enormous authority as a journal of theoretically based cultural commentary, did not publish an article on translation until my version of Derrida's lecture appeared in its twenty-seventh volume.

With the emergence of such areas of research as colonialism, translation has increasingly become a topic of discussion in cultural studies. And rightly so: the colonization of the Americas, Asia, and Africa could not have occurred without interpreters, both native and colonial, nor without the translation of effective texts, religious, legal, educational. Yet what I shall call the *theoreticism* of some research in this area, the emphasis on the construction of theoretical concepts to the exclusion of textual analysis and empirical research, has limited the attention given to translation.

Homi Bhabha, for instance, one of the most influential theorists of colonial discourse, opens his essay "Signs Taken for Wonders" by discussing the charismatic quality that the English book acquired in such British colonies as India. As Bhabha notes, it is "a process of displacement that, paradoxically, makes the presence of the book wondrous to the extent to which it is repeated, translated, misread, displaced"; to demonstrate his point, he quotes a lengthy passage in which an Indian catechist describes a huge crowd outside of Delhi reading "the Gospel of our Lord, translated into the Hindoostanee Tongue."[20] Bhabha acknowledges that "in my use of 'English' there is a transparency of reference that registers a certain obvious presence: the Bible translated into Hindi, propagated by Dutch or native catechists, is still the English book" to the colonized.[21] And this acknowledgment occasions an exploration of colonial authority, in which he relies on a productive synthesis of such poststructuralist thinkers as Derrida and Foucault. Yet the exposition remains on a very high level of generality, and absolutely no effort is made to consider what implications the translated status of the text might carry for the theory of colonial discourse that Bhabha formulates so powerfully.

An analysis of Hindi translations of the Bible is likely to reveal linguistic and cultural differences that support and deepen Bhabha's notion of the inherent ambivalence of colonial discourse. Vicente Rafael's work on Spanish colonialism in the Philippines bears out this likelihood: Rafael shows how Tagalog translations of religious texts at once advanced and undermined the Spanish presence.[22] In Bhabha's case, however, the theoreticism of the commentary preempts any close textual analysis, whether of literary texts or of translations. Within colonial studies, his work has been criticized for stressing discourse at the cost of neglecting the material conditions of colonialism.[23] Ironically, the stress on discourse does not include any attention to the discursive strategies employed in translations.

Even when cultural theorists have themselves produced translations of literary and theoretical texts, their acute awareness that no translation can communicate a foreign text in an untroubled fashion does not lead them to provide a searching examination of specific translations, whether those made by others or their own. Gayatri Spivak's translations from the work of the Bengali fiction writer Mahasweta Devi are accompanied not by any explanation of her translation choices, but by essays that draw on various theoretical concepts to illuminate the political dimensions of Devi's writing. This omission becomes more noticeable when Spivak reports a suggestive criticism of her work. After asserting that the translations are "going to be published in both India and the United States," she mentions that the Indian publisher and translation scholar Sujit Mukherjee has criticized their English for not being "sufficiently accessible to readers in this country [India]."[24] Spivak acknowledges that her English "belongs more to the rootless American-based academic prose than the more subcontinental idiom of [her] youth"; she even admits that whether Indian texts should be translated into Indian English "is an interesting question."[25] But notwithstanding a generally phrased "Translator's Note," she does not address the question with the sustained attention that she gives to Devi's themes.

What makes the language of Spivak's translations all the more intriguing is the fact that it is richly heterogeneous, far removed from both academic prose and a subcontinental dialect, hardly "straight English." Here are two extracts from her version of Devi's story "Breast-Giver":

> The boy got worried at the improper supply of fish and fries in his dish. He considered that he'd be fucked if the cook gave him away. Therefore on another occasion, driven by the Bagdad djinn, he stole his mother's ring, slipped it into the cook's pillowcase, raised a hue and cry, and got the cook kicked out.

> Then Kangali said, "Sir! How shall I work at the sweetshop any longer? I can't stir the vat with my kerutches. You are god. You are feeding so many people in so many ways. I am not begging. Find me a job."[26]

This mixture of current standard usage with colloquialism and obscenity, of Britishisms with Americanisms, of orthodox with unorthodox spelling to signal differences in pronunciation inevitably raises the question of how and to what extent Spivak's translating has recreated or transformed Devi's textual effects. Such abrupt shifts in dialect, register, and style need to be examined against the Bengali texts so that Spivak's discursive strategies can be compellingly linked to the cultural values and political agendas that she so ardently espouses in the commentaries that accompany her translations.

TRANSLATION IN TRANSLATION STUDIES

Within translation studies, discursive strategies are paid a great deal of attention, but they tend to be treated in such a way as to reveal a different form of academic anti-intellectualism: a focus on the data yielded by textual analysis at the expense of the various philosophical, cultural, and political issues raised by translation. Here the disciplinary resistance seems to be due to the empirical orientation that has dominated the field since the 1960s, driven largely by the varieties of linguistics that provide the analytical tools. Thus, research that is less empirical and more speculative, or that uses different categories of analysis which are more pertinent to cultural studies, is likely to be not merely misunderstood, but questioned for not providing detail that is sufficient or representative. In a recent survey of linguistic perspectives on translation, the linguist Mona Baker took this position in relation to my work:

> Apart from analysing poetic devices such as metre, rhyme, alliteration, and so on, Venuti draws on categories which a linguistically oriented researcher would consider too broad and too restricted to the traditional levels of vocabulary and syntax: archaisms, dialect, regional choice, syntactic inversions. A linguistically oriented scholar would typically want to provide analyses which offer finer distinctions at the levels of lexis and syntax and which also incorporate other levels of description, such as information flow, cohesion, linguistic mechanisms of expressing politeness, norms of turn-taking in conversation, and so on.[27]

Conspicuously absent from Baker's comment is any indication that I was analyzing the literary effects of literary translations, and that the selection of linguistic features was guided by a particular interpretive occasion, an effort to link the effects of specific translation strategies to patterns of reception and to cultural values.[28] Since my analysis used relatively few of the tools that linguists generally bring to translation studies, it implicitly raised the question of whether the "finer distinctions" produced by such tools are necessary for an exploration of literary and cultural issues or even for the development of translation practices. More generally, Baker's comment points to an incommensurability between two current approaches within translation studies, one informed by linguistics, the other informed by literary and cultural theory.

Indeed, from this theoretical standpoint, the results of linguistically oriented approaches can seem trivial, inconsequential not only for translation research but for translator training. What is questionable here is not the use of empirical research, which remains valuable to document and explore the factors that figure in the production, circulation, and reception of translations, but rather an *empiricism* that focuses narrowly on minute linguistic materials and practices to the exclusion of such decisive social considerations as the commission that the translator has received and the prospective audience for the translation. As Louis Althusser argued, empiricist epistemologies claim direct or unmediated access to a reality or truth, but this claim mystifies a process of "abstraction" in which essential data are distinguished from inessential on the basis of a privileged theoretical model, and a real object is reduced to an object of a particular kind of knowledge.[29] The empiricism that prevails in translation studies tends to privilege analytical concepts derived from linguistics, regardless of how narrow or limited they may be in their explanatory power. And from the vantage point of these concepts the essence of a translation is an abstracted notion of language.

This is most evident in the many university programs that take a linguistics-oriented approach to translation research and translator training. A book that receives many course adoptions in such programs is Basil Hatim and Ian Mason's *The Translator as Communicator* (1997), which brings together an array of linguistic concepts to perform close analyses of translations in different genres and media. For instance, they analyze the subtitling in a foreign-language film with the aid of politeness theory, a formalization of speech acts by which a speaker maintains or threatens an addressee's "face," defined as "the basic claim to. . . freedom of action and freedom from imposition" as well as a "positive consistent self-image" and "the desire that this self-image be appreciated and approved of."[30] Their analysis of the subtitling demonstrates that the foreign dialogue undergoes a "systematic loss" of the linguistic indicators that the characters are satisfying each other's "face-wants."[31]

The authors, however, go no further than this conclusion. "Far more empirical research would be needed," they state, "to test the generalizability of these limited findings to other films and other languages."[32] Yet one wonders about the implications of their analysis for this particular film. No consideration is given to the impact of translation patterns on characterization, narrative, and theme in the film as a whole or on the audience's potential response to these formal features. Such considerations would require rather different theoretical concepts that take into account but extend beyond the linguistic analysis, a theory of how characters are formed in film narrative, for example, and a theory of audience reception or cultural taste. In Hatim and Mason's analysis, linguistic indicators of politeness function as an empiricist essence abstracted from both the foreign film and the subtitled version.

From the translator's point of view, the empiricism that currently distinguishes the linguistic approach to translation carries at least two serious limitations. First, because this approach devises and deploys such complex analytical concepts, it always yields much more detail than is necessary to solve a translation problem, threatening to annex translation studies to applied linguistics. Here we can glimpse an instance of what Bourdieu calls "the most serious episte-mological mistake in the human sciences," the tendency "to place the models that the scientist must construct to account for practices into the consciousness of agents" who carry out those practices.[33] In translator training, this mistake transforms translators into linguists by requiring them to learn and apply in their translating a wide range of the analytical concepts that linguists have formulated. In translation research, furthermore, these concepts tend to become standards by which translations are judged. For despite Hatim and Mason's denial that their "objective had been to criticize subtitlers or subtitling," their analysis lays the groundwork for a judgment that the subtitler who produced their examples failed to establish an equivalence with the foreign dialogue: "in sequences such as those analysed," they assert, "it is difficult for the target language auditors to retrieve interpersonal meaning in its entirety. In some cases, they may even derive misleading impressions of characters' directness or indirectness."[34]

Thus, the linguistic analysis of translations is potentially laden with an uncritical prescriptivism, which reveals a second limitation: the translator is given the deceptive idea, not only that such an analysis is impartially descriptive, but that it will be sufficient for develop-ing, explaining, and evaluating translation decisions. Because such decisions are usually made on the basis of the textual effects, cultural values, and social functions that translations possess in target situa-tions, a linguistic analysis that is primarily concerned with equiva-lence will fail to encompass the factors that are so consequential for translating. Why, we might ask, do the subtitles in Hatim and Ma-son's examples necessarily give the viewer "misleading impressions" of the characters in the film? Can we not view the impressions as ef-fectively different interpretations, shaped partly by the technical con-straints on subtitling (e.g., the limitation on the number of keyboard spaces that can appear in the frame) and partly by the translator's discursive strategies as they are developed for an audience in a dif-ferent culture? In the long run, the empiricism in translation studies resists the sort of speculative thinking that encourages translators to reflect on the cultural, ethical, and political issues raised by their work.

AN INTERVENTIONIST TRANSLATION

Bourdieu remarks that "the structure of the university field is only, at any moment in time, the state of the power relations between . . . agents," so that "positions held in this structure are what motivate strategies aiming to transform it, or to preserve it by modifying or maintaining the relative forces of the different powers."[35] In Bourdieu's account, the power in the university is mediated by the different forms of capital assigned to the fields in which academics work: not only are the fields arranged hierarchically, with some (law, medicine, the sciences) assigned greater economic and cultural capital than others (the arts), but the capital assigned to the materials and practices within particular fields is also distributed unevenly. In American universities, translation undoubtedly occupies a subordinate position, not only in relation to socially powerful fields like law and medicine, but also in relation to fields that are affiliated to translation, such as linguistics, literary criticism, and cultural theory. In my argument thus far I have tried to be more precise: translation has undergone a double marginalization in which its understanding and development have been limited both by the theoreticism of influential work in cultural studies and by the empiricism of the prevalent linguistic approaches to translation studies.

It was this marginality that motivated my decision to translate Derrida's lecture. I viewed the project as a means of challenging the subordinate position and reductive understanding of translation in the American academy. To intervene effectively, however, my presentation of the lecture—not only my translation strategies, but my very choice of the text—had to answer to the two rather different conceptual discourses that have limited translation, even as I sought to transform them.

Translation has always functioned as a method of introducing innovative materials and practices into academic institutions, but its success has inevitably been constrained by institutionalized values. Foreign scholarship can enter and influence the academy, although only in terms that are recognizable to it—at least initially. These terms include translation strategies that minimize the foreignness of foreign writing by assimilating it to linguistic and discursive structures that are more acceptable to academic institutions. Philip Lewis has shown, for example, that because of structural differences be-

tween French and English, along with the translator's announced
"aim to anglicize," the first English version of Derrida's essay "La
mythologie blanche" suppresses the "special texture and tenor of
[his] discourse" by using "an English that shies away from abnormal,
odd-sounding constructions."[36] In this domesticated form, the essay
significantly influenced the English-language reception of Derrida's
thinking, which from the very start had been assimilated to American academic interests.[37] The recognizable terms that permit the foreign to enter the academy may also include authors and texts that
have already achieved canonical status, as well as issues that are currently under scholarly debate. Hence, my choice to translate Derrida's lecture was strategic: it invited recognition but at the same
time aimed to precipitate a defamiliarization that might stimulate a
rethinking of the institutional status of translation.

   Within cultural studies, Derrida has long been a canonical figure,
an author of foundational texts in the field. Not only would a previously untranslated work by him be certain to attract a large academic
readership, but it would immediately interest the editors of leading
journals. Following Derrida's recommendation, I proposed my translation to the editor of *Critical Inquiry* who quickly accepted it on the
strength of a brief summary. The lecture, furthermore, addresses the
theme of translation in the context of such currently debated issues
as racism and political repression. Derrida interprets the characters
in Shakespeare's *The Merchant of Venice* according to the code of
translation, showing how Portia aims to translate Shylock's Judaic discourse of "justice" into the "merciful" discourse that underwrites the
"Christian State."[38]

   This is an unprecedented interpretive move in the critical history
of the play, which may now be read differently by Shakespearean
scholars who are interested in theoretical approaches. Yet for American readers of Derrida the most unfamiliar move is likely to be his
own recourse to translating. He offers not only an exposition of his
interpretation, but an unusual French rendering of Portia's line,
"when mercy seasons justice," in which the word *seasons* is translated
as *relève*, the term that he used for the Hegelian *Aufhebung* to highlight the contradictions in the dialectical movement of thinking. In
Derrida's philosophical lexicon, *relève* signifies "the double motif of
the elevation and the replacement that preserves what it denies or
destroys, preserving what it causes to disappear."[39] By rendering Portia's line with a word that has acquired such a conceptual density,

Derrida indicates the assimilative force involved in her translation of Shylock's demands for justice into the Christian discourse of mercy. At the same time, he provides a remarkable demonstration that translation too can perform exactly the sort of interrogative interpretation that scholars in cultural studies have come to associate with his work.

Within translation studies, Derrida has carried considerably less weight than a linguist like Halliday or a philosopher of language like Grice. This comes as no surprise: Halliday and Grice have provided the conceptual and analytical tools that have informed the empirical orientation of much translation research, fostering ideas of textual stability and cooperative communication that have in fact been questioned by poststructuralism.[40] Nonetheless, even within translation studies, translating Derrida's lecture can be an effective intervention because he addresses relevance, a concept that came to dominate translation theory and practice during the twentieth century. Eugene Nida, for instance, a theorist who has exercised an international influence on translator training for several decades, championed the concept of "dynamic equivalence" in which the translator "aims at complete naturalness of expression, and tries to relate the receptor to modes of behavior relevant within the context of his own culture."[41] More recently, Ernst-August Gutt has developed a cognitive approach to translation based on the branch of pragmatics known as "relevance theory."[42] Gutt argues that "faithfulness" in translation depends on communicating an interpretation of the foreign text through "contextual effects" that are "adequate" because they take into account the receptors' "cognitive environment" and therefore require minimal "processing effort." The relevant translation, then, is likely to be "clear and natural in expression in the sense that it should not be unnecessarily difficult to understand."

Derrida's lecture is particularly challenging in this context because although he admits that relevance is the guiding principle of most translations, he also questions it. He calls attention to its ethnocentric violence, but also to its simultaneous mystification of that violence through language that is seemingly transparent because univocal and idiomatic. The effect of transparency in translation is illusionistic: accessibility or easy readability, what Gutt calls "optimal relevance," leads the reader to believe that the signified has been transferred without any substantial difference. Yet the fact is that any translating replaces the signifiers constituting the foreign text with another signifying chain, trying to fix a signified that can be no more than an interpretation according to the intelligibilities and interests of the receiving language and culture. Derrida goes further than simply demystifying relevant translation: he also exposes its cultural and social implications through his interpretation of Shakespeare's play. Portia's translation of Shylock's demand for justice seeks an optimal relevance to Christian doctrine which ultimately leads to his total expropriation as well as his forced conversion to Christianity. Derrida thus shows that when relevant translation occurs within an institution like the state, it can become the instrument of legal interdiction, economic sanction, and political repression, motivated here by racism.

TRANSLATING WITH ABUSIVE FIDELITY

Whereas my choice to translate Derrida's lecture aimed to establish a relevance to institutionalized thought which also questioned the subordinate position and limited understanding of translation within academic institutions, my translation strategies risked irrelevance: they were uncompromising in their effort to bring his writing into English so as to demonstrate the power of translation in shaping concepts. More specifically, I sought to implement what Philip Lewis has called "abusive fidelity," a translation practice that "values experimentation, tampers with usage, seeks to match the polyvalencies and plurivocities or expressive stresses of the original by producing its own."[43] Abusive fidelity is demanded by foreign texts that involve substantial conceptual density or complex literary effects, namely poetry and philosophy, including Derrida's own writing. This kind of translating is abusive in two senses: it resists the structures and discourses of the receiving language and culture, especially the pressure toward the univocal, the idiomatic, the transparent; yet in so doing it also interrogates the structures and discourses of the foreign text, exposing its often unacknowledged conditions.

In practice abusive fidelity meant adhering as closely as possible to Derrida's French, trying to reproduce his syntax and lexicon by inventing comparable textual effects—even when they threatened to twist English into strange forms. The possibilities are always limited by the structural and discursive differences between the languages and by the need to maintain a level of intelligibility and readability,

of relevance, for my English-language readers. I knew that my translation strained the limits of academic English because of the reactions that it received from the editorial staff at *Critical Inquiry*. Thus, I
wanted to preserve many of Derrida's telegraphic, sometimes ellipti-
cal syntactical constructions in English, but the copyeditor tended to
recommend insertions that expanded these constructions into grammatically complete units. Here is an example with the copyeditor's
insertions in square brackets:

> [It is] As if the subject of the play were, in short, the task of the trans-
> lator, his impossible task, his duty, his debt, as inflexible as it is un-
> payable. [This is so] At least for three or four reasons: [44]

Sometimes the copyeditor recommended the insertion of connec-
tive words to increase the cohesiveness of the English syntax:

> mercy resembles justice, but it comes from somewhere else, it be-
> longs to a different order, [for] at the same time it modifies jus-
> tice, . . . [45]

Derrida's lexicon is even more abusive of academic discourse. Instead of clear, unambiguous terms, he favors complicated wordplay
that cannot always be reproduced in translation because of irreducible linguistic differences. Readers of Derrida in English now ex-
pect to confront a page punctuated by foreign words, so I took
advantage of this expectation by inserting Derrida's French within
square brackets wherever a particular effect could not be easily
achieved in an English rendering. These occasions included his play
on *grâce* in the senses of "gratitude," "pardon," and "grace," as well as
his play on *le merci*, meaning "thanks," and *la merci*, meaning "forgiveness." [46] In other instances, however, I was able to imitate the wordplay in English. Thus, the French *marche/marché* [step/purchase]
became the English *tread/trade*, while in an alliterative series that required an English choice beginning with the consonant cluster *tr* the
French *trouvaille* [windfall, fortunate discovery, lucky break] became
treasure trove.

> surenchère infinie, autre marche ou autre marché dans l'escalade
> infinie [47]

> an infinite extravagance, another tread or trade in an infinite as-
> cent [48]

une de ces autres choses en *tr.*, une transaction, une transformation, un travail, un *travel*—et une trouvaille[49]

one of those other things in *tr.*, a transaction, transformation, travail, *travel*—and a treasure trove . . .[50]

The fact that my effort to reproduce Derrida's wordplay tampered with English usage also became apparent in the copyeditor's queries. In one instance, Derrida himself directs the reader's attention to a pun through a parenthetical remark:

Ceux et celles à qui l'anglais est ici familier l'entendent peut-être déjà comme la domestication, la francisation implicite ou, oserai-je dire, l'affranchissement plus ou moins tacite et clandestin de l'adjectif anglais *relevant*[51]

Those of you who are familiar with English perhaps already understand the word as a domestication, an implicit Frenchification [*francisation*] or—dare I say?—a more or less tacit and clandestine enfranchisement of the English adjective *relevant*, . . .[52]

To reproduce the pun *francisation/l'affranchissement* in English, I chose *Frenchification/enfranchisement* and avoided the expected rendering, *Gallicization*. Yet the copyeditor responded that the pun was more apparent in the French than in the English: "I only found it," she wrote, "after you alerted me to it, and only after rereading the French—and others in the office had the same experience."[53] She recommended that both French words be included within square brackets after the English ones, and I accepted her recommendation so as to retain a rendering that not only sounded unusual, but would recreate the pun.

Another of my renderings was sufficiently odd-sounding to draw similar comments from the staff. Here Derrida is interpreting Portia's famous speech on the "quality of mercy":

Elle sied au monarque sur le trône, dit donc Portia, mais mieux encore que sa couronne. Elle est plus haute que la couronne sur la tête, elle *va* au monarque, elle lui sied, mais elle *va* plus haut que la tête et le chef, que l'attribut ou que le signe de pouvoir qu'est la couronne royale.[54]

Mercy becomes the throned monarch, Portia says, but even better than his crown. It is higher than the crown on a head; it *suits* the monarch, it becomes him, but it *suits* him higher than his head and the head [*la tête et le chef*], than the attribute or sign of power that is the royal crown.[55]

The copyeditor responded that the staff had some difficulty in puzzling through the meaning of this passage. "We're unclear on *suits higher*, she wrote, while recommending more idiomatic alternatives: *It sits higher than his head? It suits more than his head?*"[56] I explained that the unusual construction results from Derrida's effort to tease out the transcendental logic in Portia's concept of mercy, a logic that is signaled here by her comparative, "becomes . . . better than." Hence, *suits higher* means that the monarch's mercy suits the divinity from which monarchy is said to receive its authority. In line with Derrida's interpretation, my rendering of this passage actually creates an instance of wordplay where none exists in the French: the phrase *la tête et le chef* is an idiom which can be translated simply as *the head*, yet I saw in it an opportunity to draw the political distinction—to which Derrida refers elsewhere in the lecture—between the king's two bodies, the king as a private person (*his* own head) and as a political figure (*the* head of the state, the crown).

The editorial staff of *Critical Inquiry*, especially the copyeditor Kristin Casady, were very supportive of my translation experimentalism: they appreciated and permitted my abuses of English as well as the *Chicago Manual of Style*, which is generally applied in copyediting articles for the journal. Among the most important editorial decisions was to retain the polylingualism of Derrida's text, often without bracketed translations and even in places where only a minute difference in spelling indicated a linguistic difference. Not only does Derrida use various languages in the lecture, but he varies the spelling of *relevant/relevante* to express his uncertainty about its status as an English or French word and thereby to point up the problem that it poses to relevant translation. Retaining the polylingualism of the lecture is essential for the strategic intervention that I had planned: it foregrounds the issue of translation in a most effective way by turning the reader into a translator.

Lewis is careful to note that an abusively faithful translation does not merely force "the linguistic and conceptual system of which it is a dependent," but also directs "a critical thrust back toward the text that it translates and in relation to which it becomes a kind of unsettling aftermath."[57] If my translation abuses the English language and an English style manual, it also has an interrogative impact on Derrida's text. This emerges, for example, in my handling of the key term *relève*, which Derrida describes as "untranslatable," and which Alan Bass left untranslated in his English versions of other texts by Derrida.[58] For the most part, I have followed their lead by retaining the French word and thus forcing the reader to perform repeated acts of translation. In some instances, however, I rendered *relève* expansively, making explicit the range of meanings that it accumulates in Derrida's discussion:

> Je tradurai donc *seasons* par "relève": "*when mercy seasons justice,*" "quand le pardon relève la justice (ou le droit)."[59]

> I shall therefore translate "seasons" as "relève": "when mercy seasons justice," "quand le pardon relève la justice (ou le droit)" [*when mercy elevates and interiorizes, thereby preserving and negating, justice (or the law)*].[60]

> le pardon *ressemble* à un pouvoir divin au moment où il relève la justice[61]

> mercy *resembles* a divine power at the moment when it elevates, preserves, and negates [*relève*] justice . . .[62]

Such expanded translations interrogate the French text by exposing the conditions of Derrida's interpretation. Because, as he observes, his use of *relève* to render the Hegelian *Aufhebung* has become canonical in academic institutions, the retention of the French term throughout my translation would silently participate in this canonization and work to maintain the relevance to Shakespeare's play of what is in fact an irrelevant anachronism, a deconstruction of Hegel. The expanded translations, however, produce a demystifying effect by revealing the interpretive act that is at once embodied and concealed in Derrida's French.

Another abuse in my translation hinges on the recurrent choice of the English word *travail* to render the French noun *travail* and the verb *travailler*. At one point, Derrida himself uses the English form *travailing* to pun on the English word *traveling*:

> Ce mot [*relevant*] n'est pas seulement *en* traduction, comme on dirait en travail ou en voyage, *traveling*, *travailing*, dans un labeur, un *labour* d'accouchement.[63]

The word is not only *in* translation, as one would say in the works or in transit, *traveling, travailing,* on the job, in the *travail* of childbirth.[64]

Following Derrida, I decided to make use of the English word *travail* but my uses far exceeded his: they amount to thirteen instances, which occur at the beginning and the end of the translation and are therefore quite noticeable to the reader. Some were determined by Derrida's characteristic wordplay, such as the alliteration of the consonant cluster *tr:*

le motif du *labour,* du *tr*avail d'accouchement mais aussi du *tr*avail *transférentiel* et *tr*ansformationnel[65]

the motif of *labor [travail],* the *tr*avail of childbirth, but also the *transferential* and *tr*ansformational *tr*avail . . .[66]

Other uses were solely my decision, such as turning *un travail du negatif* and *un travail du deuil* into *a travail of the negative* and *a travail of mourning,*[67] even though in the latter case Derrida's translator Peggy Kamuf might have chosen the more familiar word *work,* as she did in her version of his book on Marx.[68] My use of *travail* is abusive in a number of ways. It deviates not only from the practices of a previous translator, but, more generally, from current standard English, since the word has become a poetical archaism. It also constitutes a deviation from the French text, because the French words *travail* and *travailler* are neither poetic nor archaic, but very much part of current French usage.

My abusive rendering can be seen as consistent with a distinctive feature of Derrida's writing, his tendency to favor literary effects, to blur the line between philosophy and poetry. Yet the recurrence of *travail* is also interrogative of the French text, particularly since it appears in the phrases that Derrida uses to describe relevant translation. Because *travail* has acquired the status of an archaism in English, the word adds a temporal dimension to his critique of relevant translation, situating it in the past, suggesting that it did not originate with him, that in fact it has a long history in translation theory. In 1813, for instance, Friedrich Schleiermacher had in mind relevant translation when he questioned the translator who "leaves the reader in peace, as much as possible, and moves the author toward him."[69] For Schleiermacher too, relevance was suspect because it meant assimilation or domestication, an erasure of the foreignness of the foreign text by rewriting it in the terms of the receiving language and culture. More recently, Henri Meschonnic has attacked the prevalence of relevant translation because it masks a process of "annexation" whereby the translated text "transposes the so-called dominant ideology" under the "illusion of transparency" (my translation).[70] Of course, the theoretical genealogy of Derrida's critique can be no more than vaguely suggested by the recurrent use of an archaism in my translation. It is only when this abusive choice is juxtaposed to my editorial introduction, where Schleiermacher and other theorists are cited, that the historical conditions of Derrida's treatment become clearer.

TRANSLATION AND THE POLITICS OF INTERPRETATION

As this last point indicates, even if translation is regarded not simplistically as an untroubled transfer of meaning, but as an act of interpretation in its own right that works on the linguistic and cultural differences of the foreign text and thereby alters its meaning, a translation requires yet another interpretation to make explicit its own interpretive force. Thus, in translating Derrida's lecture, I wanted to suggest, on the one hand, that a more materialist approach to translation can contribute to theoretical speculation in cultural studies and, on the other hand, that a more philosophical and socially aware approach can contribute to empirical research in translation studies. But despite the fact that Derrida's texts, in any language, are generally read with the closeness reserved for literature, my translation itself cannot achieve these goals. I must still rely on a commentary attuned to the issue of translation, whether an editorial introduction or this very essay, risking the cynical charge of self-promotion that a translator always faces when attempting to describe the choices and effects of his or her work. And if this cynicism should be preempted here by a Derridean argument that a unique translation project can nonetheless exemplify the academic marginality of translation today, then my effort to criticize the circumstances of my work, its institutional trials and obstacles, faces another, equally cynical charge: sour grapes. The peculiar marginality of translation is such that not only is invisibility enforced upon it through a widespread preference for fluent discursive strategies that produce the illusion of transparency, the effacement of the second-order status of the translated text, but the translator is expected to remain silent about the conditions of translation.

As a result, my intervention can have an impact only if others take up the task of commentary, only if my version of Derrida's essay is submitted to the interpretive practices that are performed in academic institutions. It would need, first of all, to be judged worthy of inclusion in the English-language canon of his writing and so worthy of the close attention that canonicity enforces upon texts. It would then need to play a role in cultural studies teaching and research, would need to be included in reading lists and syllabuses for courses in literary and cultural theory and in philosophy. It would also need to be judged worthy of reading within translation studies, to be included among the empiricist theoretical texts that dominate translation research and to find a place in courses devoted to theory in translator-training faculties and in translation studies programs. In these institutional contexts my translation might well bring about changes because there its abusive strategies can solicit interpretation, prompting further discussion that will ultimately encompass the very institutions in which it circulates.

What institutional changes, then, can possibly be expected from translating Derrida's lecture in the way that I have translated it for my projected audiences? Perhaps the first and most crucial change is an increased visibility for the translator and the act of translation. In pursuing a fidelity to the French text that abuses current English usage and an authoritative style manual, in deviating from the choices that previous translators of Derrida's texts have made for his key terms, I have produced a translation that highlights its own discursive strategies and thereby demands to be read as a translation, as a text that is relatively autonomous from the text on which it depends. Within cultural studies, this increased visibility can alter interpretive practices by leading scholars to focus on translations the interrogative forms of reading that are now routinely applied to literary and philosophical texts, among other cultural products. Within translation studies, a more visible discursive strategy can alter translation research and translator training by leading scholars and teachers to be more receptive to innovative translation practices and to question the enormous value that continues to be placed on fluency and uncritical notions of equivalence.

Yet these changes assume that a very different approach will be taken to the interpretation of theoretical texts in translation. The ap-

proach that currently prevails is to read translated theory for meaning by reducing it either to an exposition of argumentative points or
to an account of its conceptual aporias or to both in succession. This
communicative approach, however necessary in processing any text,
assumes the simplistic notion of translation as an untroubled semantic transfer. And indeed such an approach is invited by fluent translating whereby a foreign text comes to seem unmediated by the
translator's labor of rewriting it in a different language for a different
culture. Translating that pursues an abusive fidelity resists this illusion by directing the reader's attention to what exceeds the translator's establishment of a semantic equivalence. To be sure, an excess
is present in every translation: a semantic equivalence must be established by deploying dialects and registers, styles and discourses that
add to and alter the foreign text because they work only in the translating language and culture, that make the foreign text intelligible
by linking it to language usage and cultural traditions among the receptors and thereby limit and exclude foreign usage and traditions.
Yet only a translation of abusive fidelity foregrounds—by challenging—its linguistic and cultural conditions, which include the language of instruction and research in the academic institution where
the interpretation occurs. Clearly, this form of reading translated
theory requires some knowledge of foreign languages and cultures.
But this knowledge is not enough: the reader must use it to interrogate the linguistic and cultural materials on which the translator has
drawn to rewrite the foreign text.

In the United States, a more visible translation practice can point
to the global dominance of the language that prevails in teaching
and research: English. An English translation that makes readers
aware of its abuses, namely its transformation of the current standard
dialect in its interrogative work on a particular foreign text, will ex-
pose the limitations and exclusions of the translating language,
showing that "English" is an idealist notion that conceals a panoply
of Englishes ranged in a hierarchical order of value and power
among themselves and over every other language in the world. Thus,
a translation practice can turn the interpretation of translated texts
into an act of geopolitical awareness. In fostering changes in pedagogical techniques and research methods, more visible translating
constitutes a concrete means of forcing a critical self-reflection upon
both cultural studies and translation studies, opening them to the
global asymmetries in which they are situated and with which—in

their use of English—they are complicit. A translation practice might not only advance theories of culture and translation, but join them to a politically oriented understanding that can potentially extend their impact beyond the academic institutions in which these theories are housed. This is not to say that translation, especially the translation of specialized theoretical texts, can change the world in any direct way. Rather, the point is that translation can be practiced, in various genres and text types, so as to make their users aware of the social hierarchies in which languages and cultures are positioned. And with that awareness the different institutions that use and support translation, notably publishers, universities, and government agencies, can better decide how to respond to the cultural and social effects that follow upon the global dominance of English.

NOTES

1. For translation figures, see Lawrence Venuti, *The Translator's Invisibility: A History of Translation* (London: Routledge, 1995).

2. See Lawrence Venuti, *The Scandals of Translation: Towards an Ethics of Difference* (London: Routledge, 1998), chapter 3.

3. Jacques Derrida, *Le Monolinguisme de l'autre: ou la prothèse d'origine* (Paris: Galilée, 1996), 40.

4. Jacques Derrida, *Monolingualism of the Other; or, The Prosthesis of Origin*, trans. Patrick Menash (Stanford: Stanford University Press), 19–20.

5. See especially Jacques Derrida, "Différance," in *Margins of Philosophy*, trans. Alan Bass (Chicago: University of Chicago Press, 1982), 1–27.

6. Derrida, *Monolingualism of the Other*, 40.

7. Ibid., 20, 26.

8. Jacques Derrida, "What Is a 'Relevant' Translation?," trans. Lawrence Venuti, *Critical Inquiry* 27 (2001): 174–200; see 171.

9. Ibid., 179

10. Ibid., 183.

11. Ibid., 181.

12. Ibid., 178.

13. See Simon During, ed., *The Cultural Studies Reader* (London: Routledge, 1999).

14. See Itamar Even-Zohar, *Polysystem Studies, Poetics Today* 11, no. 1 (1990).

15. See, for instance, Basil Hatim and Ian Mason, *The Translator as Communicator* (London and New York: Routledge, 1997), and Gideon Toury, *Descriptive Translation Studies and Beyond* (Amsterdam: Benjamins, 1995).

16. Pierre Bourdieu, *Homo Academicus*, trans. Peter Collier (Stanford: Stanford University Press, 1998), 94–95.

17. Ibid., 95.

18. Pierre Bourdieu, *Practical Reason: On the Theory of Action*, trans. Randal Johnson (Stanford: Stanford University Press, 1998), 78.

19. See Brian Harris, ed., *Translating and Interpreting Schools* (Amsterdam: Benjamins, 1997).

20. Homi K. Bhabha, *The Location of Culture* (London: Routledge, 1994), 102–4.

21. Ibid., 108.

22. See Vicente L. Rafael, *Contracting Colonialism: Translation and Christian Conversion in Tagalog Society under Early Spanish Rule* (Ithaca: Cornell University Press, 1993).

23. See, for example, Ania Loomba, *Colonialism/Postcolonialism* (London: Routledge, 1998), 96, 179–80.

24. Gayatri Chakravorty Spivak, *Imaginary Maps: Three Stories by Mahasweta Devi* (London: Routledge, 1994), xxiii, xxviii.

25. Ibid., xxviii. Cf. Mahasweta Devi, *Breast Stories*, ed. and trans. Gayatri Chakravorty Spivak (Calcutta: Seagull, 1997), 16, where Spivak states that "I have used 'straight English,' whatever that may be."

26. Devi, *Breast Stories*, 40, 44.

27. Mona Baker, "Linguistic Perspectives on Translation," in *The Oxford Guide to Literature in English Translation*, ed. Peter France (Oxford: Oxford University Press, 2000), 23.

28. Baker cites Venuti, *The Translator's Invisibility*, and a previously published version of Venuti, *The Scandals of Translation*, chapter 1.

29. See Louis Althusser and Etienne Balibar, *Reading Capital*, trans. Ben Brewster (London: New Left Books, 1970), 34–43.

30. Penelope Brown and Stephen C. Levinson, *Politeness: Some Universals in Language Usage* (Cambridge: Cambridge University Press, 1987), 61.

31. Hatim and Mason, 84.

32. Ibid., 96.

33. Bourdieu, *Practical Reason*, 133.

34. Hatim and Mason, 96.

35. Bourdieu, *Homo Academicus*, 128.

36. Philip E. Lewis, "The Measure of Translation Effects," in *Difference in Translation*, ed. Joseph Graham (Ithaca: Cornell University Press, 1985), 56.

37. On this issue, see Rebecca Comay, "Geopolitics of Translation: Deconstruction in America," *Stanford French Review* 15, no. 1–2 (1991): 47–79.

38. Derrida, "What Is a 'Relevant' Translation?," 183–94.

39. Ibid., 196.

40. See, for example, Mona Baker, *In Other Words: A Coursebook on Translation* (London: Routledge, 1992), and the critique in Rosemary Arrojo, "The Revision of the Traditional Gap between Theory and Practice and the Empowerment of Translation in Postmodern Times," *The Translator* 4 (1998): 25–48.

41. Eugene Nida, *Towards a Science of Translating, with Special Reference to Principles and Procedures Involved in Bible Translating* (Leiden: Brill, 1964), 159.

42. See Ernst-August Gutt, *Translation and Relevance: Cognition and Context* (Oxford: Blackwell, 1991), 31–35; for the linguistic theory, see Dan Sperber and Deirdre Wilson, *Relevance: Communication and Context* (Oxford: Blackwell, 1986).

43. Lewis, "The Measure of Translation Effects," 41.

44. Derrida, "What Is a Relevant Translation?," 183.

45. Ibid., 195.

46. Ibid., 175, 191.

47. Jacques Derrida, "Qu'est-ce qu'une traduction 'relevante'?," in *Quinzièmes Assises de la Traduction Littéraire (Arles 1998)* (Arles: Actes Sud, 1999), 35.

48. Derrida, "What Is a Relevant Translation?," 188.

49. Derrida, "Qu'est-ce qu'une traduction 'relevante'?," 46.

50. Derrida, "What Is a Relevant Translation?," 198.

51. Derrida, "Qu'est-ce qu'une traduction 'relevante'?," 24.

52. Derrida, "What Is a Relevant Translation?," 177.

53. Kristin Casady, letter to the author, 6 September 2000.

54. Derrida, "Qu'est-ce qu'une traduction 'relevante'?," 41.

55. Derrida, "What Is a Relevant Translation?," 193.

56. Kristin Casady, letter to the author, 6 October 2000.

57. Lewis, "The Measure of Translation Effects," 43.

58. See Alan Bass's discussion on this point in Derrida, "Différance," 19–20 n. 23.

59. Derrida, "Qu'est-ce qu'une traduction 'relevante'?," 42

60. Derrida, "What Is a Relevant Translation?," 195.

61. Derrida, "Qu'est-ce qu'une traduction 'relevante'?," 45.

62. Derrida, "What Is a Relevant Translation?," 197.

63. Derrida, "Qu'est-ce qu'une traduction 'relevante'?," 24.

64. Derrida, "What Is a Relevant Translation?," 177.

65. Derrida, "Qu'est-ce qu'une traduction 'relevante'?," 23

66. Derrida, "What Is a Relevant Translation?," 176.

67. Derrida, "Qu'est-ce qu'une traduction 'relevante'?," 47

68. Jacques Derrida, *Spectres de Marx: l'état de la dette, le travail du deuil et la nouvelle internationale* (Paris: Galilée, 1993), and Jacques Derrida, *Specters of Marx: The State of the Debt, the Work of Mourning, and the New International,* trans. Peggy Kamuf (London: Routledge, 1994).

69. Friedrich Schleiermacher, "On the Different Methods of Translating," in *Translation/History/Culture: A Sourcebook,* ed. and trans. André Lefevere (London: Routledge, 1992), 141–66.

70. Henri Meschonnic, *Pour la poétique II* (Paris: Gallimard, 1973), 308.

French Thinking/Thinking French—
In Translation

Laurent Milesi

INTRODUCTION

ONE WAY OF CHARACTERIZING THE RAPIDLY CHANGING PANORAMA OF English studies since the 1970s is to recognize how critical attitudes in the discipline in Britain have been influenced and reshaped by the import of ideas, concepts and thinking/writing practices and especially so-called "theories" from across the Channel (or, for other "continentals," the Atlantic). As critical agendas busily reshaped themselves in the light of these new trends which, for some, were eventually to acquire the status of new alternative orthodoxies, no real attention seems to have been paid to the phenomenon of "translation," cultural, ideological, and linguistic, that such foreign ideas underwent as they were repackaged and redeployed in a radically different academic environment—save in the form of later monographs which too often ungenerously cataloged the sins of critical misappropriations and misunderstandings usually perpetrated under the name *poststructuralism.*[1] Rather than taking a turn at fruitlessly awarding more bad marks, I would like to examine some examples of that perhaps inevitable "negligence" in/of translation—a concept which will be made to stretch far beyond the too numerous infelicities that alas also plague the reading of original French texts "in translation" (although these somehow contribute to the phenomenon I shall try to analyze)—in order to convey something of Homi Bhabha's own conception in *The Location of Culture* (1994), where "cultural translation" (partly modeled on Benjamin's and Derrida's understandings of the resistance of/to translation) is used to designate the necessity of a transposition attesting to the foreignness of languages and the staging of cultural difference.[2] I shall look at, and try to "theorize," the vicissitudes undergone by three simple yet fundamental examples of a "notion," "movement," or "idea" (and the practices it covers) which form as much our daily staple as Walter Benjamin's original example of the German and French versions of *bread* [*Brot, pain*]: (a) "theory" versus *théorie*; (b) the invention, circulation and application of the label *poststructuralism*; and (c) Barthes's much maligned polemic catchphrase *the death of the author*. Combining a loosely historicist approach with an eye for reception in this exposition, and using a Derridean angle in the subsequent attempt to negotiate the ideological gaps, I shall try to review how these migrations, (re)appropriations and implementations, fraught with unthought assumptions about their intellectual borrowings, were perhaps necessary to generate another academic "tradition" within specifically Anglo-American contexts, and shall also briefly outline how such inevitable institutional recontextualizations, "nativizations," or naturalizations can give way to more fruitful contextual transactions, where the foreign as radical other will be preserved and respected, rather than subdued or ignored.

Theorizing — or Is It *Théoriser?* — The Difference: Theory versus *Théorie*

What could be more revealing of the subtly divisive gap in presuppositions between the Anglo-American and French-speaking worlds— as an instance of the larger diversity of cultural and ideological constructions underlying various national historico-literary/critical, scientific traditions—than the overarching word *theory* "itself," which has presided over the renewal of our perception of the literary object for the last thirty to forty years? But which self?

To my knowledge, we owe the pioneering invention of the concept and, ultimately, of the method of (modern) "literary theory"— what "theory" in English started as in the subject known then as "English Literature"—to Wellek and Warren's epoch-making *Theory of Literature* (1942).[3] Starting with the acknowledgement that there is no satisfactory name in English for the "integrated study of literature"—"The most common terms for it are 'literary scholarship' [which excludes criticism] and 'philology' [misleading, as it has

shifted from the 'study of language and literature' to 'linguistics']"—
the two critics propose *literary theory* as a term to designate "the study
of the principles of literature, its categories, criteria, and the like" (as
opposed to the analyses of concrete works either as literary history or
literary criticism). Thus Wellek and Warren's "theory of literature"
subsumes both the "theory of literary criticism" and the "theory of literary history" so as to reconcile their respective insights within a
larger, more systematic framework, and operates a junction between
a historically grounded conception of literature and the need to articulate the theoretical locus/place of literariness.[4]

Of course, one takes (or should take) for granted nowadays that,
in a general sense, there is no reading or study of literature or of any
literary work which does not rest upon the ideological axiomatics of
even some rudimentary, implicit, or unconscious "theory" about language, meaning, communication, and interpretation. So why single
out these two writers' enterprise, even if their intimate background
knowledge of, and greater openness to, the different procedures and
problematics in continental humanist studies explains why one
could legitimately want to claim their 1942 work as a distant precursor for the later fashioning of "critical theory"? In fact, Wellek's famous controversy with F. R. Leavis in the latter's journal *Scrutiny* five
years before, following his review of *Revaluation* (1936) in which he
called upon the English critic to "defend [his] position more ab-
stractly and to become conscious that large ethical, philosophical,
and, of course, ultimately, also aesthetic *choices* are involved,"[5] proves
both points. Leavis's parry then had been that Wellek's critical priorities and principles were those of a philosopher, not a critic's, and
that the two disciplines were and had to be kept separate. And to this
day, despite recent, ever increasing attempts to bridge the gap and
"(re)philosophize" what literary theory has become under the um-
brella name and exercise of "critical (and cultural) theory"—though
using an adaptation of philosophical discourse which usually distinguishes it sharply from its continental equivalents—this clash between "criticism" and "theory" (what Leavis perceptively diagnosed
as "philosophy" in Wellek's critique) largely remains unsolved and
could be used as a starting point to further explore the still prevalent
underpinnings of "theory" versus *théorie* (or other continental translations for that matter), in ways that I can only schematically suggest.

Whether we are talking about German *Theorie* (cf. *Literaturtheorie*
or *Literaturwissenschaft*, that is, the science of literature, inherited

from the nineteenth-century Humboldtian model), Italian (but also Spanish) *teoria* (the former steeped in Croce's philosophico-literary aesthetics), the Russian formalists' own construction of *teoria*, or, as my focus will be, French *théorie*, the common denominator of the practices behind the word is a philosophical or at least a systematic approach, hence its reemergence within the intellectual and ideological context of continental structuralism. Thus—and given the strong philosophical background and heritage of the postwar generations of French intellectuals, most of whom attended Alexandre Kojève's history-making lectures on Hegel's *Phenomenology of Mind* in the 1930s or were more generally steeped in current (German) philosophical debates[6]—the critical analysis of literature presupposes asking questions as to the essence of literariness and its "existential" implementations as literature (for instance, Sartre's *Qu'est-ce-que la littérature?* [1947]) via the systematic and generalizable analysis of its structures, the transcendence of categories of literary discourse (unlike the traditional immanentist French flavor of "practical criticism" known as *explication de texte*—and feared and respected by many a French pupil for its subtly boring, yet terroristically forming blend of rigor and rigidity), and the critical reinscription of its products and genres within a global historico-conceptual framework.

It is therefore worth recapitulating what underpins the more distinctly continental flavor of theory, in contradistinction to how "critical theory" emerged out of the demarcation of literary theory from literary criticism, and I will do so by looking at the organization of two representative anthologies produced within one year of each other (crucially, toward the beginning of the 1980s, when several volumes on structuralism "and since" were already available,[7] and more global introductions to (modern) literary theory or manifestos were seeing the light of day or were in the making.[8]) These are: *Théorie de la littérature*, a Dutch-German-French venture edited by Kibédi Varga in 1981,[9] and *French Literary Theory Today*, a reader in translation for the benefit of the Anglo-American public collected by Tzvetan Todorov in 1982. These in turn will be contrasted with the more international, Franco-Canadian-led project directed by Marc Angenot *et al.* (with collaborations from the likes of Jonathan Culler, a French specialist operating in an American academic context): *Théorie littéraire: Problèmes et perspectives* (1989).[10]

Kibédi Varga's edited volume kicks off with a few *Généralités*, which shape the contours of the concept of a theory of literature between science, history, and methods. The collection is then divided into two parts: one focusing on the description of the literary text—with illustrations from textology (the science of the text), prosody (one sense of the word *poetics*), rhetoric and stylistics, and narratology—the other on the literary text's functioning in several wider socio-historico-ideological contexts. What the four "descriptive" methods have in common is

(a) an anchoring in a strongly methodical, systematic approach, which explains why they cumulatively usually failed to find favor in Anglo-American academe (compare the preponderant role of Jakobson, felt as *passé*, as opposed to the "later Barthes," for instance); but also, despite going in tandem with a global reinscription of their functioning within a theory of communication,

(b) the perception of a certain "monumentalization" of the literary work, albeit of a different kind than the one generated by the formalist, ahistorical readings of the schools of both *explication de texte* (inherited from Lanson) and practical criticism (I. A. Richards) or the American spin-off of New Criticism, that ultimately does away with the reader's individual sociohistorical background for "receiving" it.

Even more revealing of the orientations of continental (French) theory is Todorov's *Reader*, its architecture, and his own introduction to its contents and choices (which range from 1968 to 1978: that is, the birth and development of poetics under structuralism and the latter's mutations in the next decade). The manual falls into four parts, from the general to the more "applied," which I will gloss by recasting Todorov's own categorizations:

(a) Part I defines the broad "scope" via one single essay, by Gérard Genette, on "Criticism and Poetics" (the latter being perhaps the "master concept" that separates theory from *théorie*, as we shall see);

(b) Part II elaborates the typology of literary creation from three conjoint perspectives: Barthes on the *effet de réel* in literature; Riffaterre (known throughout the 1970s for his conjunction of semiotics with stylistics from which he worked out his model of intertextual semiotics as chief mechanism of literarity and textual production);[11] and Laurent Jenny (on form and structure);

(c) Part III explores several descriptive-analytical categories and concepts born from the interface between linguistics and narratology and poetics: Jean Cohen's "A Theory of the Figure"; Belgian linguist Nicolas Ruwet on parallelism and deviation in poetry; "A

Critique of the Motif" by Claude Brémond; and "What is a Description?" by Philippe Hamon;

(d) Part IV applies the theory or poetics to three examples of genres and models: medieval literature (Paul Zumthor); autobiography (Philippe Lejeune); (Rimbaud's) poetry (Todorov himself).

The critical focus of those essays is on the renewed conception and practice of poetics—for Todorov, a synonym for the "theory of literature" itself[12]—which is to be understood neither as a "theory of poetry" (if anything, it was applied more to prose narratives and dovetails therefore with narratology), nor more generally in the sense of a system of devices characteristic of the work of a given writer, but rather as the theory of genres and literary discursive practices. As such, it is also to be distinguished from (literary) interpretation—in a different context, one could recall T. S. Eliot's similar wish to disengage the understanding of poetry or, more broadly, literary works from the task of hermeneutics he called "explication"[13]—as its object is "the general laws which govern the functioning of literature, its forms and varieties,"[14] and, unless it is qualified and redeemed by an adjective, as with "Romantic poetics," one sees in Todorov's definitional angle why the discipline thus conceived could not implant itself on Anglo-Saxon soil as part of an attempt to challenge the monolithic institution of ideology behind the study and reading of (canonical) English literature, despite—or is it also because of?—the imbrication of conceptions of literary discourse within a stricter, more systematic exercise of post-Saussurean, Bakhtin-influenced linguistics and its manifold branchings into discourse analysis and sociocriticism which the institutional redeployment and translation of these and other continental ideas and practices could not afford to take on board.[15]

It is thus not surprising to read the following caveat in Todorov's introduction, which I would like to tacitly oppose to the slightly skewed title of Culler's otherwise excellent *Structuralist Poetics* (1975) —incidentally mentioned in a short bibliographic conclusion to Todorov's introductory presentation:[16]

> I do not find that there is much to say about the relation between poetics and structuralism. . . . Particularly in France, it was under the influence of structuralism that literary studies became open to theory; however, poetics is not a method—structuralist or other—but rather a way of looking at the facts. So, since that creates the facts, it is both an object and a discipline.[17]

Related to systematic description and categorization and perceived within the epochal movement of continental (French) structuralism—that is, the extension of Saussure's linguistic theoretical work via the Prague and Copenhagen schools, as opposed to (American) Bloomfieldian structuralism which, in conceiving syntax in a continuum from phonology, bypasses the problem of (the production of) signification—the supposedly transmethodical poetics (and the linguistic models that nourished it) was assimilated as structuralist poetics and, once the opening to poststructuralism had taken place (as "critical theory" emerged out of the radicalization of "critical practices" in modern literary theory to supersede practical and literary criticism), was "relegated" outside the confines of the emerging Anglo-American conception and practices of theory. On the contrary, *théorie* cannot satisfactorily be severed from a global inquiry into structure (beyond its structuralist "moment") and from a "poetic" conception of the literary object or of literarity. Even today, the practice of so-called "critical theory" in, say, French-speaking countries (and who would translate it as *théorie critique* and yet hope to be understood?) is by and large confined to departments of English studies and is a mirror reflection of the reimported hegemony and influence of Anglo-American academic discourses—of which several official documents occasionally emanating from the Research Assessment Exercise panel, dismissing as ill-founded the proposal of having "external" foreign assessors, give us a rather sad nationalistic reminder in this supposedly postcolonial day and age . . . .

Atypical for Anglo-American evasions of essentialist questions to literature is Jonathan Culler's essay on "La littérarité" in Angenot's more international, multiperspectival volume. Yet Culler's historical approach and framing of the concept in order to stake out the ambit of the question "What is literature/literariness?"—that is, its essential features, also in contradistinction to what is not (the) literary—implicitly confirms the critical divide I have outlined, as most of the antecedents that nourished the critico-philosophical project of defining or exploring (the limits of) literature are continental in the largest sense, ranging from French, German, to Russian formalist attempts (compare, for instance, the work of the Moscow and Leningrad schools of poetics on *literaturnost*). It would appear that the nearest that critical projects emanating from within an "English" context—that is, especially one not aware of *Francophone* issues—usually ever get to a quasi-phenomenological inquiry into literariness is via a reflection focused on "the language of literature" (poetry, narrative, etc.) and a reasoned cataloging and exploration of its major constitutive tropes (for example, irony).

WHO INVENTED "(POST)STRUCTURALISM" AND FOR WHOM?

Unearthing the always problematic "origin" of a concept may be an impossibly mythical task that would seem to disregard the now well-known Derridean warnings against such a positivistic understanding of the notion; yet mapping the history (or histories), space, and genealogies of concepts, whether in the original or in translations, would help provide valuable information about the circulation and filiations of new ideas and intellectual exchanges.

It has been generally assumed since Geoffrey Bennington's detective work in *Legislations* (1994)—itself much indebted to an earlier paper by Robert Young later published as chapter three of *Torn Halves* (1996) —that, historically speaking, the word *poststructuralism* seems to have been used in French first, in Jean-Joseph Goux's *Freud, Marx: Économie et symbolique* (1973). Incidentally, Bennington notes that "the word *already* appears in quotation marks [emphasis added]" and perhaps hastily seems to perceive the marks of citationality as the literal sign of a quotation rather than as the possibility of a tentative coinage.[18] It then gained widespread acceptance and use in the Anglo-American world after about 1979 (usually in the form of "so-called poststructuralism"), before being reimported into French with Vincent Descombes's *Grammaire d'objets en tous genres* (1983). The ironic quid pro quos of the toings and froings of an originally French source adopted into Anglo-American critical circles against the grain and inclination of all those (usually mutually antagonistic) Gallic thinkers which it helped label under one common, neatly recognizable banner,[19] then reimported back into French critico-philosophical discourses, partly justify Bennington's reticence toward the otherwise "necessary" program of investigating and writing the history and sociology of this institutionalization of a "phantom movement," whose complexities prompt an engagement with issues of nationality (notably via the question of translation).[20]

Yet there could be an alternative history of births and developments, presumably lying outside what could have come under direct scrutiny to influence the redrawing of intellectual debates in English studies, let alone any subsequent historicist recontextualizations. Quite uncannily, this alternative story of beginnings for the period label *poststructuralism* would recall the debt of its predecessor, structuralism, to anthropology. The debt is mainly to Claude Lévi-Strauss's "Structural Analysis in Linguistics and in Anthropology" (1945) and *The Elementary Structures of Kinship* (1947), but also, almost at random, his *Structural Anthropology* (1958), one year after the first landmark international encounter between anthropologists (Lévi-Strauss himself), critics (Barthes) and linguists (Chomsky, Marcellesi) that arguably sealed the official emergence of a new "method," and also his 1960 article "La structure et la forme," the first introduction of Propp's *Morphology of the Folk Tale* (originally in Russian, 1928) to a French readership which was to form one of the ferments behind the impetus toward narratology.[21] The noun *poststructuralism* was in circulation as early as 1967, in its derived adjectival form, and used by one J. Van Velsen in A. L. Epstein's *The Craft of Social Anthropology*: "I have contrasted the aims and methods of anthropologists writing in the structuralist tradition with the types of problem in which many anthropologists of a younger, *post-structuralist*, 'generation' have become familiar [emphasis added]."[22]

The date and nonliterary context are interesting in themselves: one year after the landmark conference at Johns Hopkins University which brought together for the first time in America an international perspective on continental structuralism, nine years after the Parisian affair, at a juncture when structuralism was already undergoing some revisions and criticism in France (among which may be mentioned Pierre Macherey's 1965 article "Literary Analysis: The Tomb of Structures," the strong impact of *Tel Quel* from 1966/67 onwards, the emergence of the concept of "intertextuality" (1965/66), the discovery of "another Saussure" less recuperable by an early orthodox structuralism (1964 onwards), and of course Derrida's work, from which he presented and reworked for the occasion his attack on Lévi-Strauss himself: "Structure, Sign and Play in the Discourse of the Human Sciences").[23] If I recall these historical moments and offer what could otherwise pass as naïve reconstructions waiting to be deconstructed in turn by some demonstrable examples of earlier antecedence,[24] it is because the complex mixture of palimpsestic myths of alternative origins and filiations, together with the generational *décalage* in critical debates and the silencing of other or wider intellectual contexts, all partake of the logic of thinking in translation which the inevitable adjustment and reshaping of imported theory within a foreign institutional climate testify to, and which itself needs attending to *before* observing that the history and sociology of the telluric movements of the label *poststructuralism* across the Channel or the big pond would have to take into account the nonlinear, precisely so-called "poststructuralist" construction of the "*post-*" (not unlike the future perfect modality of Lyotardian postmodernism[25])—to return to Bennington's reservations about the heuristic foundations of such a project. What got hollowed out of *théorie* through its historical assimilation and "translation" as "structuralist poetics"[26] marks the tension in the coemergence of structuralism and poststructuralism in the Anglo-American world, if not the retroactive quasi-antecedence of the latter over the former as its alleged critique, which offers an uncanny mirror reflection of the belated reimportation of the once exported theory (back) into France whereby, according to the famous maxim concluding Lacan's "Seminar on 'The Purloined Letter,'" "the sender . . . receives from the receiver his own message in reverse form."[27] As Robert Young excellently summarizes the interchange:

> As Jonathan Culler has pointed out, in the USA poststructuralism virtually did precede structuralism. This is because in many respects poststructuralism (a word that has begun to be used in France only recently) represents the American translation of that non-scientific form of structuralism that Culler himself separated off from structuralism proper in his highly influential *Structuralist Poetics* (1975). . . . Poststructuralism, in this case, would amount to a form of translation, of metaphoricity, its "post" denoting the crossing of national and conceptual frontiers that had served to separate structuralism from itself.[28]

Before timidly offering my own theoretical programme by way of conclusion, I will adduce one further instance of the institutional warping or translation of one much bandied-about catchphrase in literary-critical circles: Barthes's proclamation of the "death of the author."

THE RETURN TO THE DEATH OF THE AUTHOR

There is hardly a critical slogan, even more so than quasi-neologisms like deconstruction and *différance*, that can lay claim to having led to more interpretive extrapolations (i.e., misprision of tone and slant and erasure of ideological context within which these were operating) in crossing the murky waters from one institutional context to another, than Roland Barthes's celebrated pronouncement on the "death of the author."

Through yet another quirk of history, Barthes's polemic essay first appeared as "The Death of the Author," in *Aspen* (1967), one year before its delayed French publication as "La mort de l'auteur" in *Manteia*.[29] The anteriority of the American commission, one year prior to the May 1968 event with which Barthes's essay has often hastily been associated (and to which it certainly lent an *a posteriori* critico-revolutionary *mot d'ordre*), is recalled, together with the long-standing hostility of French *universitaires* since Barthes's first, more timid, anti-authorial formulations as early as *Sur Racine* (1963), in Seán Burke's *The Death and Return of the Author* (1992), which features a minute analysis of the French critic's essay and eventually a refutation on grounds of argumentative excess keyed to a lack of substantial logical proof.[30] Himself not immune to the exacerbations of polemic misrepresentations he accuses Barthes of, Burke quite symptomatically abides by the *letter* of the Barthesian text, failing to register all the contextual determinations of the ideological, intellectual, and institutional framework, which gave the piece its shape, tone, and thrust—and which no French reader or critic "in the know" then would have ignored or missed. For instance, the target of the attack, the so-called *critique d'auteur* that had been holding pedagogical and intellectual sway over so many decades, is not even mentioned by name—one should compare this with the then equally powerful *cinéma d'auteur*, to which the *Nouvelle Vague* of Godard, Resnais, and Truffaut was likewise strongly reacting at approximately the same time—and the tenaciously literal misunderstanding of Barthes's essay not only misses the point and range of the metaphors of the polemic tone but also how such a deliberate strategy, within the context of a long-lasting feud (the *affaire Picard* in 1965), was wielded in order to lay bare and chip away at the *critique universitaire*'s own unthought metaphorical assumptions (filiation, intentionality, exactly *who* was an author: that is, worthy of being studied under the curricular name of a representative, canonical "French literature," on which the *authority* of its authoritarian approach (the "man-and-his-work") was unchallengeably founded. Even more seriously, that the *author* meant the "realist" author—hence Barthes's alignment of the heyday of the French novel with the burgeoning of capitalism and its later academic relay by a bourgeois literary criticism—would have been contextually self-evident, even though Barthes felt the need to be explicit only once, in denouncing "the castrating objectivity of the realist novelist," to whom he opposes the lineage of *modernité*, from Mallarmé to the surrealists, then to the *nouveaux romanciers*, whose literary productions academic criticism would not have deemed worthy of the nineteenth-century label *novel*. Burke's construction of Barthes's parricidal desire to abolish the author ultimately rests on the misperception of the need then to vociferously proclaim such a "death," so as to force academic criticism to face the fact that writing practices and writers' relation to their work and the latter's "meaning" had changed, and this was not a matter of logical argumentation—after all, the *critique d'auteur* certainly never ever thought of proving the legitimacy of its own creed in the first place—but of "performative effect": castigating a monolithic, anachronistic conception of literature and criticism in the light of historically renewed practices. Through a subtle irony, Burke's ultimate dismissal, though itself patiently presented, partly resorted to the kind of argument the more dismissive rearguard, mostly academic, French criticism would choose to tap without seeing the implications of bringing such a necessity to bear on its own time-sanctioned tenets.

Conclusion: "Thinking Otherwise"

Of course our own as well as mutual misunderstandings are always somehow or other "understood": that is, eventually taken for granted but therefore also ignored and "naturalized," and their effects neutralized. Besides, as Derrida's cogent critique of the auto-affectiveness of thinking and belief in its self-presence to itself has underlined—or as John Irwin's reminder, in his intervention in the controversy around "The Purloined Letter," of the ultimate, one might say *differantial*, noncoincidence of thought with itself has reemphasized[31]—thinking will always essentially be "at odds" with itself, let alone with the other's, and will therefore always be in a more radical sense a "thinking otherwise," whether (in) French or (in) English. Yet one should not forget this added twist of translation or "translationality" at work across languages, cultures, and "national" institutions—after always already being at work *within* one's "domestic" language —even more urgently so nowadays, with the fashionable but too often glib lip-service being paid to cultural difference and the repoliticization or reethicalization of ideas, concepts, and texts.[32] Thinking will inevitably and indeed must travel in any guise, and is always "in translation" in one sense or another, as this is the double bind of its survival and operability: to be grafted and "translated" into alien socio-politico-institutional setups and surroundings which will "domesticate" and "nativize" the original contextual thrust by reorienting it elsewhere and otherwise. But paradoxically I would want to claim that the best way of achieving a desired "political" intervention is perhaps to pay heed to the original inscription and try to calculate the import of that displacement or "trans-lation" as well. This is also where the more pragmatic issue of translation and language communication and barrier comes in (as Derrida's resistant texts have tried to performatively thematize and thus force translators to address), with the necessity to be aware of differences in linguistic usage and tones, cultural practices, and modes of address, and how these contribute to challenging a specific historical climate that also needs to be grasped "for itself" in its radical alterity and in its difference. In other words, those of a now forgotten etymological fable, the ambivalence of the French *hôte*, either the one who gives (host) or the one who receives (guest) hospitality, should be fully observed in the laws of "academic," even "intellectual" exchanges, provided that the two components of its Latin forebear *hospes, hostis*: foreign, "hostile," and the Indo-European root **pet*, connoting "oneself,"[33] be themselves "domesticated" not so much in the interest of polite conversations but of transhistorical, transcultural (that is, transatlantic as well as *trans-Manche*) dialogues.

NOTES

1. See, for instance, Leonard Jackson's polemical study of the misuse of Saussure, *The Poverty of Structuralism: Literature and Structuralist Theory* (London: Longman, 1991)—to which a "companion volume" was added three years later: *The Dematerialization of Karl Marx: Literature and Marxist Theory* (London: Longman, 1994). An even less generous "reassessment," itself not beyond cardinal misunderstandings of several critical and theoretical contexts, can be found in Raymond Tallis, *Not Saussure: A Critique of Post-Saussurean Literary Theory* (Basingstoke: Macmillan, 1988).

2. Homi K. Bhabha, *The Location of Culture* (London: Routledge, 1994); see especially 228, for the statement "Translation is the performative nature of cultural communication."

3. René Wellek and Austin Warren, *Theory of Literature* (Harmondsworth: Penguin, 1949). See especially chapter 4.

4. Ibid., 38–39.

5. Quoted in *Modern Literary Theory: A Comparative Introduction*, ed. Ann Jefferson and David Robey, with contributions from David Forgacs et al. (London: Batsford, 1982), 5.

6. On this issue see, for instance, Elisabeth Roudinesco, *Jacques Lacan & Co.: A History of Psychoanalysis in France, 1925–1985*, trans. Jeffrey Mehlman (London: Free Association, 1990), especially 134–47.

7. See, for instance, Michael Lane, *Structuralism: A Reader* (London: Cape, 1970); David Robey, *Structuralism: An Introduction* (Oxford: Clarendon Press, 1973); Henryk Baran, ed., *Semiotics and Structuralism: Readings from the Soviet Union*, trans. William Mandel, Henryk Baran, and A. J. Hollander (New York: White Plains, 1976); Terence Hawkes, *Structuralism and Semiotics* (London: Methuen, 1977); Jonathan Culler, *Structuralist Poetics: Structuralism, Linguistics, and the Study of Literature* (London: Routledge and Kegan Paul, 1975); John Sturrock, *Structuralism and Since: From Lévi-Strauss to Derrida* (London: Methuen, 1977).

8. See, for instance (apart from Jefferson and Robey, eds., *Modern Literary Theory*), Terry Eagleton, *Literary Theory: An Introduction* (Oxford: Blackwell, 1983) and also Catherine Belsey, *Critical Practice* (London: Methuen, 1980).

9. A. Kibédi Varga, ed., *Théorie de la littérature* (Paris: Picard, 1981).

10. Marc Angenot, et al., *Théorie littéraire: Problèmes et perspectives* (Paris: Presses Universitaires de France, 1989).

11. See my introduction, "Inter-textualités: enjeux et perspectives (en guise d'avant-propos)," to *Texte(s) et Intertexte(s)*, ed. Éric Le Calvez and Marie-Claude Canova-Green (Amsterdam: Rodopi, 1998), especialy 14–18.

12. Tzvetan Todorov, ed., *French Literary Theory Today: A Reader*, trans. R. Carter (Cambridge: Cambridge University Press, 1982), 1.

13. See T. S. Eliot, "The Frontiers of Criticism," in *On Poetry and Poets* (London: Faber and Faber, 1957), especially 109–10. A well-known instance of Eliot's distrust of explication is provided by his misleading "Notes on the Waste Land."

14. Todorov, *French Literary Theory Today*, 2.

15. It is this phenomenon of the "sociality" of literary as well as critical texts which newly founded (post–May 1968) periodicals like *Littérature* (launched in 1971) set themselves as a program of analysis by replacing them within the global, cultural, and discursive context of a *sociocriticism* (see for example the work of Claude Duchet).

16. Todorov, *French Literary Theory Today*, 7.

17. Ibid., 3. However, see Todorov's own earlier presentation of poetics within a series of introductions to structuralism, in *Qu'est-ce que le structuralisme?*, ed. François Wahl (Paris: Seuil, 1968), 97–166; reprinted as *Poétique* (Paris: Seuil, 1973).

18. See Geoffrey Bennington, "Postal Politics and the Institution of the Nation," in *Legislations: The Politics of Deconstruction* (London: Verso, 1994), 241–42, 253–54

n. 4, and Robert Young, "Poststructuralism–The Improper Name," in *Torn Halves: Political Conflict in Literary and Cultural Theory* (Manchester: Manchester University Press, 1996), 67–83. However, the genesis of the genesis seems itself to be somewhat problematic since Young's chapter, bearing the date "1986" at its close, refers on page 17 to an earlier work by Bennington, *Dudding: des noms de Rousseau* (Paris: Galilée, 1991), and was therefore published after Young's "original" essay.

19. Compare with François Laruelle, *Les Philosophes de la différence: Introduction critique* (Paris: Presses Universitaires de France, 1986).

20. Cf. Bennington, "Postal Politics and the Institution of the Nation," 241.

21. Yet, despite his collaboration with Jakobson in an important reading of Baudelaire's "Les Chats" (1962), Lévi-Strauss remains altogether conspicuously absent from dictionaries and encyclopedias on language and semiotics in French.

22. J. van Velsen, "The Extended-case Method and Situational Analysis," in *The Craft of Social Anthropology*, ed. A. L. Epstein (London: Tavistock, 1967), 140.

23. The proceedings were published as *The Languages of Criticism and the Sciences of Man*, ed. Richard Macksey and Eugenio Donato (Baltimore: Johns Hopkins University Press, 1970), to which *The Structuralist Controversy* was symptomatically appended two years later, thus registering the focusing into intellectual consciousness of an increasing critical distance toward the structuralist method. Young, in *Torn Halves*, recalls that change in title, adding rightly that Derrida's paper "constituted the decisive intervention that in the USA produced a new critical relationship to structuralism" (70).

24. This is also what John Barth does in "The Literature of Replenishment" for modernism and postmodernism, in order to undermine the epistemological validity of categorizing or differentiating literary styles into period labels or movements which could be conveniently carved out and defined from a knowable or reconstructible origin. Cf. *The Literature of Exhaustion and The Literature of Replenishment* (Northridge, Calif.: Lord John Press, 1982), 21–39.

25. Both Bennington and Young make the parallel.

26. See Culler, *Structuralist Poetics*. Thus, in his influential examination of the complex relationship between structuralism and poststructuralism via a review of a full-scale retrospective study (Descombes's *Le Même et l'autre* [translated by L. Scott-Fox and J. M. Harding as *Modern French Philosophy* (Cambridge: Cambridge University Press, 1980)]) and an anthology edited by Josué V. Harari (*Textual Strategies: Perspectives in Post-Structuralist Criticism* [Ithaca: Cornell University Press, 1979])— which led him to wonder whether "post-structuralism [was] nothing more than the advent in due course of structuralism's auto-critical moment"—Philip Lewis could write that "in mainstream literary studies, poetics is the discipline that appropriates the method of structural analysis and pursues a comparative inquiry grounded in the construction of models" (see "The Post-Structuralist Condition," *Diacritics* 12 [1982]: 2–24; quotations on 5 and 6).

27. Jacques Lacan, "Seminar on 'The Purloined Letter,'" in *The Purloined Poe: Lacan, Derrida, and Psychoanalytic Reading*, ed. John P. Muller and William J. Richardson (Baltimore: Johns Hopkins University Press, 1988), 52–53.

28. Young, 75. The whole meticulous argument would need to be quoted in full.

29. See Molly Nesbitt, "What Was An Author?," *Yale French Studies* 73 (1987): 229–57.

30. Seán Burke, *The Death and Return of the Author: Criticism and Subjectivity in Barthes, Foucault and Derrida* (Edinburgh: Edinburgh University Press, 1992), especially 20–29.

31. See John T. Irwin, "Mysteries We Reread, Mysteries of Rereading: Poe, Borges, and the Analytic Detective Story," *MLN* 101 (1986): 1168–1215, especially 1181.

32. See Jacques Derrida, *Of Hospitality: Anne Dufourmantelle Invites Jacques Derrida to Respond,* trans. Rachel Bowlby (Stanford: Stanford University Press, 2000), especially 158 n. 1. Derrida's treatise could provide one of the (philosophical) foundations for the generalized ethics and politics of translation that this paper implicitly advocates.

33. See *Le Robert. Dictionnaire historique de la langue française,* sous la direction de Alain Rey, 2 vols. (Paris: Robert, 1992), 1:975, s.v. *hôte.*

II
THEORY AND PRACTICE—
RE-ARTICULATIONS

Teaching Deconstruction:
Giving, Taking, Leaving, Belonging, and the Remains of the University

Simon Morgan Wortham

The Remains of the University
and the Study of Culture

In a recent essay on "Literary Study in the Transnational University," J. Hillis Miller tries to account for the hostility shown by some practitioners of a certain kind of cultural studies toward what is perceived as "high" theory and, in particular, deconstruction. Describing the emergence of cultural studies as a quasi-discipline, he remarks:

> Insofar as cultural studies still depends on the traditional idea of culture as the production in a subject or subjectivity of an identity produced through indoctrination by a nation-state or by a subculture such as an ethnic or gender community . . . it was necessary to resist the questioning by deconstruction of all the key concepts necessary to this idea of culture. These include identity, agency, the homogeneity of a given culture, whether hegemonic or minority, the definition of an individual by his or her participation in a nation or community, the unbreakable tie of a text or any other assemblage of signs to its context. The questioning by theory of these concepts often needed to be sidestepped in order for the project of cultural studies and related new disciplines to get going. These key concepts are glued together by a reinstalled referentiality that can no longer afford to be put in question and remain in question.[1]

For Miller, a cultural studies of this sort relies on, at the very least, a minimal degree of retention of such unquestioned "referentiality" as a condition of its need to thematize, narrativize, or interpret various texts, events, and artifacts according to a wider "context" (whether this be described as "historical," "social," or "cultural") to which these phenomena remain unbreakably tied. A "context" such as that outlined by Miller would of course need to be accorded, at bottom, a basic level of coherence for the analysis to get underway. Moreover, insofar as—for Miller—this "context" would thereby establish a more or less generalizable framework within which might be understood the shaping of identity in particular instances, thus facilitating traditional ways of determining objects of cognition and knowledge, it could be considered to work so as to reanimate conventional ideas of the "self" or "agency." In assuming that there is always a "context" for every "text," in a way that could be comprehended in the above terms, a cultural studies of the kind described by Miller would reinstall the particular as an expression or exemplar of a more clearly determined situation or setting (history, nation, culture, society, ideology) which, in turn, might be considered to fuel critical misrecognition or reduction of the effects and implications of "transnationality" or "globalization." Furthermore, in this case, the supposed exemplarity of the particular in its identity with the general would inevitably tend to prompt an account of, as Miller himself puts it, the "production in a subject or subjectivity of an identity" produced by a culture, whether it be hegemonic or minority: the assumed culture of nation-state or, as is more often emphasized nowadays, a subculture existing in some sort of relation to more dominant cultural practices and trends. In addition to this reinscription of knowledge in relation to the human subject, the founding of a certain kind of cultural study upon long-standing models of cognition, as described above, would reestablish cultural studies practictioners working in this way as themselves knowing *subjects*. From this perspective, then, Miller would doubtless see certain aspects of the critical landscape of cultural studies—its not infrequent commitment to "identity politics" over the years, its shift of emphasis toward the participatory agency of subjects within contemporary popular culture, even some versions of the debate about the ethics of cultural studies—as set up to reinstall the coextensivity of subjects of knowledge and knowing subjects in a way that would depend uncritically on deeply structured relations of reference, identity, and agency.

Miller therefore views cultural studies as, in the last analysis, based on an unquestioning reversion to more orthodox humanistic themes and modes of inquiry that he considers out of step with the "post-modern" or "posthistorical" moment. This prompts doubts, for Miller, about the political effectivity of cultural studies in general. Clearly Miller's anxieties in this regard resonate with Bill Readings's own misgivings concerning the effort to renew or reanimate political radicalism, which in *The University in Ruins* (1996) he takes as an important issue in the orientation of cultural studies.[2] For Readings, the end of the epoch of the nation-state brought about by the unstinting globalization of late capitalism and the apparently irresistible rise of transnational corporations has been accompanied generally by a process of depoliticization characterized by "the loss of belief in an alternative political truth that will authoritatively legitimate oppositional critique."[3] This is partly because the de-referentialization of culture that happens alongside the weakening of the nation-state itself begins to erode the distinction between cultural participation and exclusion, Readings tells us. But it is also because the modern or "posthistorical" bureaucratic state is no longer fashioned on the basis of the traditional concepts and politics of national identity, instead reproducing itself only in terms of a "non-ideological belonging."[4] The "managerial state" of the late twentieth- (and now early twenty-first) century promotes only a highly diluted simulacrum of social inclusion along the lines of "a corporate identity" whereby participation occurs at the price of becoming an (efficient) operative. This tends to wear away the established discourse and rhetoric of the subject or the citizen, recasting almost beyond recognition an historically specific ensemble of notions of contract and right. Readings suggests that the emergence of this nonideological or, as it were, apolitically determined "unipolar" state "marks a terminal point for political thought." As "posthistorical" human societies develop, the institution of the nation-state no longer occupies the center of our contemporary nexus or system of power relations but "is now merely a virtual point that organizes peripheral subjectivities within the global flow of capital."[5] The previously fundamental relationship between the state and the individual (understood variously in terms of long-standing conceptions of right, contract, and so forth) is more or less dismantled as the era of "translationality" or "globalization" takes hold, and it is in these terms that the question of political inclusion or exclusion with regard to the (political) center becomes misleading if not obsolete. This situation is just as relevant for the university. With the onset of the logic and discourse of excellence,

notions of communicative transparency within the more or less unified community of the university advocated by the German Idealists—or indeed the transactional models of communication within a
horizon of consensus envisaged by the likes of Habermas—become
increasingly untenable, even though the "generalized spirit of performativity" (Lyotard) characterizing excellence installs a supposedly cast-iron principle of translatability. This paradox occurs because the paradigm that customarily organizes and regulates the
relationship between individual disciplines and the institutional formation of knowledge in general, according to long-standing notions
of the shared ideals, principles, culture, and language of the academic community, is closely linked to the very same conceptual
framework of identity and unity that fashions the individual as a particular yet exemplary expression of the nation-state. For Readings, of
course, this framework is irredeemably eroded in the "posthistorical"
setting of the nation-state's decline. It is in precisely this setting,
then, that the university is in "ruin," and this "ruin" cannot be addressed or resolved by any sort of traditional politics, since this would
rest upon ideas and practices that the situation itself renders obsolete.

The impact upon Miller's recent work of Readings's description
of the ruined university of excellence is perhaps most pronounced,
therefore, where Miller develops his account of certain types of cultural study as somewhat out of step with the contemporary "postmodern" or "posthistorical" moment as one of "ruin" and "remains."
(This is the case despite the fact that, whereas Miller underlines what
he sees as the persistence of notions of reference and identity within
the institutional and disciplinary formation of cultural studies, Readings places the emphasis instead upon a crisis of orientation in cultural studies as it is faced with the de-referentialization of culture and
the problem of cultural participation this entails.) Indeed, in contemplating the "remains" that may survive (on condition of) this situation of "ruin," Miller might well have resorted to Readings's idea
of a "*pragmatic scene of teaching*"[6] to offer an alternative to the image of
cultural studies that emerges from his own work: that is, of cultural
studies' structural reliance upon the coextensivity of the knowledge
of cultural subjects, on the one hand, and knowing subjects of culture, on the other. In *The University in Ruins*, Readings advocates the
decentering of teaching today. This decentering entails just such a
"*pragmatic scene of teaching*" as one which dispenses with the idea of

the transmission of messages between preconstituted subjects understood as more or less automomous or sovereign (in a traditional liberal, humanistic education, this locates the teacher as authoritative magister, and the student as—notwithstanding—a free citizen free to partake of academic freedoms) in favor of a notion of "teaching and learning as sites of *obligation*,"[7] whereby "in place of the lure of autonomy, of independence from all obligation" comes an insistence that "pedagogy is a *relation, a network of obligation*."[8] Readings suggests that such teaching involves a thoroughly dialogic interaction that radically interrupts or suspends orthodox notions and practices of agency, identity, and communicability. Indeed, an example of such orthodoxy is detected in the Saussurean model of communication:

> Teaching should cease to be about merely the transmission of information and the emancipation of the autonomous subject. . . . First of all, the scene of teaching should be understood as a radical form of dialogue. This is not a Habermasian claim for communicative rationality in which the dialogues of teachers and students are really divided monologues. . . . The dialogue does not thaw and resolve into a monologue, nor is it controlled by the sender as a formal instrument in the grasp of the writing subject, like Mallarmé's use of the *mise en page*. . . . The listener is not an empty head, as in the line drawings that illustrate Saussure's account of communication. Saussure would have communication be the passage of a message from a sender to a receiver who is silent. . . . Dialogue would then be merely the exchange of roles between two persons, so that the first sender becomes in turn the empty receiver, and so on.[9]

Miller's "Literary Study in the Transnational University" would suggest the following kind of argument: to the extent that cultural studies (as both an archive of academic study and a disciplinary procedure) draws upon and reactivates a formal analogy between knowledge of subjects and the subject of knowledge, it will be inclined to recreate something like this Saussurean model of communication in the classroom, despite various attempts to undertake or promote radical sorts of dialogue, plurality, openness, inclusivity, and exchange. Indeed, it might be interesting to recall this sort of argument when rereading the work of Bill Readings: although the analysis works somewhat differently here, we do find in Readings that the effort to rethink the scene of teaching is situated alongside a number of misgivings concerning the critical, disciplinary, or indeed political effectivity of cultural studies in the context of the university's "ruin" as well as in the "posthistorical" setting of "transnationality" or "globalization."

If theorists of the effects of "globalization" or "transnationality" such as Readings and Miller remain critical of the project of cultural studies, and if their work calls upon us to rethink its institutional and pedagogical strategies and ambitions, then such a rethinking nevertheless requires further reflection and development. In part, this is due to the fact that Miller's (and to a lesser extent, Readings's) depiction of cultural studies has been taken by some as far too partial and at times a bit ill informed, failing to account fully for variants in the field as well as new work and perspectives within cultural studies that in fact operate to question and transform rather than reinforce the very same kinds of traditional concepts and procedures with which Miller in particular tends to associate the "discipline" in general. Above and beyond this criticism, however, the intellectual or critical "positions" with which these critics might themselves be associated beg a further kind of questioning. Both these critics have worked, written, and researched in fields strongly influenced by what is sometimes called "high" theory, and more specifically their analyses and perspectives obviously owe a debt to deconstruction and to the traditions of thinking upon which it draws. In offering strong analyses of some important aspects of cultural studies, not least its institutional, disciplinary, and pedagogical set-up, the work of Readings and Miller therefore calls us to reflect on the relation of deconstruction to teaching, its thinking and practice of teaching, especially in relation to the interplay with "culture." Via a return to Derrida, we will therefore discuss the import of "teaching deconstruction" in view of the problem of "culture." Close attention to Derrida's work (and his teaching) may well provide us with a way of imagining precisely the kind of "network of obligations" in the classroom or lecture hall to which Readings gestures, whereby teacher and student remain embroiled upon the difficult, aporetical ground of teaching as an event both within and beyond "tradition" which one can neither simply take nor leave. However, moving beyond the choice that is implied in the work of Readings and Miller (between viewing cultural study as either largely an ineffective symptom of or a rather sterile backlash against "posthistoricality" and "globalization"), my own essay will trace a perhaps more productive approach to the institutional, disciplinary and pedagogical instability of "culture" within Derrida's work on culture and the gift. Here, via Derrida's reading of Mauss, we find that the founding of cultural discourse or interpretation upon the "concept" of the gift founds the possibility of teaching today upon an unteachable situation, which might, nonetheless, give rise to a teaching in, of, or for the university that "remains."

TEACHING, CULTURE, AND THE GIFT

This essay will therefore proceed by attempting to show that, for Derrida, the theory and discourse of "culture" which has characterized an important feature of academic study in the humanities for some while now, inevitably, and somewhat centrally, raises the question of teaching. In *Given Time* (1991), Derrida suggests that the interdisciplinary study of "culture" in fact rests upon the idea or motif of the gift as that which provides a way for academic discourse in the humanities and the social sciences to transcend or subsume more straightforward forms of "cold economic rationality" by asserting the "symbolicity" of this very same "rationality."[10] For Derrida, as we will see, the work of Marcel Mauss constitutes a turning point in the historical development of this sort of study. Moreover, in thereby attempting to *give* an *account* of the gift, this very same kind of academic investigation leads to the experience of a fundamental aporia, since the gift—if there be any—must necessarily be diminished and even annulled at the moment it is accounted for. As Derrida points out, acknowledgment or recognition of the gift unavoidably involves giving something back, thus effectively subjecting the gift to a certain type of economic exchange that militates against its very idea. This implies that the study of culture, from which all sorts of accounts proceed, in fact rests upon that which, in a sense, must remain unaccountable. However, this aporetical situation not only intimates that the teaching of "culture" itself happens in an unteachable situation (as we will see, a similar sort of problematic also surrounds deconstruction itself); it also raises questions of the responsibilities (or, indeed, the irresponsibility) of any such teaching, which I will suggest need not only be negatively marked, but might be affirmed as opening on to a new experience or possibility of responsibility, or of the "ethical."

In two essays, then, by Jacques Derrida—"The Time of the King" and "The Madness of Economic Reason," collected together in *Given Time*—it is the discussion of the relationship between gift and exchange found particularly in Mauss's *The Gift* that is seen to spark a vast shift from traditional forms of economism (those predicated on more rudimentary base-superstructure or foreground-background divisions), through anthropology and sociology, structuralism and linguistics, to contemporary cultural study and interdisciplinary work generally in the humanities. For Derrida, Mauss's insistence in this study on the centrality of the concept of the gift epitomizes the pivotal moment at which social thought tries to transcend or exceed "cold economic rationality" by asserting economic reason's "symbolicity"; thus affording, as Derrida puts it, "an account of religious, cultural, ideological, discursive, esthetic, literary, poetic phenomena," all organized under the general rubric of the "economic."[11] (Readings would doubtless view the interdisciplinary discourse of "culture" as a weak substitute for the erosion of long-standing notions of communicative transparency discerned by German Idealists within the more or less unified horizon of the university.) Resorting to the gift as a key question within economic thought and reason, then, allows academic discourse ultimately to imagine access to "*total social fact*"—or, in effect, culture[12]—by rethinking, disposing, and deploying the "economic" within the problem of the gift.

Now in *The Gift*, Mauss argues that gifts (in archaic societies in particular) function to establish complex systems and networks of exchange, reciprocity, debt, obligation, status, and deferment. However, while Derrida acknowledges the concept of the gift as "related to economy," he nevertheless asks "is not the gift, if there is any, also that which interrupts economy? That which, in suspending economic calculation, no longer gives rise to exchange?"[13] In other words, for the gift truly to exist or to be given, reciprocity, obligation, debt—as particular formations of the general principle of exchange—must be absolutely dispensed with or forgotten. The gift once identified as gift inevitably bears "the mark of a duty, a debt owed, of the duty not-to . . . even not to give back," although of course the acknowledgment of a gift as gift cannot avoid giving something back, in the form of the acknowledgment itself (this need not even take the form of gratitude since, as Derrida points out, a gift can amount to "hurting, to doing harm" because it "puts the other in debt").[14] Hence, recognition of the gift "gives back, in the place . . . of the thing itself, a symbolic equivalent"[15]—just as Mauss gives a symbolic equivalent, his book *The Gift*, in recognition of the gift that ostensibly it is about, but which according to Derrida it also effectively annuls through the particular kind of exchange (between the gift and *The Gift*) taking place.

Thus the gift, as soon as it is acknowledged as gift (via academic parlance, wisdom, or teaching, for example), leads by way of patterns of real and symbolic investment to property rights and relations which ruin it *as* gift. For the gift to be possible, the "ritual circle of the debt"[16] incurred by giving must therefore undergo what Derrida terms "effraction" or interruption, in a time that, paradoxically and impossibly we might think, constitutes itself as an instant. This—perhaps unattainable—spontaneity is nevertheless vital because the gift, if it is to exist at all, cannot exist in a time characterized by deferral, by temporal lag or delay, through which patterns, cycles, circles of investment, accumulation, deferment, debt, and return unavoidably return. Yet formulating the concept of gift involves a recognition — "someone *intends-to-give* something to someone"[17]—which obviously requires or takes a time. To this extent, as Derrida is well aware, the philosophical contemplation of and return to the problem of the gift—even the knowing *giving* of a formula that suggests the gift's possibility/impossibility—leads us not away from methodological problems (those associated with Mauss, for example) but brings us straight back to the heart of them. Crucially, this would furthermore suggest serious implications for teaching (that is, for *giving* an *account*) in the era of the interdisciplinary study of culture (on the aporetical "grounds" or impossible yet necessary condition of the gift).

The paradox of the gift as acknowledged by Derrida therefore threatens to trap cultural and critical discourse in a circle or cycle whereby the problem is compounded in the very process of unraveling and *teaching* it. As Derrida himself notes, the very context of his paper "The Time of the King" is characterized by "an unsigned but effective contract between us [addresser:addressee/donor:donee: the speaker and his audience, but now also the writer and the reader], indispensable to what is happening here, namely that you accord, lend, or give some attention and some meaning to what I myself am doing by giving, for example, a lecture."[18] Even if dissatisfaction is expressed on receipt of the gift (the *teaching*) Derrida gives the donee (audience/reader)—"even if in a little while we were to argue or disagree about everything"—nevertheless sufficient "good faith" is shown or enough respect and "credit" paid in the event of such a teaching that it fulfills the terms of a contract, a calculated exchange. Yet this return to the logic of contract, and to the "ritual circle of debt," generosity, and gratitude that typifies and surrounds conventions of public speaking and teaching in the academic setting, annuls any gift Derrida might hope to give, subsuming the much regarded and wished-for "object" of analysis (namely the gift itself, which, as we have said, would also seem to establish the conditions of possibility of teaching in an age of the interdisciplinary study of culture) under the dense fabric of intellectual exchanges, investments, and approbations that intrinsically oppose it.

It is this very problem (a problem of *teaching*) that Derrida struggles with toward the end of his lecture. Here, he insists, "If one must *render an account* (to science, to reason, to philosophy, to the economy of meaning) of the circle effects in which a gift gets annulled, this account-rendering requires that one take into account that which, while not simply belonging to the circle, engages in it and sets off its motion": that is, the gift itself, which exists both within the economic circle, contracted almost inevitably "into a circular contract" or logic of exchange, but which crucially also appears as the "first mover of the circle," the prior or suppositional term of the "someone *intends-to-give* something to someone" upon which the circle or cycle, the whole economy, spins.[19] It would seem that what Derrida is saying here is that the paradoxical and unresolvable conditions of possibility/impossibility of the gift produce themselves as a kind of incalculable madness, generating an irrational excess in excess of the circle's economy, this "otherness" harboring the potential perhaps for a way out of the circular trap in which criticism seems to be caught in regard to the problem of the gift. And yet to *render an account* to someone or something (reason, philosophy, the economy of meaning) of this excess would surely entail a return to the logic of contract and calculation which this excess exceeds but also relentlessly "sets off [in] motion." Indeed, Derrida in the same passage describes this "account-rendering" in terms of "the contract between us, for this cycle of lectures," recognizing once more the ironic impossibility underlying the conditions of possibility of his lectures, his teaching, on the gift. Subsequently, Derrida wrestles with the need to render an account, if only of the possibility of a simulacrum of the gift, which in turn entails for him a question of desire: what impels

Derrida toward this account-rendering? Why would he wish to commit himself, to obligate himself, to the impossible task of rendering an account of the gift?

The question is in one respect arrived at naturally, since as we have seen, the issue under discussion provides a model, a paradigm or analogue for the difficulty of academic discourse and practice (or teaching) itself: *giving* an *account.* But, of course, the problem is given a further twist when we recall that, for Derrida, contemporary academic knowledge in the humanities—insofar as it deploys a discourse of culture in a characteristically interdisciplinary institutional setting—tends to be set off specifically by the gift itself. Cultural criticism or cultural studies, when speaking of the economic in ways which go beyond cold economism, must necessarily be speaking of the gift, since according to Derrida it is the category and concept of the gift that has allowed cultural study to maneuver itself into this position, to open its discursive formation of the economic as the discursivity (and, thereby, the interdisciplinary economy) of the economic. For the study of culture, the gift is always inseparable from the economic since without it the economic could not be transposed into and spoken of according to its own terms of "culture." Culture as an object of study or the organizing term of (inter)disciplinary activity in the humanities might therefore be thought to facilitate an academic discourse founded on the category of gift, which itself will therefore be required—even if this is not explicitly acknowledged—to work within the context of, to have recourse to, and thereby implicitly to *give an account of* the gift. And of course Derrida has drawn our attention to the impossible (impossibly tangled and fraught) conditions of such a process. Although again we need to note that this impossibility lies at the origins of the possibility of cultural criticism, since to say anything at all about the economic, and by extension about anything at all (since the object of cultural criticism is ultimately "*total social fact*" located within the "symbolicity" of the economic), it must somehow speak of the gift.

Hence, mirroring the problem of the impossible yet necessary possibility of the gift for contemporary cultural criticism and study, Derrida contemplates the paradoxical calling which urges him "to answer . . . for a gift that calls one beyond all responsibility";[20] that is to say, a gift which at once insistently calls for and (in absolute terms) renders impossible (a) *response* and *responsibility.* Thus, to pursue the difficult question of the gift, even of the excess and irresponsibility of the gift, nevertheless again compels Derrida to move *responsibly* within the circles of credit, debt, deferment, respect, generosity, and gratitude/reward that constitute the economy of academic teaching, discourse, and community: this returns him and us to the impossibility of simply *giving* an account, of course.

The issue of (ir)responsibility therefore arises at the moment Derrida finds himself struggling under the burden of a need to account for the tantalizingly unattainable object of his interest (the gift), which is unavoidably "other," the necessary yet impossible "other" at the heart of his discourse (as well as at the core of cultural discourse); but which, it seems, is ceaselessly displaced and lost in the very process of naming, identifying, speaking of it, *teaching* it. In "Violence and Metaphysics" Derrida's reading of the philosophy of Levinas turns upon similar issues. In this essay Derrida pursues the problem of otherness identified in Levinas's claim: "'If the other could be possessed, seized, and known, it would not be other.'"[21] The unattainability, by definition, of otherness within (academic) discourse and knowledge both sparks and frustrates the language and concept of the other, to the extent that the *phenomenon* of the other cannot encounter the other without friction and violence (just as cultural theory cannot encounter, know, or teach the gift as its founding principle without the experience of aporia, confusion, and conflict). And since the other *as* other cannot truly be included or spoken of within a discourse of the other, the friction or violence generated by any given discourse produces only a kind of violence against itself; just as the gift-account, since it requires the very same acknowledgment that entirely undermines it, suffers similar kinds of self-inflicted damage, perplexity, and disarray. Thus Derrida remarks, "Discourse, therefore, if it is originally violent, can only *do itself violence*, can only negate itself in order to affirm itself."[22] However, this violence against itself is of course necessary for discourse to produce itself, to sustain itself, to be and to speak. Such oddly productive violence characterizes the antagonistic simultaneity of recognition and neutralization of the other within discourse (a simultaneity of the kind we have located in a study of culture predicated upon the gift).

In "Violence and Metaphysics," however, it would seem difficult to ignore or repress the violence of a discourse of the other (that, is of discourse *itself* which must always—impossibly—give itself to something, someone, or some other) without risking compounding the very same kinds of discord and turbulence that set the problem in motion. Even if we might imagine from a reading of Levinas that violence could be abolished by recognizing and respecting the irreducible alterity of the other, nevertheless such "eschatology which animates Levinas's discourse would have to have had kept its promise already, even to the extent of no longer being able to occur within discourse as eschato*logy*."[23] The possibility of an end to violence can only be stated through discourse: that is, through violence.

If the gift, as the sign of the symbolicity of the economic upon which the era of the interdisciplinary study of culture is founded, "calls one beyond all responsibility," then nevertheless the obligation to render an account, to answer for, to *teach*, entails a violence that a critical discourse of culture would seem to effect as a condition of its response (to the call of the gift). And for which the question of responsibility or of the "ethical" inevitably arises.

TEACHING DECONSTRUCTION

Given that Derrida himself implicitly allies the question of the discourse and study of "culture" to a problem of teaching, with teaching thereby being found to be insistently or relentlessly "in" deconstruction, how might we account for the teaching given *by* deconstruction?

In all the literature written over the last twenty or thirty years concerning deconstruction as a philosophical or literary-critical practice, relatively little *concerted* attention has been devoted directly to the question of deconstruction and teaching, or, to go further, deconstruction as teaching, as perhaps *a* teaching.[24] In one respect this is unsurprising, since it has often been the case that "deconstruction" has been presented and defended by its best proponents as neither a traditionally constituted philosophical system tending toward its own coherence and closure, nor an easily reproducible, stabilizable method of inquiry or analysis, nor a readily communicable or transposable "object" of cognition. As is well known, involved and complicated discussions have abounded in the critical attention paid to the writings of Jacques Derrida concerning the strongly complexified status, for deconstruction, of the "concept" and the "example,"[25] of the relation of the particular to the universal, of transcendentality, singularity, iterability, repeatability, communicability, and so forth. Thus, the usual instruments of learning and teaching, and indeed many of the methods and assumptions underlying them, seem so thoroughly brought into question by deconstruction itself that it is no easy matter to explain how deconstruction might actually *determine* itself pedagogically, although undoubtedly in an obvious sense "deconstruction" is taught all the time.

Of course, many of the published writings of Jacques Derrida have often stemmed from work done in seminars or lectures given on specific occasions, with the singular and performative aspects of such events often being carefully preserved and, indeed, presented as a condition of the thinking that takes shape in Derrida's various texts. Not least due to his involvement with the Groupe de Recherche sur l'Enseignement Philosophique (GREPH) from the mid-1970s onwards, Derrida himself has written directly at some length on the question of teaching, although insights into Derrida's thoughts about how to teach deconstruction itself—if indeed any such thing were possible—are perhaps to be considered rare. Alongside the comments we have already looked at in *Given Time* (which, although they deal in some manner with wide-ranging questions surrounding the issue of teaching, nevertheless fall well short of a *statement* of the general relationship of deconstruction to pedagogy in all its forms), those pursuing the question of deconstruction and pedagogy might find a starting (and perhaps a stalling) point in the opening section of "The Double Session," with "quotations on the blackboard . . . pointed to in silence."[26] Alternatively, there is some discussion in *Living On: Borderlines* concerning the topic of the institution, language, and teaching.[27] One might also turn to Derrida's various analyses of the thought of Hegel, Nietzsche, and Heidegger in its relationship to pedagogy and to educational institutions, particularly where questions of the language, politics, and thinking of nationality and nationalism are concerned.[28] And in wider terms, of course, it should be recognized that a fairly constant interest in the university and in the institutional context of deconstruction itself runs throughout Derrida's writings, culminating most obviously in essays such as "Mochlos" and "The Principle of Reason,"[29] as well as suggesting itself in those texts that concern the setting up of the International College of Philosophy or the work of the GREPH. Nevertheless, amid these various writings, some of them clearly strategic or pragmatic in design, it remains possible to say that a clear and fully sustained statement on deconstruction's actual relation to teaching has still not readily been forthcoming. Is this responsible or irresponsible, on Derrida's part? I think one can speculate that this situation may provide a way for Derridean deconstruction to experience more fully fundamental problems and questions associated with teaching itself. That is to say, the performative dimension of teaching as an *event* in Derrida's work (as well as of writing and of speaking) allows deconstruction to *assume* rather than simply declare or resolve the pedagogical issues and problems with which it must necessarily concern itself. While bearing these broader comments in mind, then, I want to concentrate for the remainder of this essay upon two particular texts by Derrida, "Otobiographies" and "*Geschlecht* II: Heidegger's Hand," where—in some way or other—the question of teaching does raise its head (or rather, where it turns an ear, or raises a hand). This happens, in these texts, so as to engage once more issues of culture, community, communicability, and belonging, on condition of which academic and cultural discourse may well take place, today or in the past, but also according to which it may also experience certain de- or transformations within the university that remains.

DECONSTRUCTION AND ACADEMIC FREEDOM

Before coming to some particular remarks by Derrida on the topic of teaching and academic freedom—a topic that must inevitably reengage questions of the subject, agency, knowledge, responsibility, and pedagogy, as well as of (academic) culture and community—I want to begin by establishing a setting for these remarks in terms of the overall focus of the essay "Otobiographies: The Teaching of Nietzsche and the Politics of the Proper Name." Here, Derrida moves around and within the question of (a) teaching in the (proper) name . . . of Nietzsche. However, Nietzsche as a proper name, with all the effects a proper name induces, itself implies and underscores not just *a* teaching, but a plurality of teachings: teachings of and for Nazism, but also of Derrida and of deconstruction (among many others). For Derrida, the politics of the proper name and the question of teaching in the name (of Nietzsche) takes us to a "place of a very dense crisscrossing of questions" where "we must approach selectively, moving between the issue of the pedagogical institution, on the one hand, and, on the other, those concerning life-death, the-dead-the-living, the language contract, the signature of credit, the biological, and the biographical."[30] Derrida indicates that we might pursue in these very densely crisscrossed questions a rethinking of the relations of a Nietzschean legacy and the cultural and educational institutions of Nazism, in a perhaps more restricted sense; but also that we will inevitably be called to touch upon wider problems concerning the relationships between scholarly and pedagogical mastery, the authority and legacy of the signature and the proper name, and the possibility or necessity of receiving or hearing any (such) teaching "otherwise," with the ear of the other. In this essay, then, Derrida confronts the doubleness of teaching as, on the one hand, the supposed manifestation and perhaps inescapable effect of authoritative, self-crediting self-presentness where the pedagogue or magister is concerned; but also, on the other hand, of teaching as unavoidably a *différant*, anachronistic, untimely address to an "other," and indeed a response called forth by an "other," which—here, in Derrida's attention to Nietzsche's writing—inevitably occurs precisely as an effect of the supposed manifestation of self-presence and self-identity on the part of the magisterial teacher. Derrida writes this of Nietzsche's "autobiographical" and somewhat didactic text *Ecce Homo*: "The life that he lives and tells to himself ('autobiography,' they call it) cannot be *his* life in the first place except as the effect of a secret contract, a credit account . . . an indebtedness . . . it cannot be honoured except by another." Thus, "he does not live presently," and "it is by doing violence to himself that he promises to honor a pledge in the name of his name, in his name and in the name of the other," even in the form of " 'I and I who recite my life to myself.' "[31] Since the question of the effects of an authoritative, self-crediting pedagogy and the complex problem of teaching's legacy and return here supplement one another according to a logic of the interlacing of *différance*, Derrida shows that we are called upon to witness, in Nietzsche's *Ecce Homo* and other texts, the complicated interplay between the living and the dead. The proper name alone inherits the credit opened up by autobiography (a "life of . . . "), for example, and this proper name is a name of death. More widely, it might be suggested that this interplay between the living and the dead, and between the legacy and the proper name, in fact structures the histories and relations of the academic institution itself. Certainly, as Derrida goes on to show, it is this interplay between the living and the dead (between so-called living and dead languages and living and dead cultures, as well as living and dead masters) which imposes itself precisely on academic institutions of the sort specifically described and critiqued by Nietzsche, raising the issue of a thinking of the state in the age of Enlightenment. In the specific case of Nietzsche's understanding of his contemporary educational institutions as vehicles of the state, what is evident is a disfigurement of the mother tongue accompanying a return to a dead paternal language. As Derrida writes: "Not only is the State marked by the sign and the paternal figure of the dead, it also wants to pass itself off for the mother—that is, for life, the people, the womb of things themselves. . . . How an umbilical cord can create a link to this cold monster that is the dead father or the State—this is what is uncanny."[32] For Nietzsche, then, his interest in the state obviously entails thinking the state "otherwise" in relation to what Derrida has described as a statist problematic of education within modernity since the time of Enlightenment.

Leaving aside the broader concerns of Derrida's essay, concerns which nevertheless impose themselves on everything he has to say from the outset, Derrida prefaces his discussion with some very interesting remarks. At the beginning of "Otobiographies," itself a text originally presented as a lecture at the University of Montreal in 1979 and followed by roundtable discussions in which a select assembly of distinguished colleagues participated, Derrida has this to say:

> I would like to spare you the tedium, the waste of time, and the subservience that always accompany the classic pedagogical procedures of forging links, referring back to prior premises or arguments, justifying one's own trajectory, method, system, and more or less skillful transitions, reestablishing continuity, and so on. These are but some of the imperatives of classical pedagogy with which, to be sure, one can never break once and for all. Yet, if you were to submit to them rigorously, they would very soon reduce you to silence, tautology, and tiresome repetition.[33]

For Derrida, it is neither that the academic conventions of a more or less orthodox pedagogy can simply be ignored, surpassed, or abandoned, nor that they permit themselves to be unquestioningly defended and thereby unproblematically reproduced. Rather, any teaching necessarily partaking of pedagogical tradition that tries none the less to remain wholeheartedly devoted to an unsupplemented reinscription or conservation of the method or the system that allows and enables it to set out will inevitably dwindle into circularly self-justifying practices that actually inhibit and eventually pre-

clude everything to do with the *event* of (a) teaching: of teaching as a
singularly performative activity and a finally incalculable form of address to—but, perhaps more so, *from*—the other. One can therefore
neither simply take nor leave "classic pedagogical procedures," and
in fact one must to some extent both take (partake of) and leave
them at one and the same time in order for teaching to take place at
all. (On closer inspection, then, Derrida's remarks would in fact
seem to raise important questions concerning the possibility of a responsible standpoint on quite difficult and complex issues.) In the
face of this complication of otherwise easily polarizable positions on
the issue of pedagogical tradition, Derrida therefore proposes a
"compromise" to his audience. This has to do with a deconstructive
procedure that presents its practitioner as engaged in some sort of
settling of accounts on a number of problems (however ironic or impossible this may seem, it is of course also unavoidable), rather than
aspiring to the teaching of "truth" as such. Derrida anticipates that,
for some, such an approach will seem too "aphoristic or inadmissi-
ble," while others will accept it as "law," and yet others will "judge [it]
to be not quite aphoristic enough." While it would be easy enough to
translate such categorizations into very familiar groupings, perspectives, or positions regarding Derridean deconstruction in general,
what is perhaps more interesting here is that, on the basis of just this
"compromise," whereby deconstruction presents itself as neither just
entirely inside nor outside "classical pedagogy," Derrida begins to
question or, one might even say, *recalculate* the possibilities of academic freedom in the very process of what would seem to be an appeal to it.

   Derrida insists that since he does not wish to "transform myself
into a diaphanous mouthpiece of eternal pedagogy,"[34] a fountain of
self-proclaimed truth, untrammeled authority, and self-sustaining
mastery (Derrida himself already having indicated the inevitable at-
rophying of any such teaching, but also its unavoidable persistence
to some extent), his "compromise" or procedure is therefore one
that would seem to somewhat liberate his audience or the "students"
of his teaching, so that "whoever no longer wishes to follow may do
so." "As everyone knows, by the terms of *academic freedom*—I repeat: a-
ca-dem-ic free-dom—you can take it or leave it," he says.[35] Here, Derrida not only alerts our attention to the somewhat contradictory
elements inscribed within our usual evocations of pedagogical tradition, which stress both teacherly authority and freedom of inquiry.

More than this, a certain ironic tone becomes evident, underlying what seems to be a quite deliberately repeated and emphasized insistence on academic freedom itself. For Derrida has already shown that any worthwhile teaching (such as deconstruction, for instance), positioned in an ambivalent or equivocal relation to "classical pedagogy," neither simply frees nor binds the event or activity of (a) teaching in relation to (a) tradition. Derrida's (teaching of) deconstruction in regard to the teaching of Nietzsche obviously cannot offer a straightforward choice to the audience or student of Derrida, between unencumbered intellectual freedom, on the one hand, or absolute bondage to pedagogical mastery, on the other. Just as Derrida, by his own admission, can neither simply take nor leave "classical pedagogy," and (for that matter) since any teaching worth the name must both take and leave it simultaneously, so those that heard Derrida speak at Montreal in 1979 would, similarly, finally be bereft of any such choice forming the basis of a conventional appeal to academic freedom. To agree with everything Derrida would have to say, to "take" deconstruction in undiluted form, would be to absolutely submit to and thereby necessarily obliterate its teaching: that is, ultimately, *to take leave of it*. On the other hand, to absolutely reject or wholly take issue with, to entirely take leave of Derrida's discussion or approach from the outset would necessitate, quite impossibly, either a complete departure from the conventions of academic exposition which Derrida insists constitute the minimal level of intelligibility of his (or indeed any other) learned address, or otherwise would manifest an absolute defense of "classical pedagogy"—in which case any dispute with Derrida, any supposed "taking leave" of him, could never take the form of an absolutely diametrical opposition, for reasons he himself already presupposes and makes clear. One can therefore never simply "take it or leave it" in regard to Derrida's lecture, or for that matter in regard to the teaching of deconstruction, perhaps even teaching itself, in general. Thus, it is not just that "classical pedagogy" and "academic freedom" as clearly identifiable categories or forms constitute contradictory or somewhat opposed elements that vie with one another, bringing an awkward tension to bear on accepted notions and norms concerning scholarly tradition and convention. Rather, it is that *both* "academic freedom" and "classical pedagogy" are themselves traversed or crosscut by differential traits that, actually, paradoxically bind them together according to the logic of the supplement, of the remainder, or of the double bind.

It is this kind of recognition that orients Derrida's reading of Nietzsche's *On the Future of Our Educational Institutions* (1872). Here, Derrida observes that Nietzsche's recommendation of the very strictest linguistic discipline, "as a counter to the kind of 'academic freedom' that leaves students and teachers free to their own thoughts or programs," is not intended simply to "set constraint over against freedom."[36] Rather, for Nietzsche, it is possible to discern a more fundamental type of constraint underlying conventional appeals to academic freedom in the university, one which consists precisely in the fact that such constraint, as Derrida puts it, "conceals and disguises itself in the form of laisser-faire."[37] "Through the said 'academic freedom,' it is the State that controls everything" Derrida remarks in discussing Nietzsche's text. "In fact," he notes, "the autonomy of the university, as well as of its students and professor inhabitants, is a ruse of the State." From this point of view, "[Nietzsche's] lectures can thus be read as a modern critique of the cultural machinery of State and of the educational system that was, even in yesterday's industrial society, a fundamental part of the State apparatus."[38] Such a perspective, emerging here from "Otobiographies," might be linked to Derrida's discussion of a statist problematics of education after Enlightenment, which Derrida himself associates with one of the principal proper names in the philosophical tradition: namely, Hegel. A fuller discussion of this problematics, found in the essay "The Age of Hegel," is one in which Derrida undertakes a patient and detailed historico-sociological analysis of the complex interplay between particular kinds of liberal and enlightened discourse on the one hand, and, on the other, the "mobile, subtle, sometimes paradoxical dynamic" of the given forces of civil society that in fact also emanate from, flow into, and circulate within certain missives Hegel writes to a representative body of the Prussian State: the Ministry of Spiritual, Academic, and Medical Affairs (which Derrida terms a "State bureaucracy in the process of organizing the nationalization of the structures of philosophical education by extracting it, based upon a historical compromise, from clerical jurisdiction").[39] This is a correspondence, then, in which one can detect a very determined discourse concerning educational institutions "in the age of European civil service,"[40] as Derrida puts it, being traversed by the differential traits that organize and distribute the complex relations of academic freedom and institutionalized constraint within an emerging statist rationale taking shape in the wake of the Enlightenment. Deconstruction's reading of the philosophical tradition's relation to educational institutions and their statist problematics in the age of Enlightenment therefore establishes a setting in which Nietzsche's (and indeed Derrida's) suspicion of any appeal to "academic freedom" might be understood in terms of a rigorous rethinking of the complexly intertwined relations between academic freedom, orthodox pedagogy, and politico-institutional constraints. We cannot just "take" or "leave" these phenomena, their concepts and effects, without such a rethinking—which itself would neither simply partake nor take leave of them. One important implication here might be that the aporetical condition of (a) teaching (of deconstruction, for example), whereby one can neither simply *take it* nor *leave it*, itself provides a setting in which to use Derridean deconstruction—even as it thinks the *prehistory* of "postmodernity" or "globalization," a prehistory that is obviously entwined with the era of the nation-state: the traditions of which, however, one might nevertheless neither simply *take* nor *leave*—to imagine the kind of dissensual academic community advocated recently by critics like Bill Readings and J. Hillis Miller. This would be a community not simply bounded by a horizon of consensus and sustained by the sort of communicative rationality advocated by the German Idealists or, more recently, Habermasian thought; nor would it be a community underpinned by freedom of dissent as a notion indissociable from traditional claims to academic freedom—a notion which in fact presupposes at the more fundamental level an entirely common and shared understanding of academic protocols and conventions. Dissensus of the kind that leaves all those engaged in the scene of teaching unable simply to either take it or leave it obviously implies a complicated network of relations and obligations that nevertheless *leaves open* the question of responsibility or of the "ethical," precisely because, in the very event of teaching, such a question remains irreducible to the rationality and rational ground of autonomous subjects, or of the autonomous subject.

MONSTROSITY AND THE PERFORMATIVE

I want to conclude by returning to the performative dimension of deconstructive teaching discussed earlier. In his essay "Literary Study in the Transnational University," J. Hillis Miller revisits the well-known encounter of Derridean deconstruction with the speech-act theory of J. L. Austin. As Miller notes, for Austin a speech act "depends for its efficacy on an elaborate context of protocols, rules, institutions, roles, laws, and established formulae. These need to be in place before the performative utterance is made."[41] Comprehensibility therefore depends on a complexly preconstituted framework establishing the conditions of formulation, transmission, and reception of any communication. However, this Austinian performative also presupposes the preexistence of a self as agent able to recognize, comprehend, and perform to the "context" in which speech acts can meaningfully take place. For Miller, the "self" or subject as agent and, indeed, the idea of a delimitable and coherent "context" to which a speech act might be said to "belong," are characteristic features of the entire ensemble of concepts and categories that the experience of "transnationality" or "globalization" calls into question.

In contrast, then, Miller describes an "alternative kind of performative" which "creates the norms and laws that validate it." Each such performative "constitutes a happening that changes decisively the surrounding context. It responds to a call or demand from an 'other' that can never be institutionalized or rationalized."[42] Hence the call of the "other," which in this formulation brings the speech act into being, would have to preexist any subject or agent of cognition or communication. Here Miller, in affirming that the very idea of a speech act in this formulation is therefore a catachresis, is called on to quote Derrida: "As Derrida puts it, such a speech act is a catachresis that 'while continuing to work through tradition emerges at a given moment as a *monster*, a monstrous mutation without tradition or normative precedent.' "[43]

If deconstruction not only affirms but engages in just such an "alternative kind of performative" in its teaching, or indeed *as* a teaching, then via Derrida's "Otobiographies" we have already described how, precisely by "continuing to work through tradition," it nevertheless gives rise to "mutations" (*leaving* as *taking, taking* as *leaving*) that also interrupt or exceed "tradition" or "normative precedent." But the word *monster*, italicized for emphasis here, must surely be seen as a strong and somewhat shocking term to deploy when describing such "mutations." Does deconstruction in its teaching or as a teaching really give rise or give birth to *monsters*? What can the "monstrous" or the "monster" really mean, raising its head or its hand (or turning an "other" ear) in the midst of the teaching of deconstruction?

In "What is Called Thinking?" Heidegger embarks on a thought of the gift, and a thought of the hand, that would in turn render thinking itself irreducible to the dictates of utility, trade, and technics that in various ways underpin all activity governed by the requisites of capital. Obviously this thought of the gift and of the hand would therefore necessitate, in this very same setting, a thinking of the problem of university teaching itself. Heidegger writes:

> The hand reaches and extends, receives and welcomes—and not just things: the hand extends itself, and receives its own welcome in the hand of the other. The hand keeps. The hand carries. The hand designs and signs, presumably because man is a (monstrous) sign.[44]

In establishing some sort of relation between "man" and monstrosity, this passage provides the basis for a number of reflections that arise in Derrida's essay, "*Geschlecht* II: Heidegger's Hand." Here, Derrida evokes and explores the weight and burden of the word *Geschlecht* in regard to the German philosophical tradition after Enlightenment, and particularly in relation to the work of Heidegger himself. For Derrida, *Geschlecht* is a more or less untranslatable term that nevertheless variously comes to mean "sex, race, species, genus, gender, stock, family, generation or genealogy, community,"[45] according to a number of somewhat fraught contexts that determine its sense and usage at different moments in this tradition. In broader terms, then, Derrida is seeking in this essay to embark once more on a series of reflections concerning philosophical nationality and nationalism in German, not least as part of a serious engagement with the problem of Heidegger's relation to Nazism that is to some extent put aside here, but treated more fully in texts like *Of Spirit* (1987). Derrida negotiates the term *Geschlecht*, therefore, in order to try to think and move among various notions of belonging that, in the German philosophical tradition since the Enlightenment, determine different accounts of the national (both in the sense of national and of racist or biologistic ideologies), as well as accounts of linguistic idiomaticity, and of the relations of humanity and animality that might also be taken to determine belonging where *Geschlecht* is concerned. It goes without saying that, for any essay which wants to evoke the topic of (the politics of) Heidegger's teaching (including, since it could hardly be excluded, the Rectoral Address of 1933) and its relation to a wider philosophical tradition, these are very deep waters indeed. Nevertheless, if it is possible both to recognize and set aside for a moment the obvious political stakes of any such discussion, one interesting aspect of Derrida's essay is the way in which it takes a number of Heidegger's texts to provide a setting for a closely woven set of questions having to do with nationhood, humanistic learning, the *Geschlecht* of the human, and the monstrosity of "man" in the hand that signs, carries, extends itself to the other and (thereby relatedly) teaches. These questions would clearly impose themselves on the issue of the future of the university and the humanities, and of the (ruined) relations of teaching, learning, culture, community, and nation-state in the age of global capital, that have so interested critics like Bill Readings and J. Hillis Miller in recent times.

Heidegger's hand—the hand that raises its head or hand in "What is Called Thinking?"—is avowedly monstrous. This is the hand that crafts, gives, signs, and teaches in ways that interrupt or exceed all the various activities that characterize the bureaucratic and technocratic regimes of the modern university as the place of science and technics serving the wider interests of capital. But, asks Derrida:

> Why "monster"? . . . What is *un monstre?* You know the polysemic gamut of this word, the uses one can make of it, for example concerning norms and forms, species and genus/gender: thus concerning *Geschlecht.* I shall begin by privileging here another course [*direction*]. It goes in the direction, the *sens,* of a less known sense, since in French *la monstre* (a changing of gender, sex, or *Geschlecht*) has the poetico-musical sense of a diagram that *shows* [*montre*] in a piece of music the number of verses and the number of syllables assigned to the poet. *Monstrer* is *montrer* (to show or demonstrate) . . . . *Le monstre* or *la monstre* is what shows in order to warn or put on guard.[46]

In the very context of questions of "norms and forms," of belonging and community—questions that have imposed themselves within and upon the thinking of the academic community ever since the days of German Idealism—Derrida finds a particular sense or type of monstrosity inscribed within the very discourse or thinking of *Geschlecht.* Here, to show, to demonstrate, to alert attention, to warn, to instruct, or to *teach* is monstrous. Why, monstrous? Turning to part of a well-known poem by Hölderlin, "Mnemosyne"—which Heideg-

ger returns to in "What is Called Thinking?"—Derrida gives us to
read Hölderlin via the translation by Becker and Granel, the translators into French of "Was heisst Denken?":

> We are a "monster" void of sense
> We are outside sorrow
> And have nearly lost
> Our tongue in foreign lands

Leaving aside that which would lead him back too rapidly to questions of nationality and nationalism, Derrida concentrates on the
"'we, monster'" of this evocation.[47] (Here, it should be noted that certain effects attend his decision to read the French translation, since
"Ein Zeichen sind wir, deutungslos," the line from the poem on
which Derrida concentrates, is more frequently translated as "we are
a meaningless sign." The sign may be not just meaningless but also
"monstrous," yet it is surely monstrous *as* sign.) Whether this "we" to
whom our attention is drawn by Derrida is taken to indicate "man,"
humanity, nation, or some other sense of *Geschlecht*, the monster that
signs, "shows," or "warns," is singularly striking:

> since, showing, signifying, designating, this sign is void of sense (*deu-
> tungslos*). It says itself void of sense . . . we are sign—showing, inform-
> ing, warning, pointing as sign toward, but in truth toward nothing, a
> sign out of the way . . . in a gapped relation to the sign . . . display
> [*montre*] that deviates from the display or monstration, a monster
> that shows [*montre*] nothing. This gap of the sign to itself and to its
> so-called normal function, isn't it already a monstrosity of monstra-
> sity, a monstrosity of monstration?[48]

Setting to one side for a moment the various ways in which Derrida
tries to locate this interrelation of monstrosity and sign in the
broader framework of the development of Heidegger's thought, the
monstrosity of the sign as described here would nevertheless seem
to resonate with and reinvoke just the "alternative kind of performative" outlined by Miller. Instead of just pointing toward and remaining in the grip of "an elaborate context of protocols, rules,
institutions, roles, laws, and established formulae" which, in rather
static ways, "need to be in place before the performative utterance is
made," this alternative kind of performative "creates the norms and
laws that validate it" and thereby necessarily shows in the (monstrous) form of showing nothing. Such monstration is therefore

monstrous in the "gapped relation" of the sign to itself and to its "so-called normal function," which of course has to do with the log-ics of presence and reference. Paradoxically, however, this monstra-tion would at the same time obviously continue "to work through tradition" (to borrow Derrida's phrase), since Derrida himself shows how the very question of monstration and monstrosity arises in the vicinity of questions of *Geschlecht* (of belonging and commu-nity, of (national) culture, of species and genus, of "man," human-ity, and animality, and of "norms and forms") that not only characterize a long-standing philosophical tradition, but that may even be thought to supply the very conditions of possibility for a thinking and realization of the Enlightenment university itself. Akin to the idea of "monstration" Derrida pursues via a reading of Hei-degger's essay, then, the "alternative kind of performative" Miller associates with Derridean deconstruction would similarly work "through" tradition—here, more specifically, a tradition of *Ge-schlecht* or "belonging" to be discerned both in the "ruins" and in the "remains" of the university today. Yet it is important to recall that the performativity we are associating with the (Heideggerian) hand that shows and teaches as a de(con)struction of tradition is one that, none the less, "emerges at a given moment as a *monster*, a monstrous mutation without tradition or normative precedent" (to reprise Derrida once again). Not only would this facilitate (or, in-deed, render inevitable) "mutations" proliferating in excess of the bureaucratizing and rationalizing forces of the scientific and tech-nocratic university and indeed, the legacies of "belonging" that are tied to notions of (national) culture. It would also give a clue and a cue to the aporetical problem of teaching deconstruction as un-avoidably the teaching of that which nevertheless remains virtually unteachable *as such*.

Such monsters as we are describing are the monsters of man or of man's hand. Not least, this is insofar as they both embody "other-wise" and thoroughly deform the various projects of *Geschlecht* which in fact underpin the essential traditions of the university and of the nation-state since the Enlightenment. These manmade monsters, monsters of man, might be taken and affirmed as fertile mutations that productively distort the long-standing endeavors of humanistic study. Examples of such mutations, of such monsters (giving-taking-leaving-belonging) may be found in the experience of teaching de-construction that remains in the university's remains.

NOTES

1. J. Hillis Miller, "Literary Study in the Transnational University," in J. Hillis Miller and Manuel Asensi, *Black Holes/J. Hillis Miller, Or, Boustrophedonic Reading*, trans. Mabel Richart (Stanford: Stanford University Press, 1999), 83.

2. Bill Readings, *The University in Ruins* (Cambridge: Harvard University Press, 1996), 102. *The University in Ruins* was the subject of heated debate in the pages of *Critical Inquiry* during 1998–99 between Dominick LaCapra and Nicholas Royle. In his essay "The University in Ruins?" (*Critical Inquiry* 25, no. 1 [1998]: 32–55), La-Capra raised a series of objections and concerns concerning the generality and, indeed, the accuracy of Readings's description of the university's plight, as well as questioning the validity and robustness of the book's critical or theoretical "grounds." Royle's response, "Yes, Yes, the University in Ruins" (*Critical Inquiry* 26, no. 1 [1999]: 147–53) sought to defend Readings's thesis, and drew attention in particular to the performative dimensions of *The University in Ruins*, whereby a certain tone and mode of address Royle felt LaCapra had overlooked in his reading of the book undermined the notion of, as LaCapra put it, "critical intellectual citizenship (a category Readings enacts in his own way without thematizing it)" (54). This notion of "critical intellectual citizenship" was one that LaCapra had posited so as to challenge Readings's insistence upon the end of the university and the nation-state as the grounds for the production of recognizable forms of intellectual practice. La-Capra's response to Royle, "Yes, Yes, Yes, Yes . . . Well, Maybe" was published in the same issue of *Critical Inquiry* (154–58).

3. Readings, *The University in Ruins*, 47.

4. Ibid., 48.

5. Ibid., 111.

6. Ibid., 153. Unless otherwise stated, all emphases in quotations are present in the original.

7. Ibid., 154.

8. Ibid., 158.

9. Ibid., 154–55.

10. Jacques Derrida, *Given Time: 1. Counterfeit Money*, trans. Peggy Kamuf (Chicago: University of Chicago Press, 1992), 42.

11. Ibid., 42.

12. The association Derrida suggests between, on the one hand, the institution of cultural criticism or of an academic and quasi-disciplinary discourse of "culture," and various explorations of "*total social fact*" located within the "symbolicity" of economic reason, on the other, might well be reexamined via Bill Readings's discussion in *The University in Ruins* of Antony Easthope's *Literary into Cultural Studies* (London: Routledge, 1991). Published around the time that saw cultural studies acquire, in Readings's terms, "professional disciplinarity," Easthope's book is described by Readings as follows: "In place of the 'old paradigm' of literary studies, Easthope offers a 'new paradigm' of Cultural Studies, which appears in order to replace the entire swath of disciplines in the humanities and social sciences as a generalized 'study of signifying practice.' . . . The new paradigm is characterized above all by resistance

to all attempts to limit its field of reference" (98). Of course, *Readings* is quick to note that "Easthope's is not the only way of thinking about Cultural Studies" (99), and indeed that "We cannot provide an account of what it is to do Cultural Studies that is theoretically self-consistent" (97). Nevertheless, Easthope's book may be considered at least a symptom of the forces of re- and dereferentialization and, indeed, the play of totalization and detotalization that assume such a pivotal place in the disciplinary histories of cultural discourse and debate.

13. Derrida, *Given Time*, 7.

14. Ibid., 12.

15. Ibid., 13.

16. Ibid., 23.

17. Ibid., 10.

18. Ibid., 11.

19. Ibid., 30–31.

20. Ibid., 31.

21. Jacques Derrida, "Violence and Metaphysics: An Essay on the Thought of Emmanuel Levinas," in *Writing and Difference*, trans. Alan Bass (London: Routledge and Kegan Paul, 1978), 91.

22. Ibid., 130.

23. Ibid., 130.

24. Alongside the more well-known writings of Paul de Man, Gayatri Spivak, and Bill Readings, other contributions to the question of deconstruction and teaching include Tim Caudery, ed., *Literary Pedagogies After Deconstruction: Scenarios and Perspectives in the Teaching of English Literature* (Aarhus: Aarhus University Press, 1992) and Peter Pericles Trifonas, *The Ethics of Writing: Derrida, Deconstruction and Pedagogy* (Lanham, Md.: Rowman and Littlefield, 2000). However, perhaps one of the best known and most productive—although now rather overlooked—books dealing with the question of deconstruction and pedagogy is Gregory L. Ulmer's *Applied Grammatology: Post(e)-Pedagogy from Jacques Derrida to Joseph Beuys* (Baltimore: Johns Hopkins University Press, 1985). Ulmer approaches the question of Derrida's relationship to pedagogy most explicitly via a discussion of his involvement in the GREPH from the mid-1970s onwards, while also concentrating on Derrida's essay "The Age of Hegel" (see 1–43 in *Demarcating the Disciplines: Philosophy, Literature, Art*, ed. Samuel Weber [Minneapolis: University of Minnesota Press, 1986] and other scattered remarks of relevance in texts by Derrida like *Dissemination* [1972] and *The Post Card* [1980]. Ulmer's main concern is to explore the possibilities of a grammatological pedagogy along Derridean lines. One interesting feature of this book, however, is to reconceive of "the scene of teaching" (a phrase given some emphasis by Bill Readings in *The University in Ruins*) in terms of the possibilities of certain kinds of theatricality. Such an approach might be contrasted interestingly with the interconnected work of Samuel Weber on institutions and on theatricality. See the reissued edition of Weber's *Institution and Interpretation* (Stanford: Stanford University Press, 2001) and his forthcoming *Theatricality as Medium*. For an introduction to Weber's work that begins to explore linkages between the question of the institution and the effects of theater, see my essay " 'To Come Walking': Reinterpreting the Institution and the Work of Samuel Weber" published in *Cultural Critique* 48

(2001): 146–199. See also my *Samuel Weber: Acts of Reading* (Aldershot, Hants: Ashgate, 2003).

25. For an invaluable discussion of the status of the "example" in Derridean deconstruction, especially insofar as it facilitates a rethinking of the political, see Michael B. Naas's "Introduction: For Example," which introduces Jacques Derrida's *The Other Heading: Reflections on Today's Europe*, trans. Pascale-Anne Brault and Michael B. Naas (Bloomington: Indiana University Press, 1992), vii–lix.

26. Jacques Derrida, "The Double Session," in *Dissemination*, trans. Alan Bass (Chicago: University of Chicago Press, 1981), 177.

27. Jacques Derrida, "Living On: Borderlines," in *Deconstruction and Criticism*, ed. Geoffrey Hartman (London: Routledge and Kegan Paul, 1979), 92–94.

28. See, for example, Derrida's "The Age of Hegel"; "Otobiographies: The Teaching of Nietzsche and the Politics of the Proper Name" in *The Ear of the Other: Otobiography, Transference, Translation: Texts and Discussions with Jacques Derrida*, ed. Christie V. McDonald, trans. Peggy Kamuf (Lincoln: University of Nebraska Press, 1988), 1–38; and "*Geschlecht* II: Heidegger's Hand," in *Deconstruction and Philosophy: The Texts of Jacques Derrida*, ed. John Sallis (Chicago: University of Chicago Press, 1987), 161–96—discussed elsewhere in this essay.

29. Jacques Derrida, "Mochlos," in *Logomachia: The Conflict of the Faculties*, ed. Richard Rand (Lincoln: University of Nebraska Press, 1992), 1–34, and "The Principle of Reason: The University in the Eyes of its Pupils," *Diacritics* 13, no. 3 (1983): 3–20.

30. Derrida, "Otobiographies," 22.

31. Ibid., 9, 10, 14.

32. Ibid., 34–36.

33. Ibid., 3–4.

34. Ibid., 4.

35. Ibid., 4.

36. Ibid., 33.

37. Ibid., 33.

38. Ibid., 33.

39. Derrida, "The Age of Hegel," 4.

40. Ibid., 11.

41. Miller, 179.

42. Ibid., 179.

43. Ibid., 179. Here, Miller quotes from Jacques Derrida, "Deconstruction and the Other," in Richard Kearney, ed., *States of Mind: Dialogues with Contemporary Thinkers* (New York: New York University Press, 1995), 172.

44. Quoted in Derrida, "*Geschlecht* II: Heidegger's Hand," 168. In this essay Derrida cites the translation by Fred D. Wieck and J. Glenn Gray of Heidegger's *What is Called Thinking?* (New York: Harper and Row, 1968).

45. Derrida, "*Geschlecht* II: Heidegger's Hand," 162.

46. Ibid., 166.

47. Ibid., 167.

48. Ibid., 167.

Naïve Modernism
and the Politics of Embarrassment

Susan Hegeman

Reader beware. What follows has a lot to do with three
disquieting affective states: naïveté, embarrassment, and shame. Of
course, these states are not painful or unnerving in the same ways. It
is the nature of naïveté that it is un-self-conscious. Whereas the naïf
might feel only the discomfort (and exhilaration) of confusion,
shame brings with it the pain of utter self-consciousness—the pain,
perhaps, of the naïf suddenly made to feel the fool. Embarrassment,
on the other hand, is vicarious: the transitive experience of shame, of
watching the naïf caught in a moment of self-consciousness. This is
the dynamic by which these states are most commonly brought together in intellectual life: naïveté is immature, it is superstitious, it is
insufficiently theoretical; as intellectuals we struggle against the
shame of being called to account for our ignorance, our innocence,
our lack of subtlety and self-consciousness, even as we avoid the embarrassment of confronting such flaws in others.

In this essay, I will risk embarrassment (or at least a detour
through it) in order to experimentally recuperate naïveté in a particular form, at a particular period in intellectual history, which I will
call "naïve modernism." The purpose of deploying this concept is
multiple. First, I want to refine some ideas about modernism as a period and a movement. Second, I want to challenge a common conception of the way intellectual life was organized in this period, and
thus comment upon some current assumptions about the historical
relationship between intellectual theory and practice.

Overlapping with the period called modernism is the emergence
of the modern university, with its emphasis on specialized fields of

knowledge, arranged in what we have come to think of as traditional disciplinary formations. While it is possible to see these developments as features of a more generalized modernist culture, in the United States at least the "age of academe" has more commonly been seen as antithetical to the vibrant culture of modernist arts and letters in several respects. Some see this moment as initiating the retreat of the "public intellectual" from the bohemian world of arts and letters into the cozy (or suffocating) and apparently irrelevant confines of the academy. For others, such as C. P. Snow, this was the moment of the emergence of unbridgeable disciplinary gaps between the "two cultures" of the sciences and the humanities.[1] In the account that follows I would like to juxtapose some unlikely characters—on the one hand academically oriented social scientists and on the other a bohemian modernist novelist—to show the limits of both of these assumptions.

NAÏVETÉ

If, as I have indicated, naïveté is a state of un-self-consciousness, then on the face of it a conjunction between naïveté and modernism seems untenable. As an aesthetic movement, modernism is usually associated with an extreme self-consciousness both about the form and medium of artistic expression and about the relationship of art to the state of the world: its relationship, in particular, to the condition of modernity itself. Indeed, it is often noted that Western modernity, the historical condition about which the modernists are said to be so concerned, is also notable for its self-consciousness, indeed characterized by a sustained self-awareness of its own historicity. Yet I think the idea of a naïve modernism is useful if we see it, to begin with, in parallel to naïve realism, or the unreflective assumption that a given representation is transparently mimetic of reality. Naïve modernism, then, would be the similarly unreflective view that a representation, practice, or theory is transparently connected to what is modern.

This idea is most readily recognizable in the context of certain commercial and popular styles such as art deco, which sought to translate the experience of speed and machinic power into the design of everyday objects. The effect here was modern, even modernist, but art deco couldn't be said to be particularly self-conscious in the sense that, say, cubism concerned itself with problems of form, or modernist art more generally posed itself critically and self-consciously against modern commercial culture. But I think the term is applicable more widely, and perhaps also more usefully, to objects besides explicitly popular expressions of modern style. It is also helpful for understanding some of the diversity of expression contained within the term *modernism*. We commonly accept the premise that authors such as F. Scott Fitzgerald and Willa Cather (to take examples from U.S. literature) might be modernists despite their apparent lack of interest in formal innovation in the manner of, say, Joyce, Proust, or Faulkner. But I think some parallel arguments must be made for texts that were in their moment recognized as somehow embodying the spirit of the modern, but which do not now seem to be similarly challenging or representative of modernism as a whole. My tentative hypothesis is that one reason why some explicitly modern texts fail to continue to excite is because of a naïve relationship to the modern that translates badly across the decades. One such text is Sherwood Anderson's *Many Marriages* (1923), a book I will discuss at the end of this essay, and which will return me to the theme of embarrassment.

Another site for thinking about naïve modernism is in the social sciences of the early twentieth century. Here, there is some difficulty in applying a term like *modernism* to the wider field of early twentieth-century intellectual history. Formally, the social science of this period is a realist discourse, engaged in what David Hollinger calls a "cognitivist" approach to apprehending the world. Such an approach would seem on the surface to suggest an intellectual gulf between scientists and modernist artists: "The one purports to assign meanings cognitively, by finding out what is the case, while the other purports to perform this service through the creation of myths. Hence we may speak of two figures—two clusters of ideal characteristics—as the Knower and the Artificer."[2] The division here is too neat, and Hollinger himself eventually concedes that these two discretely drawn types, with their "rival prescriptions for the foundations of culture," are in fact often fused in the work of many thinkers and artists of the turn of the twentieth century. Nevertheless, he is entirely right to reveal a strange feature of many interpretations of modernism, which have tended to emphasize anti-rational aesthetic experimentation at the expense of attention to the twentieth century's strong "faith in the cultural capacities of the *wissenschaftliche* knower."[3]

What I find especially useful here, however, is not the idea that scientific rationality was important to the culture of modernism, but the idea of the pervasive *faith* in science, because it is this idea of faith that shows a way to resolve the apparent dichotomy between the arts and sciences. In the place of this strongly drawn division, we may now recognize a commonality among a great many of the diverse intellectuals of the modernist period—whether scientists or modernist aesthetes. If there was a strong cultural faith in the promise of science to transform the present, there was a comparable faith among modernist artists—great producers of manifestoes and slogans, and of injunctions to revitalize seeing, language, painting, poetry, music, life, society, and all the rest—that their projects would bring about similar monumental changes. In other words, the modernist moment might be characterized alternatively as a moment of faith in intellectual endeavors generally and their capacity to create profound change.

For Perry Anderson, a central element in his "conjunctural" periodization of modernism is the "imaginative proximity of social revolution."[4] Certainly, the decades surrounding the turn of the twentieth century saw the Russian revolutions of 1905 and 1917, the chaos of World War I, and the beginnings of struggles for colonial independence. But the industrialized West also experienced other dramatic changes in culture and daily life—in transportation, communication, and in sexual morality and gender relations, for example—that could also be called revolutionary. Add to this the emergence and rising cultural power of whole new cadres of experts and professionals—another veritable revolution in class structure, in which expertise became the key to admission to cultural elites—and one begins to understand the full contours of this revolutionary context, in which intellectuals saw (or, *pace* Anderson, imagined) themselves as centrally situated in the radical ferment taking place around them.[5]

But we must also consider the possibility that there is something in the very nature of this imaginative proximity to revolution and its attendant intense conversions and passions that leads, in effect, to its own undoing. Fredric Jameson describes this possibility as follows:

> [In the moment of modernism] one did not simply read D. H. Lawrence or Rilke, see Jean Renoir or Hitchcock, or listen to Stravinsky, as distinct manifestations of what we now term modernism.

> Rather one read all of the works of a particular writer, learned a style
> and a phenomenological world. D. H. Lawrence became an abso-
> lute, a complete and systematic world view, to which one converted
> ... The crisis of modernism as such came, then, when suddenly it be-
> came clear that "D. H. Lawrence" was not an absolute after all, not
> the final achieved figuration of the truth of the world, but only one
> art-language among others, only one shelf of works in a whole dizzy-
> ing library. Hence the shame and guilt of cultural intellectuals, the
> renewed appeal of the Hegelian goal, the "end of art," and the aban-
> donment of culture altogether for immediate political activity.[6]

Just as a revolutionary passion for one kind of aesthetic or phenomenological vision could succumb to another, or to calls, such as
those so common in the 1930s, for an abandonment of art in favor of
political struggle, so finally could political struggle as a kind of final,
literal form of the imaginative proximity to revolution ultimately give
way to a retreat from politics as well.

This is a common narrative of the postwar moment, where the
transition to the Cold War involves a litany of disillusioning events—
the Hitler-Stalin pact, bureaucratized mass murder in Nazi Germany,
the incineration of Hiroshima and Nagasaki, the Moscow show trials—that shattered a general belief in the very idea of transformative
visions. This is the point of Daniel Bell's famous assertion of the "end
of ideology," in which we in the mature and sensible postwar
"West"—in contradistinction to the Russians and postcolonial Asians
and Africans—are argued to have simply (and perhaps a bit wist-
fully) outgrown our immature and emotional attachments to the
grand idea.[7] It is also that of Susan Sontag's cultural identification of
a mid-century "piety without content," in which, "in the backwash of
broken radical political enthusiasms," intellectuals instead became
"fellow-travelers" of religious faith, fully unbelieving but nevertheless
"nostalgic" for the feeling of sacredness.[8]

It is important to note the element of *tristesse* in the accounts of
the likes of Sontag and Bell, for it seems characteristic of the intellectual climate of the postwar, particularly among liberals, to both
refuse the now suspect commitments of their predecessors and in-
dulge in some nostalgia for those earlier moments of faith and passion. As Harold Rosenberg observed, the enormous emphasis placed
on the topic of alienation in the popular social science of the 1950s
(in, for example, David Riesman's *The Lonely Crowd* [1950], William
H. Whyte's *The Organization Man* [1956], and C. Wright Mills's *White*

Collar [1956]) could be seen centrally as a reflection of the situation of intellectuals, whose working lives in various organizations seemed to rub uncomfortably against some of their central values and beliefs.[9] Thus, even while inhabiting positions of significant political and social authority, and while elaborating postideological and consensual accounts of American history and society, Cold War intellectuals still managed to see themselves as outsiders.[10]

Obviously, our current concerns about intellectual life are haunted by the preoccupations of both prewar modernism and its postwar late modernist aftermath. In particular, the issues of alienation and nostalgia for the earlier modernism both seem to be in full force: alienation, in recurrently expressed concerns about the status of the "public intellectual" and the reification of (the rest of) intellectual life into a narrow academic professionalism and nostalgia, in various calls to regard this or that modernist hero as a model of intellectual commitment.[11] But I think concomitant with these residual impulses of the cold war, we have also never completely gotten over a fundamental *embarrassment* over the modernists, particularly in regard to their exaggerated sense of the cultural importance and power of intellectuals and ideas, and their spurious and even dangerous expectations of dramatic social and cultural change.[12]

What I find so interesting about this relationship of naïve modernist and embarrassed postmodern sophisticate is the way that it brings affect back into the problem of historical thinking. T. J. Clark has suggested that for the postmodern subject "modernism is our antiquity . . . as overgrown and labyrinthine as Shelley's dream of Rome."[13] While Clark's work brilliantly demonstrates the historical and conceptual gulf that separates us from the modernists, this sense of incommensurability nevertheless seems to break down in the context of our own experiences of intellectual history, where the intellectual generations that preceded us are not understood to have lived a fully other kind of social and cultural existence, but are rather more like our parents and grandparents, the embarrassing and error-prone people who bore us and whom we, in turn, must forebear.

So let us turn now to the modernists' apparent error, the source of postmodern embarrassment. I have already suggested that one feature of modernist naïveté is modernist intellectuals' sense of their own power to transform the world, art, perception, and so forth. One manifestation of this sense, which I think we may now see as virtually definitive of "naïve modernism," was the relatively common assumption of that period that intellectuals' efficacy lay in the realm of exposing truths of one kind or another, an exposure which was often assumed to have quick and impressive effects. This version of Enlightenment is, of course, the logic of the talking cure, in which the sheer revelation of some repressed trauma is sufficient to exorcise a patient's emotional pain. That this idea had strong popular resonance, perhaps especially in the United States, is indicated by its repeated cultural deployment throughout the first half or so of the twentieth century, in, for example, Alfred Hitchcock's psychological thrillers, such as *Spellbound* (1945) or, later, *Marnie* (1964), whose plots center on the detection of some trauma in a character's past. In these narratives, and countless others like them, psychological catharsis joins seamlessly with dramatic catharsis, as the patient is confronted with the truth of his or her own history. In the dénouement, the patient falls into a swoon (the sign of Truth's powerful effects), only to awaken cured: exorcised of the ghosts of the past and in the loving arms of the doctor-detective.

This strategy of curing through the revelation of truth had significant counterparts in early twentieth-century American social science, particularly in its more public forms. While Thorstein Veblen's acerbic analysis in 1899 of the mores of the American bourgeoisie in *The Theory of the Leisure Class* bears the stamp of this technique (or is it a desire?), perhaps its purest practitioner was the sociologist, later turned cultural anthropologist, Elsie Clews Parsons. A fascinating figure who managed to coexist in the worlds of Greenwich Village bohemia, Columbia University, Washington political circles, and high-society New York, Parsons deployed her social scientific voice to significant popular effect in books such as *The Family* (1912) and *The Old-Fashioned Woman* (1913), and in the pages of the radical journals of Greenwich Village. In these venues, she advanced important arguments for women's suffrage, trial marriage, birth control, and a host of other controversial feminist issues, in large part through the elaboration of a simple argument: that modern American customs and ideas of propriety were no less irrational and superstitious than their comparable rituals and beliefs in other, supposedly primitive, settings. In her witty, confident, and fact-filled prose, Parsons scandalously compared the custom of giving wedding gifts to bride-price, debutante balls to the profligate potlatches of the tribal Northwest coast, and the sex-segregated world of upper-class New York women to that of Turkish seraglios.[14] In estranging custom in this way, Parsons' intention was to render it obsolete: "Primitive ideas are always grave and always troublesome—until recognized. Then they become on the one hand powerless to create situations, and on the other, enlivening."[15] Rationality, in other words, would turn the weight of tradition—which fell particularly hard upon women—into a series of amusing anecdotes about the colorful customs of Americans in the Gilded Age.

In advancing this social version of the talking cure, in which the lingering ghosts of irrelevant custom and outmoded belief were revealed and therefore imagined to be exorcised, Parsons was only slightly in advance of many of her contemporaries in the social sciences who were increasingly concerned with a problem sometimes called "cultural lag." This term, first coined by the sociologist William Fielding Ogburn in 1922 (that watershed modernist year), referred to the discontinuity between the ultramodernity of American technological and economic development and its apparent backwardness in regard to customs, religion, and moral standards. This was the moment of national alcohol Prohibition and of the notorious "monkey trial," in which a high school biology teacher was put on trial in Tennessee for teaching evolutionary theory.[16] Though these examples of "cultural lag" had their roots in deep political and cultural conflicts between north and south, rural and urban, center and periphery—that is, in the very conditions that could be said to be central to the production of modernist culture[17]—they were generally seen by (urban and northern) intellectual elites as thoroughgoing failures of rationality. The pragmatist philosopher John Dewey articulated the problem as follows:

> About physical conditions and energies we think scientifically; at least, some men do, and the results of their thinking enter into the experiences of all of us. But the entrenched and stubborn institutions of the past stand in the way of our thinking scientifically about human relations and social issues. Our mental habits in these respects are dominated by institutions of family, state, church, and business that were formed long before men had effective techniques of inquiry and validation. It is this contradiction from which we suffer to-day.[18]

For Dewey the solution to this contradiction was nothing less than a second "great scientific revolution" of social science, which "will

ensue when men collectively and cooperatively organize their knowledge for application to achieve and make secure social values; when
they systematically use scientific procedures for the control of
human relationships and the direction of the social effects of our
vast technological machinery."[19] In other words, the ultimate goal of
this rationalization of culture was social engineering.

Parsons' flair for pointed cultural comparisons and Dewey's
hopes for a culture managed by social scientists can be seen to have
converged in the work of some of the more popular and important
American anthropologists of the period. Though anthropologists
did not typically concern themselves with modern cultures, the anthropologists associated with Franz Boas at Columbia University
(among whom Parsons would become a prominent member in the
later years of her career) were unique in the frequency with which
they directly applied their observations of other cultures to what they
understood to be modern problems. Indeed, Boas himself dedicated
much of his long career debunking the cultural and biological
premises of scientific racism by marshaling evidence from the ethno-
graphic record to destabilize common popular views of normativity.

Most notably, Ruth Benedict (a student of Parsons, Boas, and
Dewey) and Margaret Mead (Benedict's student) inherited from
their teachers a fascination with the social talking cure. In her most
famous work, *Coming of Age in Samoa* (1926), Mead invoked the
Samoan counter-example to show how the very category of "adolescence" was a peculiarly Western invention—and a peculiarly American site of concern. Mead did not suggest, as Parsons might have,
that this observation about the cultural specificity of the problems of
adolescence was alone sufficient to dispel the frustrations of American girls. Rather, her point was that adolescence was a cultural,
rather than a biological phenomenon, and therefore amenable not
only to intelligent apprehension, but to change.

This latter view, that the biological realm of humanity is im-
mutable while the cultural is malleable, may be one of the central
conceptual differences that makes modernism seem like our antiquity. It is not only that we now live in a world in which cloning, gene
therapy, in vitro fertilization, and sex-change operations have made
the biological matrix of humanity seem increasingly open to tinker-
ing, but culture seems increasingly *less* amenable to alteration. Popu-
larly, culture is often seen as synonymous with "heritage," an
inescapable part of an individual's fundamental identity, something

that ought to be preserved and protected, something that is passed down from generation to generation. Indeed, going back to Mead, her assessment of why American culture produced adolescent crises and why Samoan culture did not presents a daunting picture of the difficulties inherent in trying to mold culture. American girls suffer at adolescence, Mead suggested, because they were modern: subjects of a morally and culturally complex society, in which they were confronted with difficult choices and divergent expectations.[20] How on earth, wonders the contemporary reader, does one confront this issue, which is of course modern alienation itself? Mead's answer— hopeful, progressive, and at base a legacy of the educational philosophy of John Dewey—was that we must educate young women for the challenges and choices inherent to living in a complex society. What we might cynically see as preparing them for the suffering to come, Mead saw as a pragmatic agenda for change.

Benedict was even more optimistic than Mead about the malleability of culture. In her most influential book, *Patterns of Culture* (1934), Benedict compares very different cultural sites to consider how culture is related to individual behavior, and to show how the very same behavior in different cultural contexts can be seen either as the quintessence of normality or grotesque maladjustment. The result of this comparison is a powerful attack on behavioral normativity. Benedict concludes, "Those who function inadequately in any society are not those with certain fixed 'abnormal' traits, but may well be those whose responses have received no support in the institutions of their culture."[21] Interestingly, however, Benedict's hero of maladaption is not a figure trapped in the "wrong" culture, but Don Quixote, a man out of time. Though certainly a figure unsupported by the "institutions of [his] culture," he is an even clearer example of cultural lag. Thus, one of her final messages is that the perception of abnormality can exist as a product of society's changing cultural standards, or, conversely, as a result of its failure to adapt its norms and moralities to new social conditions. Her conclusion here is explicitly Deweyan, in favor of what she calls "social engineering": "No society has yet attempted a self-conscious direction of the processes by which its new normalities are created in the next generation." Indicating the kind of cultural power she imagined the truth-telling social scientist might wield, Benedict argued that irrational adherence to "traditional arrangements" could be done away with, or at least "adapt[ed] . . . to rationally selected goals."[22]

The American anthropologists' practice of critique by cultural comparison was theoretically influential and illuminating on any number of grounds, and often had implications and effects far exceeding the terms of the given study. For example, Boas's work was significant to a shift in the thinking of important black intellectuals, notably W. E. B. Du Bois, away from racially based conceptions of black identity to culturally based views.[23] Equally impressive, and indicative of the authority of modernist intellectuals, was the extent to which Boas's name was invoked in black elite circles of the period, standing in for scientific authority in many anti-racist polemics. The same is of course true of Margaret Mead, whose widely disseminated public persona as a daring young female anthropologist (a kind of intellectuals' Amelia Earhart) probably had more effect in changing Americans' views of women's roles in society than her sharply drawn contrasts between America and Samoa ever could. Of course, the social scientists themselves saw their power in rather different terms, as producers of powerfully transformative social visions. It is telling in this regard that both Mead and Benedict later had serious misgivings about their use of intercultural comparison. In the context of potential U.S. involvement in World War II, both began to worry that this gesture's powerfully estranging effects in regard to modern Western society was "malicious" and conducive to moral uncertainty and lack of political resolve.[24]

As I have said, it is often noted that the time surrounding World War II, especially the dropping of the A-bomb and the revelation of the Nazi genocide, represented the end not only of a great many people's attraction to "social engineering" but of their certitude over the inevitable triumph of rationality. These events would then of course also signal the end of what I am calling naïve modernism, as well. But I think it important to emphasize (especially in the context of current calls for solidarity in the face of one national crisis or another) that this loss of faith in the transformative powers of estrangement had already begun for many, such as Mead and Benedict, *before* the war. Quite simply, such intellectual strategies of addressing the lags and absurdities of contemporary society began to look treasonous in the context of war mobilization, running counter to the propagandistic requirements for cultural and political unity. In other words, the rejection of these strategies also had their roots within a specific political climate, one that was extended and exacerbated by the cold war.

A few more words need to be said about this context. In tandem with the common accounts of the betrayals of idealism and rationality instigated by World War II is another common argument that modernist engagement with the world ended with the flight of intellectuals from a bohemian, urban public sphere into the sinecures of the academy.[25] However, a far more important development in the structure of intellectual life actually preceded the enormous postwar growth in U.S. universities: the flight of intellectuals (both academic and nonacademic) into government work. This trend began in earnest with Roosevelt and his New Deal bureaucracy, extended through the war years (when both Mead and Benedict worked for Washington), and into the cold war, with the full efflorescence of a government-industrial-academic partnership, in which scientists, political and economic theorists, linguists, historians, anthropologists, sociologists, psychologists, and so forth, worked both directly and indirectly in the service of U.S. foreign policy, the military, foreign aid and "development," and the welfare state. In the postwar years, then, we witness the emergence of an important division in intellectual life, not between the academic and the "public intellectuals," and not even between the sciences and humanities, but between those intellectuals connected in some way with the government and those, whether in the academy or elsewhere, who were—or felt themselves to be—largely detached from this huge Cold War enterprise.[26]

This distinction helps clarify a number of things. First, it further breaks down the idea of the "two cultures," for there were scientists whose work fell outside of the purview of the Cold War effort, just as certainly as there were scholars in the humanities who were very much part of the government's ideological machine (one thinks, for example, of Arthur Schlesinger, Jr., who was a virtual propagandist for the Kennedy administration). The division between those intellectuals involved in government-related work and those uninvolved is also the context of much of the Cold War rhetoric of intellectual life well through the 1980s, in which the pragmatic, mature, *Realpolitik* of the technocratic elite came to seem the favored stance over and against the "ideological," childish, emotional, bleeding-heart, utopian fantasies of the prewar intelligentsia, as well as their apparent heirs, the Vietnam war protesters and the postwar academic left.[27]

This context also helps explain why there is, finally, no significant difference between the positions of the slightly liberal magazine-based New York Intellectuals and the more overtly conservative academic New Critics: despite their differences of institutional location and their starting ideological positions, they fundamentally coincided in the view that aesthetic concerns took precedence over "ideological" ones.[28] Unable to partake of the technocratic mentality, they were equally unable to adopt the discredited "ideological" positions of the prewar period. Their only refuge, it seemed, was to imagine themselves as the repository of ethical detachment—as embodying the moral outside to the ugly cold war world.

I have already argued that this position of exteriority was both exaggerated and to some extent self-imposed.[29] Adorno's famous dictum that "to write poetry after Auschwitz is barbaric" was misused by some to connote the obsolescence and irrelevance of both art and its intellectual champion: the impossibility in the Cold War present of meaningful cultural activity of any form—excepting, perhaps that which preserved the "innocent" culture of prewar modernism.[30] The idea of the impossibility of culture—particularly an engaged, transformative, and transformable culture—had its appeal for many. Art and art criticism could be definitively located in a realm separate from politics, and the artist and critic were allowed to celebrate the achievements of modernism, freed from the embarrassment of the earlier modernists' naïve faith in the possibility of participating in profound cultural and historical changes.

Yet for Adorno, the Holocaust did not represent some horizon of possibility of cultural work, so much as an *intensification* (the "final stage") of the ongoing dialectical struggle between "culture and barbarism."[31] In other words, poetry was "barbaric" for Adorno much in the same sense as when Walter Benjamin had suggested that "there is no document of civilization which is not at the same time a document of barbarism" (when would the writing of poetry *not* be "barbaric"?).[32] The point I want to make here is that the rejection of a naïve modernism was thus not only the rejection of the embarrassments of innocence—a rejection of intellectuals' historical inability to anticipate the horrors of the Holocaust, the gulag, or the atomic bomb. It was also a rejection of the kind of thinking and politics that required a belief in the possibility of dramatic social and cultural transformation, for good or ill. It was a rejection of the imaginative proximity to revolution every bit as much as it was a resistance to the complex dialectics of modernism, of culture and barbarism, that Adorno undertook to explore. Nor was this rejection solely a matter of discipline, unique and specific to the humanities, the sciences, or the social sciences. If cultural creators and scholars refused political engagement (Clement Greenberg and the abstract expressionist painters he championed are here exemplary) then it was equally true that many of the revolutionary impulses that had animated a Veblen or a Parsons were unavailable to many social scientists. Yet like any such repression of history, this produced its own partial memory—and this, then, is my more complete account of the phenomenon of cold war nostalgia for a kind of intellectual excitement and power specific to an earlier moment.

SHAME

Rather than explore this nostalgia (well exemplified by books such as Russell Jacoby's *The Last Intellectuals* (1987) and in much of the work of Christopher Lasch), or indeed recount the ways in which subsequent generations of intellectuals undertook to reimagine their social role, I would like to turn backwards again to the moment, context, and rhetoric of naïve modernism in order to ask what this moment offered, and indeed might still offer us, for thinking about the relationship between thought and practice in intellectual life. I wish to return, as it were, to the repressed. In doing this, I must also press deeper into that most painful of affects that, finally, unites naïveté and embarrassment: shame.

In this case, my example is a novel, Sherwood Anderson's *Many Marriages* (1923), a fascinating text for thinking about both naïveté and its attendant embarrassments.[33] It is also a document of the changing sexual morality of early twentieth-century America and of a bohemian sexual radicalism that sought to challenge heterosexual relations in ways that paralleled other kinds of radicalisms, including the aesthetic and the political. Anderson was a distant member of the sexual bohemia that included such figures as Parsons, the anarchist Emma Goldman, and Floyd Dell, author of *Love in the Machine Age* (1930). In its moment, *Many Marriages* was considered a novelistic contribution to the critiques of marriage generated by such writers; interestingly, it was also one of Anderson's best-selling works. In the 1920s United States, a place and time famously "sex obsessed" and riven with concerns about marriage's status as the traditional institution of heterosexuality, family, and even state order, Anderson's vision achieved a significant audience.

The plot of *Many Marriages* is a familiar one, in which a modestly prosperous small-town washing-machine manufacturer named Webster decides to leave his wife Mary, and begin an affair with a stenographer in his office. This basic story of office romance would, of course, be reiterated throughout the popular culture of the twenties and thirties, in such codebreaking films about office flirtation as *Red-Headed Woman* (1932) and *Baby Face* (1933), and in melodramatic works like Christopher Morley's novel *Kitty Foyle* (1939). But here, the story of office infidelity is not the typical warning about sexually predatory working girls, but rather centrally about the man—the boss's—wildly ecstatic midlife crisis, in which the breakup of the marriage and the beginning of this new romance is portrayed in highly ritualized terms as largely a matter of Webster's consciousness. Indeed, through the workings of this new romance, Webster suddenly feels himself freed to challenge and question every feature of his existence, extending from the character of his relationship with his grown daughter to that of his relationships with his fellow townspeople. It is, in this sense, a highly appropriate book for thinking about the broad implications of the idea of the imaginative proximity to revolution.

But before returning to this issue I wish first to address a far more local problem regarding *Many Marriages*, which, if my reactions are any gauge of those of my fellow critical readers, may help to explain why this book is now so seldom read with any serious attention. *Many Marriages* is, quite simply, an excruciatingly embarrassing book to read. I would not be the first to note that Anderson's prose style and heavy-handed symbolism can be embarrassing. In fact, both of Anderson's best-known protégés William Faulkner and Ernest Hemingway made this point—the latter rather laboriously so, in the parodic *Torrents of Spring* (1926), Hemingway's novel-length exercise in slaying the father. But I think the embarrassment in reading *Many Marriages* goes beyond whatever stylistic infelicities one finds in Anderson's prose. Indeed, the embarrassment here is the kind that makes the reader (or at least me) physically squirm, cover one's eyes, and shout out to a character to stop behaving so shamefully.

What is the source of this book's ability to invoke physical discomfort? Let us begin with the prose. Here is a passage in which Webster muses about his daughter's emergence into adulthood: "It was a strange and terrible fact, but the truth was he had never thought much about his daughter, and here she was almost a woman. There was no doubt she already had the body of a woman. The functions of womanhood went on in her body. He sat, looking directly at her. A moment before he had been very weary, now the weariness was quite gone. 'She might already have had a child,' he thought. 'Her body was prepared for childbearing, it had grown and developed to that state' " (20). What is happening here, in Anderson's laborious reiterations, is a hyperliteralization—indeed, a gynecologization—of the rather obvious point that the daughter "was almost a woman." Though he risks a diminution of the reader's trust in the narrator's subtlety and handling of nuance, sometimes Anderson just won't let us alone until we grasp all the embarrassing implications of the obvious.

Nor is this technique of insistent repetition confined to the prose alone; indeed, it is also central to the plot and characterization of the novel. In enacting the break from his wife, Webster invents a set of complex rituals, the most prominent one involving a homemade altar consisting of a picture of the Virgin, and several yellow candles set in holders adorned with tiny figures of Christ on the cross. Before this impromptu altar (in which the image of the Virgin is partly an icon of his wife, Mary, before their marriage), Webster paces naked, wondering (perhaps legitimately) about his sanity, and recalling his past (85–86). The scene in which his wife and daughter walk into this sanctuary, and are, as Anderson puts it, "completely frightened and cowed," is embarrassing enough, but it is not as bad as Webster's recollection of the courtship of his wife—which, still naked, he recounts to his daughter in this bizarrely sacralized bedroom setting.

Webster's story of how he first met his wife when they were both houseguests of mutual friends begins like a (very tame) pornographic scenario. Mary had arrived at the house tired from a long train trip, and had undressed to take a nap. Webster and the son of the house had been out in the woods, and, upon returning home, undressed to take baths. By mistake, the unclothed young Webster encountered the other naked houseguest in her room. Partly, it is suggested, because Mary was still rather sleepy, she didn't register much surprise at Webster's embarrassing intrusion, which Webster interprets as indicating some kind of bond of intimacy that had developed between them in this brief accidental encounter. But when Mary finally comes to her senses, she begins to sob mournfully out of what Anderson identifies as "shame." I think the conventional response to such scenes of accidental exposure—particularly ones that carry a certain freight of sexual threat—would be to ignore the act, or to otherwise deflect from it. Indeed, Webster notes that his young host, who witnessed this scene, was "embarrassed," and never spoke of the incident again. But Webster's response to this scene of shame and embarrassment is otherwise: Webster repeats the act, running back, still naked, into the bedroom where Mary lies sobbing on the bed, and tries to comfort her—thereby creating a kind of nude tableau, to be fully witnessed, once again, by his hosts, and presumably heightening the girl's distress. Moreover, this uncomfortable scene repeats itself in the novel when his wife and daughter encounter Webster in his nakedness before the altar, and also when he tells this story to his daughter.

Certainly, these reiterations do nothing to alleviate the sense of embarrassment for the reader, which I think comes from two features of the scene: it has the painful feeling of ritual gone bad; a repetition compulsion with disturbing overtones of sadism and exhibitionism. Then there is also the matter of public exposure. This kind of sexual shame requires the embarrassment of witnesses, or else it is simply the rather harmless business of Webster prancing naked in front of his picture of the Virgin. It is even suggested that Mary is not particularly disturbed when he first intrudes on her privacy; rather, her shame descends upon her after the fact, in anticipation of the audience that must necessarily exist for it. Speaking now in terms of social convention, the only solution to this kind of reiterated scene of sexual shame is another kind of public ritual that legitimates the heterosexual encounter: marriage.

It is here where we might begin to think about Anderson's sexual politics, for I think he is suggesting that shame is central to the problem with contemporary heterosexuality. As the sanctioned affect of Victorian sexual hypocrisy, shame is the snake in the garden, intruding upon and spoiling the perfect romantic-sexual connection between Mary and Webster in that sleepy moment when they first lay eyes on each other's naked forms. Also as in the *Genesis* story, it is Webster's future wife who can be understood to have made this scene go wrong, to have cried out in her shame, and then to have failed to overcome this affective state when Webster returns to her room to comfort her. Because Webster did not ease Mary's shame, his gesture of returning to her room is not one of healing her sorrow or recapturing their bliss, but of compulsive reiteration. As a result, Webster and Mary's marriage is permanently, and fatally, attached to this experience of shame, especially for Mary, who resists sexual intimacy with Webster (we are told she regards sex as a matter of procreation). Webster, for his part, responds in two ways: through the time-honored technique of taking a lover, and through his naked antics in front of his mirror. This latter behavior allows Webster to detach sexuality from marriage and re-ritualize it in such a way as to separate it from the affect of shame. For her part, Mary quietly—and in this narrative, almost incidentally—kills herself.

As readers, we too are brought along to experience this destructive shame. Indeed, it is in this light that I think we may be able to reread both the embarrassment of this book, and the deliberate and painful reiterations that so often provoke that sensation. Rather than being the ham-fisted stylings of a truly awful writer, I think Anderson's repetitions are intended to confront readers with their own embarrassment, to insist that they vicariously experience the affect of shame. In this respect, the reiterations and other ritual aspects of *Many Marriages* can be seen as analogous to working through a trauma, and toward a purgation of this powerful emotional state. But I think Anderson's commentary on shame lies beyond this narrative attempt at psychoanalysis. Perhaps not surprisingly, it lies in another, deeply perplexing feature of the novel, namely in the novel's treatment of Mary's fate.

We are let into Mary's consciousness enough to know that she regards her husband's behavior toward her as violently aggressive. According to her, his first naked encounter with her was not a moment of transformative possibility, but of "rape"; and his sexual conversations with his daughter about this and other events is another "rape," a shameful reiteration of that past violence (154). In other words, it is all too easy to read Webster's own liberation from shame as a deeply callous self-liberation from whatever guilt he feels—or fails to feel—for the violence he has done to Mary. She can easily be read as the sacrificial victim of Webster's own rather ecstatic liberation. Then too, the contemporary reader is more than a little unsettled by Webster's lip-smacking fascination with his own daughter's sexuality, which is justified in the narrative as Webster's attempt to alter his relationship to his daughter from that of father to "man"—thereby further dismantling a marriage in which a shame-filled sexuality was socially sanctioned through procreation. In this respect, we might be tempted to ascribe to the book a disturbing (if familiar) patriarchal version of sexual liberation that comes at the expense of women. Indeed, Anderson's vision can be seen to simply extend into matricide what Ann Douglas has nicely labeled the "matrophobia" of so many modernist writers, obsessed with distancing themselves from the Victorian mother as the central symbol of hypocritical gentility and outworn tradition.[34]

But before relegating the book entirely to the dustbin of older forms of sexism, I'd like to extend further what I see to be Anderson's analysis of shame. Psychological theorists of the affect of shame have observed that it emerges very early in human psychical development, roughly coterminous with the infant's ability to recognize itself as distinct from its caregivers. Thus, on the basis of her reading of this research, Eve Sedgwick trenchantly suggests, "Shame, as opposed to guilt, is a bad feeling that does not attach to what one does, but what one is."[35] If Mary and Webster's marriage is constituted by shame, then so, in some fundamental sense, is Mary herself: she is formed narratively in the moment in which she sees her own nakedness in the eyes of others. We may reasonably see this interpellation as a moment of terrible violence for the subject in question, but perhaps this is also the terrible truth behind her suicide. The only way to truly abolish shame is to destroy the subject, or rather the kind of subject that Mary so clearly represents: bourgeois, married, sexually repressed.

In Mary's place, the novel offers us two figures, the daughter, who joins her father in remaining curiously unmoved by her own mother's suicide, and Natalie, Webster's new lover, a curiously silent figure seen almost exclusively through Webster's eyes. Natalie is a specimen of a new kind of feminine figure, the working girl, who would become a *tabula rasa* for sexual and social fantasies of the period, because of her class position and a still prevalent sexual mythology that saw working women as a species of amateur prostitute. The first thing we learn about Natalie is that she is in some interesting sense beyond shame, sexual or otherwise. The daughter of a German saloonkeeper and a drunken Irish mother given to loudly abusing her in public, Natalie can keep no secrets from the town that knows far too much about her private life. Fully a creature of the public realm—a "girl of the streets" in a very special sense—Natalie has, we are told, kept her soul clean; that is, she has somehow never allowed shame to enter into her personality. She is receptive; indeed, she is, in Webster's view, a house with wide-open windows.

There is a great deal to be said about the house imagery of this book—imagery that it shares, indeed, with a number of other works of the same time, notably Jean Toomer's *Cane* (1923). As in *Cane* and also in Anderson's earlier *Winesburg, Ohio* (1917) the house is a figure for both the human psyche with its complex interior spaces, and for the private and domestic ethos that prevents full human expression— including the expression of true fellow feeling. Houses, in this book, are "prisons" (118) and "tombs"—and Webster imagines himself rescuing people from them. He also imagines himself floating up and along the second stories of the houses (as in, say, the perspective of an elevated streetcar), so as to fully see the lives within; and he imagines "new and marvelous cities" where "the doors to all the houses were wide open," and where its occupants, if not present, might leave pleasant welcoming little snacks for unknown visitors (167). This imagery is, of course, highly sexual. But I want to emphasize that as a social vision it is much more than a critique of bourgeois privacy and domesticity; rather, it is broadly utopian. When Webster first contemplates having an affair with Natalie, his romantic reverie is interrupted by two people who claim to share in his distracted emotional state: a worker in his own factory and a black hobo. In other words, sexual liberation here is not portrayed as individualistic, but rather suggests fellowship between strangers, even between those representing very different social positions. What Webster imagines, from the liminal position of a man fully in the grips of romance, is love under the stars and in the streets (where he so often meets Natalie) but also love that is not exclusive and dyadic, but rather creative of wider communal bonds.

If all of this sounds like some hippie utopia of unbounded collective eroticism, so be it. Certainly, Anderson would not be the last person to see sexual shame as a terrible psychic burden or to wonder about the possibilities of creating communities through new kinds of bonds of love, erotic or otherwise. But I think he did offer something important in his conjoining of these two ideas, in seeing shame as a central affect of late nineteenth-century bourgeois marriage and therefore as a central impediment to conceiving of other relationships of community, family, nurturance, and love. If shame, finally, is constitutive of both the late nineteenth-century bourgeois subject and of the painful moment that distinguishes such subjects from one another, then what Anderson is calling for here is nothing less than the renovation of this subject, as part of a thoroughgoing renovation of human community as a whole.

EMBARRASSMENT, AND ALL THE REST

The strangeness of Anderson's vision should offer us further proof of Clark's point about what has become for us the essentially alien quality of modernist thought and art. Though many of us are familiar with the general grounds of Anderson's critique of bourgeois marriage (it is a repressive institution designed to control sexuality, procreation, and the transmission of property), in so many ways his habitus is not ours, not the least of which being his capacity to imagine the old Victorian world quietly killing itself off in order to leave a completely new one in its place.

That we are embarrassed by such a work, by such a naïve and even cruel view of change, is clear. But what does this embarrassment mean? Are we embarrassed by this view because it is cruel, part of Adorno's dialectic of culture and barbarism, or because it imagines the process of realizing a radically altered futurity? And if embarrassment is a kind of empathy, a sharing of another's shame, where is Anderson's shame, and our empathy? On the one hand, I believe we do see something of ourselves in Anderson, perhaps in his shameful exposure as a "bad" writer, or in his unmasking as one who would wish that the cultural lags and hypocrisies and stupidities of his old world would just die—or better, like Mary, do the bloody work on its own and kill itself off. On the other hand, it is clear that embarrassment is not solely empathetic in its relationship to shame; it is simultaneously superior, condescending, and distancing. When we are embarrassed by Sherwood Anderson, as when intellectuals since the late modernists have been embarrassed by their naïve predecessors, we imagine that we know better than to fall into error, that we possess a superior understanding of the workings of history to those who saw themselves as potentially revolutionary subjects.

The problem, then, with the affect of embarrassment in relation to an earlier form such as modernism (naïve or otherwise) is that it also presupposes a curious kind of historical relationship: one in which the embarrassed party is able to feel simultaneously close enough to be implicated in the historical party's shame, and distant enough to feel superior. Historiographically, this is not a satisfying

NAÏVE MODERNISM AND THE POLITICS OF EMBARRASSMENT 175

position to take. Far better, I think, would be to insist upon the kind of estrangement Clark engages in—the kind of estrangement that also, by the way, characterized the central critical gesture of so much of the modernist social science I touched upon. In other words, rather than think about modernist intellectuals as our embarrassing older relatives, I think it high time that we see them more as inhabitants of postmodernity's version of the Romantics' Rome, as having lived in an altogether other place and time, in which the context of intellectual labor was radically different from that of the present.

So what of shame? I suppose there is a place for it as a kind of historical thinking, in which the subject experiences the barbarities of the past bodily, in the capillaries of the face. But, extending from Sedgwick, who identifies shame as a key component of recent struggles surrounding identity politics, I wonder about the extent to which shame inhabits and characterizes virtually all of the recent battles surrounding intellectual life in the United States: not only "political correctness," but also discussions over the fate and duties of public intellectuals, the so-called culture wars, science wars, and so forth.[36] This kind of shame, and shaming, seldom seems to me useful or interesting or even very corrective.

If shame is constitutive of the subject, or more specifically the turn-of-the-twenty-first-century intellectual subject, then perhaps we are stuck with it. On the other hand, perhaps this is where the renovation of a little naïveté might be in order: a naïveté that unsticks this subjectivity long enough to allow us to think the thoughts necessary for a new moment. It is true that barbarity might ensue, but then, so might culture.

NOTES

1. See Russell Jacoby, *The Last Intellectuals: American Culture in the Age of Academe* (New York: Basic Books, 1987); and C. P. Snow, *The Two Cultures and the Scientific Revolution* (Cambridge: Cambridge University Press, 1959).

2. David A. Hollinger, "The Knower and the Artificer," *American Quarterly* 39, no. 1 (1987): 40.

3. Ibid., 43.

4. The "imaginative proximity of social revolution" is one of three conjunctural elements Anderson names in a periodization of modernism, the other two being the persistence of the *ancien régime* and its support of institutionalized arts (academicism), and the emergence of new technologies including the airplane, radio, and telephone (324–25).

5. Harold Perkin calls the emergence of what some have described as the "professional-managerial class" the great "social revolution" of the postindustrial world; see his, and Barbara and John Ehrenreich, "The Professional-Managerial Class," in *Between Labor and Capital*, ed. Pat Walker (Montreal: Black Rose, 1978), 5–48; and also Robert H. Wiebe, *The Search for Order 1877–1920*, ed. David Donald (New York: Hill and Wang, 1967), 111–32.

6. Fredric Jameson, *Signatures of the Visible* (New York: Routledge, 1990), 75–76.

7. Daniel Bell, *The End of Ideology: On the Exhaustion of Political Ideas in the Fifties* (New York: Collier, 1962), 393–407.

8. Susan Sontag, "Piety without Content," in *Against Interpretation* (New York: Dell, 1966), 250.

9. Harold Rosenberg, "America's Post-Radical Critics," in *The Intellectuals: A Controversial Portrait*, ed. George B. de Huszar (Glencoe, Ill.: Free Press, 1960), 525.

10. For discussions of consensual models in history and the social sciences in the Cold War, see David W. Noble, "The Reconstruction of Progress: Charles Beard, Richard Hofstadter, and Postwar Political Thought," in *Recasting America: Culture and Politics in the Age of the Cold War*, ed. Larry May (Chicago: University of Chicago Press, 1989), 61–75; and Terence Ball, "The Politics of Social Science in Postwar America," in *Recasting America*, 76–92.

11. On anxieties about professionalism, see Bruce Robbins, *Secular Vocations: Intellectuals, Professionalism, Culture* (London: Verso, 1993); for examples of nostalgia, see Christopher Lasch, *The New Radicalism in America, 1889–1963: The Intellectual as Social Type* (New York: Alfred A. Knopf, 1965); Frank Lentricchia, *Criticism and Social Change* (Chicago: University of Chicago Press, 1985); and Jacoby, *The Last Intellectuals*.

12. For a related discussion, see Fredric Jameson, *Postmodernism; or, the Cultural Logic of Late Capitalism* (Durham: Duke University Press, 1991), 55–66.

13. T. J. Clark, *Farewell to an Idea: Episodes from a History of Modernism* (New Haven: Yale University Press, 1999), 3.

14. Elsie Clews Parsons, *The Old-Fashioned Woman: Primitive Fancies About the Sex* (New York: G. P. Putnam's Sons, 1913), 22–23, 27, 37.

15. Ibid., v.

16. William Fielding Ogburn, *Social Change with Respect to Culture and Original Nature* (1922; New York: Viking Press, 1950).

17. See Jameson, *Postmodernism*, 307.

18. John Dewey, *Philosophy and Civilization* (1931; Gloucester, Mass.: Peter Smith, 1968), 328.

19. Ibid., 329–30.

20. Margaret Mead, *Coming of Age in Samoa: A Psychological Study of Primitive Youth for Western Civilization* (1928; New York: Morrow, 1961).

21. Ruth Benedict, *Patterns of Culture* (1934; Boston: Houghton Mifflin, 1989), 270.

22. Ibid., 270–71.

23. Arnold Rampersad, *The Art and Imagination of W. E. B. Du Bois* (New York: Schocken Books, 1990), 228–33; and see also Thomas C. Holt, "The Political Uses of Alienation: W. E. B. Du Bois on Politics, Race, and Culture, 1903–1940," *American Quarterly* 42, no. 2 (1990): 301–23; and George Hutchinson, *The Harlem Renaissance in Black and White* (Cambridge: Harvard University Press, 1995), 62–77.

24. Susan Hegeman, *Patterns for America: Modernism and the Concept of Culture* (Princeton: Princeton University Press, 1999), 162–63.

25. Again, see Jacoby, *The Last Intellectuals.*

26. For a nuanced look at the Cold War divisions between anthropologists in the United States, see Thomas C. Patterson, *A Social History of Anthropology in the United States* (New York: Berg, 2001).

27. For examples and discussions of these distinctions, see Noam Chomsky, "The Responsibility of Intellectuals," in *The Dissenting Academy*, ed. Theodore Roszak (New York: Vintage, 1968), 254–91; and see Bell, *The End of Ideology.*

28. See Hegeman, *Patterns for America*, 171–76.

29. Ibid., 158–92.

30. Theodor W. Adorno, *Prisms*, trans. Shierry Weber Nichelsen and Samuel Weber (Cambridge: MIT Press, 1981), 34. For an important discussion of Adorno's understanding of the Holocaust, and of his various misinterpreters, see Michael Rothberg, *Traumatic Realism: The Demands of Holocaust Representation* (Minneapolis: University of Minnesota Press, 2000), 25–58. Rothberg is particularly helpful in discussing the work of George Steiner, for whom Adorno's reference to the Holocaust became the launching point for a nostalgic dismissal of contemporary culture.

31. Adorno, *Prisms*, 34.

32. Walter Benjamin, "Theses on the Philosophy of History," in *Illuminations*, ed. Hannah Arendt, trans. Harry Zohn (New York: Schocken, 1969), 258.

33. Sherwood Anderson, *Many Marriages* (New York: Huebsch, 1923); hereafter, page references to this work are cited in the text.

34. Ann Douglas, *Terrible Honesty: Mongrel Manhattan in the 1920s* (New York: Farrar, Straus and Giroux, 1955), 8.

35. Eve Kosofsky Sedgwick, "Queer Performativity: Henry James's *The Art of the Novel*," *GLQ: A Journal of Lesbian and Gay Studies* 1, no. 1 (1993): 12.

36. Ibid., 14.

Interpellations:
From Althusser to Balibar

Suzanne Gearhart

> *interpellation* . . . 1. The action of appealing to or en-
> treating: pleading, intercession. *Obs* . . . .
> 2. A summons, citation. *Obs.* . . .
> 3. The action of breaking in upon with speech or
> otherwise; interruption. *Obs.* . . .
> 4. *Sc. Law.* Prevention, hindrance. . . .
> 5. The action of interrupting the order of the day
> (in the French or other foreign legislative Cham-
> ber) by asking from a Minister an explanation of
> some matter belonging to his department.
> —*The Oxford English Dictionary*

> *interpellation:* 1. Action d'interpeller, d'adresser
> vivement la parole à quelqu'un. V. **Apostrophe.**
> 2. (1789) Demande d'explications adressée au
> gouvernement par un membre du Parlement en
> séance publique. *Répondre à une interpellation.*
> —*Le Petit Robert*

THE WORD *INTERPELLATION* ITSELF CALLS OUT FOR EXPLANATION HERE, since it is not commonly used in English. As the *OED* indicates, it has in fact more obsolete meanings in English than active ones. The *OED* also states that the word became obsolete in the fourteenth century and did not come back into English until the nineteenth century— and then by way of French and what *Le Petit Robert* indicates is a par- liamentary use of the word, beginning in 1789. French, like English, retains this parliamentary meaning of formally asking for an explanation from a public official or member of the legislature. It also has the additional popular connotation of brusquely or aggressively calling out to someone, either to greet, question, or perhaps even insult him, not in a legislative session but in the street. When a person with authority, a policeman, for example, does the calling out, *interpellation* can mean to stop and question a potential suspect, and in this instance the word also retains the obsolete English meaning of a summons. Not, however, a formal summons as in a legal document but an aggressive act of summoning that immediately stops the person being interpellated in his tracks and puts him in his place, under the gaze and authority of the interpellator or the system of authority embodied or represented by the interpellator. This popular meaning is the one evoked in Louis Althusser's celebrated discussion and dramatization of interpellation in "Ideology and the Ideological State Apparatuses," which of course introduced the word into contemporary theory.[1] It is due to Althusser that *interpellation* now has a theoretical-political significance, and, through translation and interpretation, supplementary meanings in English, once again by way of French. It is perhaps still one more sign of what used to be called the French invasion of English and American humanistic studies.

For a generation of critical theorists indebted to Althusser, interpellation has overwhelmingly negative connotations. For to be interpellated is to be subjugated to the authority of an exterior system. It is to become a cog within the apparatuses of interpellation, an entity whose place and function are determined by the system. It is, in the specifically Althusserian sense, to be a product of ideology or, I would add, a product of the nation, of language, of culture, or of any other exterior system that determines who or what one is and what one's place is. It is to be subjugated to relations of power and so thoroughly enclosed within and determined by them that one is most often not even aware of the systems that interpellate, subjugate, and imprison, not aware of one's lack of freedom to maneuver within or step outside them. It is even to be under the illusion that one has freely constituted oneself as a subject, when in reality subjectivity results from being interpellated, put in one's place, made a product and function of ideology (or culture, nation, or language). To be interpellated is thus to be summoned, determined, and subjugated as a subject—to be always the subject of someone or something.

The problem of interpellation is of course at the center of Althusser's widely influential essay, an essay that is itself at the very core of his critical legacy. Although Althusser's concept of interpellation has often been discussed, I would like nonetheless to add to and redirect the discussion by considering the term not exclusively within the critical framework of Althusser's own work and the problems he directly addressed but also within a slightly different critical framework that has been suggested by the recent work of Etienne Balibar.[2] This enlarged framework could be regarded as a reflection of the political and cultural transformations that have occurred and that are still occurring in what (for lack of a better term) we call the contemporary, postcolonial world. This is a world in which previously colonized nations and previously colonizing nations are nevertheless still confronting conflicts and problems derived from their very different but interrelated colonial histories, problems that affect the internal and external relations they continue to have with each other and with what in each of them indicates the continued and even increasingly constitutive presence of their ex-colonial other within them: for example, what remains "French" within and as an integral part of Algeria and what remains "Algerian" within and as an integral part of France.[3]

Our self-consciously postcolonial and increasingly transnational world is quite different from the one in which Althusser's theory of interpellation takes shape, and by situating the concept of interpellation and questioning the philosophical-political context in which it takes form, crucial limitations in Althusserian theory will become clear. But the point of my analysis is not only to bring these limitations to light and to confront them. It is also to argue for the continuing relevance of Althusser's concept of interpellation: not only to the critical evaluation of contemporary cultural practices, but also to the invention or reinvention of cultural practices that could address the processes of exclusion associated with both nationalism and colonialism and the forms of violence produced by and within both, a violence which continues to plague the contemporary world, no matter how postcolonial and post- or transnational it is claimed to be.

The debates about interpellation have for obvious reasons tended to center on the question of whether some form or other of interpellation is inevitable and therefore impossible to resist or undermine. Or whether, on the contrary, interpellation in its most general form as the ideological determination of the subject as subjugated can and/or must be resisted and undermined. But in either case, what is being assumed is that interpellation is an entirely negative concept and process totally incompatible with the idea of human agency or human freedom. My goal in this essay is not simply to oppose this negative view of subject formation but rather to use the concept of interpellation as a critical tool that would make it possible to articulate slightly different questions from those that tend to dominate contemporary critical debates on globalization, nationalism, transnationalism, and culture. This does not mean that my purpose in this essay is to attempt to correct a concept of interpellation that I feel has been widely misunderstood. Nor is it to propose that the concept of interpellation has now become a kind of theoretical master term that can be applied to questions relating to contemporary cultural issues. Rather, I would argue that the different meanings and assumptions associated with the concept of interpellation need themselves to be interpellated, not before a policeman or parliamentary authority—or their academic equivalents—and not because they are suspect, but rather because their critical potential has not yet been articulated or exploited.

Three closely related components of the concept of interpellation as it is most commonly used today in a theoretical context invite questioning. The first concerns the identity of the interpellator. In his essay on "Ideology and the Ideological State Apparatuses," Althusser characterizes "interpellation" as a "summons" or "summoning," and in doing so lays the foundation for the now generally accepted understanding of interpellation as a process of "subjugation." But this characterization of interpellation is based on the idea that the subject is on some fundamental level always being interpellated by a "policeman" or someone playing the role of an authority of some sort, an enforcer of the legal/ideological system doing the summoning. My question is, how is Althusser able to assume this? And if, as he admits, it is not always the case that interpellation is a negative summoning, since it can also be a greeting to a friend, why is an aggressive summoning the primary, fundamental case for him, the one that really matters?[4] What principles or assumptions permit him to identify the policeman as the primary interpellator? And if those assumptions can be questioned, is it possible, and if so, how, to identify who or what "interpellates" subjects besides the police? Subjects that are not simply and in all instances stopped, interrogated, and subjugated to the authority of the system?

The second question concerns the interpellated. Althusser tells us that this is the place of a "sub-ject," that is, of a subject created by and through interpellation and simultaneously deprived of freedom and autonomy by being created in this way. But if we cannot be sure that the interpellator always has the role of a policeman, then the idea that the subject of interpellation is always subjugated becomes problematical as well. The question, then, would not be just how subjects could avoid being interpellated by the police (or their equivalents) and thus free themselves of the subjugated subjectivity constituting and imposed on them. It would also be how to imagine other forms and scenes of interpellation, forms that produce or are implicated in different forms of subjectivity. Subjects that are not simply or in all instances sub-jugated.

Finally, the third question has to do with the process of interpellation itself. I have said that if interpellation is always modeled after the interpellation of a suspect by the police, it must be characterized as a general process of the constitution/subjugation of the subject, a subject constituted in order to be subjugated, not so much to the authority of the individual policeman per se as to the process of interpellation/subjugation itself. But if the places and functions in the scene of interpellation of both the interpellator and the interpellated are questioned and are found not necessarily and in all instances to be the places of policeman and suspect, then the entire process itself needs to be rethought.[5]

Questioning the problem of interpellation and the place of the interpellator and interpellated would inevitably lead us to a critical reconsideration of all of the work of Althusser. And if such a task were undertaken, I would argue that it would benefit greatly from a careful investigation of the recent work of Etienne Balibar on nationalism, racism, exclusion, and violence. In much of the ensuing analysis I follow closely Balibar's analysis and argument, but I also highlight the role played by interpellation and language in Balibar's thought and relate his different perspective on these issues to Althusser's own. The problem will not simply be to "update" what some might see as the slightly overused or worn-out concept of interpellation, however much it might seem to belong to a different, "structuralist" or perhaps even early "poststructuralist" era, which most would probably agree are both now irrevocably finished. It is true that what is seemingly of more import today are not the problems of language, "writing," text, discourse, or "phrases" that were central concerns of what has been rightly or wrongly labeled structuralism or poststructuralism, but rather the term *culture* itself, understood as a set of practices shared by specific, definable groups. For some it has seemed that once the problem of "culture" began to emerge (or actually, to reemerge) as a or the central critical concern, then the issues of discourse, text, and language were magically superseded and made irrelevant. As if a new post-poststructuralist, or even a new anti-structuralist and anti-poststructuralist era had been inaugurated. My position is somewhat different.

I would claim in fact that the move away from discourse and language to culture is more apparent than real in contemporary cultural studies in general and that one of the most critical elements of Balibar's work is the way he focuses on language as an explicit cultural and political issue, even if it is not a structuralist notion of language on which he relies. Although they are no longer as explicitly and conscientiously addressed by others, questions of language, writing, and discourse are in fact still as central, if not more central today, than they were during periods dominated by structuralist and poststructuralist theories. For as an application of the concept of interpellation to culture itself would indicate, one of the principles, if not the dominant principle that determines cultural groups is the fact of language. To be interpellated in or as a cultural subject is almost always to be addressed as a member of a specific linguistic-cultural group, and to be a member of such a group is to be interpellated in and by language itself before being interpellated by any authority or power using language to summon or subjugate.

Perhaps then a fourth question about interpellation should be raised: what assumptions do we make about language when we assign a particular character to interpellation? And if it can be shown that these assumptions can be challenged, what are the implications for the notion of interpellation itself? What alternate scenes of cultural interpellations might be imagined, for example, if the assumptions about language that structure Althusser's primary scene of interpellation were to be challenged? What would it mean to be interpellated not as a subjugated subject but otherwise? Or what would it mean if other potential forms of interpellation could be found even within the Althusserian scene of interpellation itself, even within what is presented entirely as a process of summoning and subjugating?

As any reader of his essay will undoubtedly recall, Althusser illustrates his concept of interpellation by means of what he calls his *petit théâtre théorique,* that is, by means of a brief narration and dramatization of a scene he imagines taking place in a city street. The scene in question, Althusser writes,

> can be imagined along the lines of the most commonplace everyday police (or other) hailing: "Hey, you there!"
>
> Assuming that the theoretical scene I have imagined takes place in the street, the hailed individual will turn round. By this mere one-hundred-and-eighty degree physical conversion, he becomes a *subject.* Why? Because he has recognized that the hail was "really" addressed to him. . . . It is a strange phenomenon."[6]

It is through his staging and interpretation of this little, everyday theatrical scene, and especially of the "strange phenomenon" of the person responding to the "Hey, you there!" he believes is addressed to him that Althusser defines interpellation as the process through which the subject is simultaneously created and subjugated.

As this brief passage already makes clear, the "summons" is for Althusser the paradigmatic form of hailing. Even though he notes parenthetically that any "other" form of hailing could serve equally well as an example and also admits that the person doing the hailing could just as well be a friend,[7] he clearly indicates that the fundamental nature of hailing, the form of hailing that concerns the subject and constitutes the subject as subjugated, is always the same. It is not the greeting of a friend or colleague but primarily an essentially aggressive or repressive act in whatever context it takes place and whatever form it takes. Or perhaps in a spirit closer to that of Althusser's analysis, it could be said that even when it takes the form of a greeting and is apparently the sign of friendship, it also subjugates the subject to the authority of the interpellator even as it constitutes the subject as friend.

For most of Althusser's readers and, one could even argue, for Althusser himself, this scene also implies that there is seemingly no resistance that can be offered by any subject to the effects of interpellation, because, though the scene depicts a sequence of actions in order to illustrate the impact of particular cultural practices on individuals, "in reality these things happen without any succession." In other words, before the policeman/friend calls out, culture has already preformed the individual. Culture has "always-already interpellated" him as a subject.[8] Culture in this sense could be considered the policeman of the policeman, the authority behind his authority, the general system of formation and subjugation that makes possible specific acts or performances of subjugation. And if subjugation were the only or essential problem of interpellation, Althusser's essay could rightly be characterized as a "limit text" of interpellation, one that itself virtually negates the possibility of historical agency and portrays "a world without the possibility of resistance or even change."[9] It could even be taken as a text that interpellates its readers and thus subjugates them by demonstrating both analytically and performatively that there is no escape from subjugated subjectivity, from culture, from ideology.

Althusser's "little theater" of interpellation, which seems to allow for no possibility of escape, resistance, or even change, is itself constructed and structured, however, not only according to a particular system of power relations but also, as is the exchange described as taking place in the street, as a fact or performance of language. More specifically it is constructed by a certain concept of language which was to a significant extent borrowed from Lacanian psychoanalytic theory. I do not mean to suggest that Althusser's relationship to Lacan's thought was simple or self-evident, nor do I wish to ignore the controversies that have surrounded it. But Althusser's borrowings were largely from Lacan's theory of language as a symbolic system, a theory that was itself indebted in ways that were anything but simple to the structural linguistics of Saussure.[10] It could be argued that Althusser's particular interest in this aspect of Lacanian theory underpins the scene of interpellation as he imagines it. For what he borrowed from Lacan was, as Balibar succinctly puts it, an idea of language "as a closed totality, the expression of a community similarly closed in on itself . . ." that could be argued to be Romantic in origin, but which has been "perpetuated even in our own day" in the guise of structuralism.[11]

My point is that one of the most basic assumptions underlying Althusser's scene of interpellation is that the two performers in the scene share the same language, and, therefore, that the scene not only takes place "in ideology" (or "in culture"), as Althusser asserts, but also *in language*. When I say "in language" I mean not only that the two actors are assumed by Althusser to share the capacity to use language, understood as a capacity common to all human beings, but rather that they are assumed to share a particular language, that is, a particular *national* language—the language that is spoken or yelled in the street by a policeman when he acts in an official capacity and that the policeman in the scene constructed by Althusser presumes will be understood by anyone who is present on national territory. It is a seemingly innocent or neutral assumption that I would argue has significant implications for his entire analysis of ideology and culture. Put a foreigner, a nonspeaker of French into the scene along with the policeman, and interpellation does not occur in the same way or perhaps at all.[12] If it doesn't occur, the interpellated subject does not respond to the summons and does not turn, does not recognize himself and is not thus recognized as a subject. The implication of this observation is clear: Althusser's "little theoretical theater" ignores the role of the national language and thus of the nation itself in constructing subjectivity, even if the scene at the same time still suggests, seemingly despite Althusser's explicit intentions, that the nation does play a role, perhaps even one of the primary and dominant roles in his theater.[13]

This critical evaluation of the role of language in Althusser's scene of interpellation is one of several issues raised by Balibar's discussion of Althusser's key essay. From a perspective both sympathetic to and critical of Althusser's version of Marxist theory, Balibar comments explicitly and at some length on Althusser's theory of interpellation in his essay on "The Nation Form" and in connection, precisely, with the idea of the nation.[14] Balibar concurs with Althusser's conclusion that in contemporary bourgeois society the principal ideological element has ceased to be "the family/church dyad" and has become instead the "family/school dyad," as Althusser argues in "Ideology and Ideological State Apparatuses."[15] But Balibar goes on to make two critical remarks on Althusser's essay:

> First, I shall not say that a particular institution [such as the family or the school] in itself constitutes *an* "Ideological State Apparatus": what such a formulation adequately designates is rather the combined functioning of *several* dominant institutions. I shall further propose that the contemporary importance of schooling and the family unit does not derive solely from the functional place they take in the reproduction of labour power, but from the fact that they subordinate that reproduction to the constitution of a fictive ethnicity— that is, to the articulation of a linguistic community and a community of race implicit in population policies. . . . In this sense, there is only *one* dominant "Ideological State Apparatus" in bourgeois social formations, using the school and family institutions for its own ends . . . and the existence of that apparatus is at the root of the hegemony of nationalism.[16]

The implications of this passage are that in the scene of interpellation Althusser himself constructed in order to understand the workings of culture and ideology, he ignored and thus failed to theorize nothing less than the "hegemony" of nationalism. This is an especially serious limitation since the scene in question unconsciously illustrates an element of that hegemony by presupposing the existence of a common, national language, one shared and spoken by both the interpellator and the interpellated, the policeman and his suspect, the subjugating agency and the subjugated subject.

One possible explanation for Althusser's seeming lack of interest in the issue of nationalism and the national language could lie in his orthodox Marxist view that culture and ideology are determined in the last instance by an economic infrastructure—even if it could be argued that Althusser is also quite rightly cited as a Marxist thinker who perhaps more than any other recognized the (relative) autonomy of the cultural sphere. This is what Balibar seems to suggest when he writes that "the contemporary importance of schooling and the family unit does not derive solely from the functional place they take in the reproduction of labour power."[17] But in his essay, I would argue, Althusser *did* in fact in large part seek to derive the importance of schooling and the family unit from their function in the reproduction of labor power, given that for him the purpose of the reproduction of the culture or ideology of capitalism was to ensure the reproduction of capitalism itself. In other words, as Balibar also argues, "It is quite impossible to 'deduce' the nation form from capitalist relations of production."[18] This impossibility helps explain why Althusser, who sees these relations as fundamental, proposes no analysis of the problem of nationalism and does not even recognize it as a problem when he constructs his "little theater" or scene of interpellation.

But if a perspective on the question of nationalism such as Balibar's represents a more or less explicit critique of the scene of interpellation constructed by Althusser, it also can involve—and in Balibar's case, it could be argued, it does involve—an appropriation or a reappropriation of interpellation as well. This becomes clear when Balibar argues that nationality is not "only an idea or an arbitrary abstraction," not merely a political value that is inculcated by the national ideological apparatus.[19] Rather, it "integrates this inculcation into a more elementary process (which we may term 'primary') of fixation of the affects of love and hate and representation of the 'self.' "[20] Indeed, nationalism could not function the way it does, could not produce national subjects, subjects subjugated to the nation form, if it did not first address or *interpellate* subjects, if it did not determine and give form to the affects of love and hate of national subjects: if it did not thus also form individuals in terms of certain images or representations, no matter how fictive, of themselves and of others.

If interpellation were only subjugation, nationalism would have only a negative form, the subordination of all individuals to the national group (and "nation-form") or even to the apparatus responsible for the formation and creation of individuals and their representation of themselves as subjugated national subjects. Balibar claims that what makes the nation form hegemonic, affecting not just relations with others but also relations with and within oneself, is that it inscribes subjectivity itself "in a sense of belonging in the double sense of the term—both what it is that makes one belong to oneself and also what makes one belong to other fellow human beings. Which means that one can be interpellated, as an individual, *in the name of* the collectivity whose name one bears."[21] In other words, when we are interpellated as national (or cultural) subjects, we are interpellated by nationalism; but this also implies that interpellation is necessary to the very functioning of nationalism as a hegemonic apparatus that coordinates and subordinates all possible alternative forms of subjectivity in and to a single "nation form."

But language of course is not the only "principle of closure"[22] defining national belonging or community belonging. There exists another principle of the nation, one that we might have thought or wished had been left behind in history, and, with the allied victory over Nazism in World War II, destroyed once and for all: an ideological construct, which despite its long and complicated history, is generally seen today as an unacceptable founding or determining principle of the nation. It is the principle of "race," or what Balibar calls "the fiction of a racial identity" or simply "fictive ethnicity," a "fiction," no matter how abhorrent, that is still a "reality" of contemporary nation-states to the extent that the ideology of nationalism inscribes it within specific everyday practices and therefore makes it "real" for all of those defined by these practices.

In the end, however, even within explicitly "racist" forms of the nation, the principle of "race" alone does not suffice to define the national community or provide it with a foundation and serve as an ultimate guarantee of its existence. One reason is that migration and

intermarriage have throughout history constantly transgressed the
boundaries that are projected by the principle or ideology of "race."
Another is that within any given ethnic community, class differences
tend to become caste differences and in doing so come into conflict
with the "fiction" of the national, "racial" community.[23] Race is the
fiction of a homogeneous, "biological" people evoked to negate the
actual diversity and heterogeneity of all peoples.

Balibar never argues, however, that "racism is an inevitable consequence of nationalism"[24] or that all nationalisms are primarily or
exclusively racist. But he does argue that racism is a necessary "*supplement of nationalism* or more precisely *a supplement internal to nationalism*, always in excess of it, but always indispensable to its constitution and yet always still insufficient to achieve its project."[25] Given
the contradictions inherent within the principles of language and
race and their general insufficiency, Balibar shows how the linguistic
principle invoked or simply presumed by national ideology to guarantee the closure of the national community and the exclusions that
result from it has inevitably to be supplemented by the principle of
the "racial" community. This is because the linguistic principle,
though it links together a people in an immediate, concrete, "performative" way, also means that a given people is always "open" or
rather, from the standpoint of nationalist and racist ideologies, is always *too* open to the outside and to outsiders—the second generation immigrant "inhabits the national language (and through it the
nation itself) in a manner as spontaneous, as 'hereditary' and as im-
perious, so far as affectivity and the imaginary are concerned" as the
so called "native son."[26] Thus "native sons" must find supplementary
means for distinguishing themselves from "non-natives," and do so
by evoking and representing themselves in terms of some additional
form of "fictive ethnicity." But, for reasons that have already been
given, the "racial" principle of national closure alone is also insufficient even from the standpoint of nationalism itself, and therefore it
too needs to be supplemented by another principle of closure—the
principle of a natural, "native" language community.

In other words, a critical analysis of nationalism is not possible if
one separates the two principles of closure, the linguistic and the
"racial," the seemingly more benign principle of "language" (and the
views of culture linked to it) and the more obviously lethal principle
of "race," an apparently open principle of "good nationalism" from
the closed, exclusive principle of "bad nationalism." In reality, "good"

and "bad" principles continuously intersect and overlap in the creation of nationalist ideology, and the principle of language is therefore potentially as problematic, as exclusionary, as the principle of "race." But I would argue that for precisely that reason, there is no form of national belonging that is not rooted in interpellation, "for every interpellation is of the order of discourse,"[27] and every nationalism, whether "good" or "bad" (or both at the same time) is in principle discursive or linguistic as well as fictively "racial," "religious," or "ethnic." A critical analysis of the "nation form" thus would seem to be inconceivable if one remains strictly within the limits of Althusser's theory (and theater) of interpellation, that is, within a theoretical framework that focuses on an abstract idea of language as a closed system and ignores the issue posed by what could be called the sociohistorical fact of language, the fact that "language" only exists in the form of different and intersecting national languages, that is, in the form of the diverse languages spoken by different peoples and the diversity of ways of speaking any given language. But this means that the problem of the nation form cannot be separated from the problem of language, now understood in part in a performative sense as the means of interpellating individuals/subjects as nationals.

Still another aspect of Althusser's contradictory debt to structuralism lies in what could be termed the systematic and therefore closed character he ascribes to culture and ideology, when, for example, he argues that we are always already "inside" culture and ideology, and, even more, that what "seems . . . to take place outside" of ideology or culture "really takes place inside of it."[28] The implications of this point with regard to the scene of interpellation are highly ironic, for though the scene clearly implies for Althusser that the relationship between the policeman and the "individual" subject he interpellates is one of subjugation and repression, and though, as the scene is constructed and framed, the policeman himself is represented as hostile and aggressive, as Althusser constructs and frames the scene, he also implies that the act of interpellation is by definition or by nature one of *inclusion* both in language in general and in a specific national language community in particular.

That this inclusion in language has effects other than repression and subjugation in the scene Althusser constructs becomes obvious if one asks what happens when we no longer assume that the interpellator and the interpellated share the same national language. At that point, the scene of "inclusion" in a linguistic community, no matter

how oppressive or repressive the summons may be, becomes a scene
of "exclusion" instead—the individual or subject who does not respond to the hailing is identified as not belonging to the national
community. And, for that reason, most likely becomes even more suspect as an excluded other. From Althusser's standpoint the scene of
interpellation illustrates the thesis that culture "interpellates individuals as subjects" and in doing so includes them in a community of
speaking subjects. But from another standpoint, the same scene
seemingly illustrates or could illustrate the thesis that the nation interpellates individuals as *national* subjects, and in doing so *includes
some* but also *excludes others* from the national-linguistic community.

It could be argued that the exclusion of particular subjects and
groups of subjects from the linguistic community of the nation is one
of the most obvious effects of nationalism and national hegemony.
Even those who would loudly deplore this exclusion might view it as
a logical consequence of the character of the language community
itself, in whose terms discrimination between those who speak a
given language and those who do not speak it is seemingly natural
and inevitable. However, the unity and the closure of language, like
the "fictive ethnicity" of a people, is in fact not given naturally but
has to be constructed or imagined and is constantly and unceasingly
constructed by nationalism and the different "nation-forms" themselves. Thus the real issue is not only that the language community
includes some and excludes others. It is that it absolutizes those exclusions and inclusions, that it constructs languages as totally independent, closed systems and in doing so not only "excludes" all
ostensibly "foreign" languages but also all of the *patois*, the jargon,
and the class languages—in short, the unassimilable "foreign" elements *within* the national language itself—which both constitute and
at least to a certain extent need to be repressed from within the "national" language.

In other words, the idea that the nation is a linguistic community
in which everyone shares and is defined by a "mother tongue" denies
that it is only through a process of "internal translation" that the (fiction of) the national language can be constructed.[29] It also makes it
possible to assert that any language needing to be translated into the
national language in order to be understood lies "outside" the national language and is totally distinct and cut off from it. That the
"national language" is not the monolithic totality posited by nationalist ideology is especially evident, however, on all national "borders,"

that is, at those locations where translation becomes necessary in order for subjects not just to interpellate but also to communicate with each other. But in reality, such borders not only coincide with the exterior physical borders of the nation-states but are also found in their cities and rural areas, that is, at those sites where translation imposes itself as a necessary instrument of communication, and where, as a result, the "fictive"—that is, the real, albeit constructed—nature of the national language community becomes apparent. I would say that borders are found wherever "little theaters" of interpellation contain and in fact are constructed in terms of scenes of translation.

Still another insight that could be drawn from a critical consideration of Althusser's scene of interpellation concerns the gender of the interpellated subject. The fact that it is seemingly a matter of indifference to Althusser whether the subject of interpellation is masculine or feminine (or that he seems frequently to assume that the subject in question is in fact always masculine)[30] could be interpreted in more than one way. It could obviously be taken as the sign that Althusser, as a "white, male, European theorist," is the victim of a phallocentrism that was certainly common in his day and that is still not all that uncommon in our own. Or it could be the sign that his perspective is dictated by a Marxism that subordinates the question of gender to that of class. But it is important to see that such indifference to "gender differences" and the troubles they cause, or rather, to the problem of the subordination of one gender to the other, can also be understood in terms of nationalism, which, Balibar argues, dictates that it is always "the symbolic difference between 'ourselves' and 'foreigners' which wins out and which is lived as irreducible"[31]— with the result that the issue of gender, like other forms of difference, is always treated by nationalist ideology as "reducible" or secondary and therefore something that does not need to be directly addressed and confronted in itself. A sign that a critical approach remains acritically "nationalist," even if it develops a critique of nationalism, is that it too accepts this reduction of gender or simply ignores the issue entirely. At least, this is one way of interpreting what Balibar means when he writes of "the secret affinity" between nationalism and sexism.[32]

In short, Althusser's scene of interpellation is a scene of national interpellation, a scene of the interpellation of the individual as a national subject, even though Althusser in this essay certainly gives no indication that he realizes his theater is constructed in such a way that exclusively masculine national subjects, subjugated or not, play the roles of either interpellator or interpellated. Nonetheless, it might seem that Balibar's critical reformulation and extension of key Althusserian insights runs up against certain limitations, not concerning the question of gender, which as we have seen Balibar does address critically, but rather having to do with the extension and nature of the nation-form itself. In other words, it might seem that to the extent that nationalism is also a matter of interpellation and not just inculcation, there is in Balibar's terms no alternative to nationalism, or, to borrow from Althusser, "there is no 'outside' " of nationalism.

It could be objected at this point that it is not really that difficult to overcome the impasse of nationalism, because even if nationalism is in some sense unavoidable, as Balibar's work suggests, there are nonetheless at least two models for the nation, only one of which is nationalist in the "bad" sense—in the sense that it is founded explicitly on exclusion. According to this model of the nation, "the people," defined as an *ethnos,* that is, as a community based on the idea of an extended kinship among its members, is the subject of the nation. According to the other, "good" (or at least "better") sense of the nation, "the people" is also considered to be the subject of the nation, but "the people" defined as a *demos* rather than an *ethnos,* that is, as the collective subject of political representation, decision making, and rights.[33] The hegemony of nationalism, so the argument might go, would be primarily a product of the dominance of the "bad" definition of "the people" over the "good" one, of the idea of "the people" as *ethnos*—that is, as a specific ethnic group or "race"—over the idea of "the people" as *demos*—that is, as a group that is constituted through the free choice of its members.

If this were so, a relatively simple choice would thus confront us. We could choose the nation (or the subject) and the exclusions that it seemingly inevitably has generated and continues to generate on the basis of "race." Or we could choose the "*cité,*"[34] (or the citizen) that is, the "city" in the sense of the *civitas* or the *polis,* terms which were used in the ancient world to designate not only an urban space but also the form of association created by a free people and which might be called in this context a different "little theater." It would be a choice that would be no choice at all. Or at least, that is what we would hope.

This view of the problems posed by the hegemony of nationalism neglects the history of the *cité* itself, however, which is one of exclusion no less than is the history of the modern nation-state—or at least, this is what Balibar argues when he observes that "the '*cité*' of antiquity (especially the Greek '*cité*,' from which the very notion of the 'political' is derived) fundamentally *excluded* by *including*, and even, one could go so far as to say, by imprisoning women, children, and slaves [that is, all those who were not considered to be free] in the 'domestic' sphere.' "[35] The exclusion of women, children, and slaves in ancient Greece through their imprisonment in an interior, domestic space, moreover, also mirrored or was mirrored by exterior exclusions. The distinction between the (native) "citizen" and the "foreigner" is fundamental to the nation, which "is still (still wants to be) a '*cité*,' "[36] but it was already fundamental to the ancient *cité* as well, "by definition."[37] Thus even the original form of democracy was based on a principle of exclusion, and the same can be said of the contemporary state, which excludes "by *disaffiliating* all or part of those whom class struggles and social movements more generally had progressively included in the network of social rights."[38] But exclusion in the modern nation-states also consists of not according full or any rights to illegal immigrants, whose work in the more developed countries "includes" them in those societies while at the same time they are "excluded" to the extent that they are denied legal status and protection under the law. The result is what Balibar argues has become a virtual *apartheid* in all of the developed nations.

In short, the terms *ethnos* and *demos* are intertwined throughout the ancient and modern histories of the city-state and the nation-state and thus inseparable in theory as well, because citizenship and "fictive ethnicity" both imply some form of exclusion. Thus the claim that is common to virtually all modern nation-states—the claim that the equality and freedom conferred by citizenship are equivalent to one's status as a national—is not just the expression of a commitment on the part of the nation-state to strive for the increasing equality and freedom of its citizens but also of a limitation imposed on equality and freedom that is accepted in advance as their fundamental condition. It is a limitation initially imposed on those perceived as not being part of the nation but which can very quickly lead to restrictions on the rights and freedom of those who ostensibly are. In short, if to be interpellated as a citizen is to be interpellated as a national, then to be interpellated as a national is to be interpellated as a subject of the hegemony of the nation.

Politics alone, then, cannot necessarily lead us outside the scene of interpellation, because "politics is not a superstructure,"[39] but is embedded in the practical life of the nation, which is itself subjected to the hegemony of nationalism. Similarly, there is no unassailable principle that would permit us to distinguish citizenship from the range of other cultural practices, with the result that even the practices of citizenship are seemingly destined to produce and to reproduce what, borrowing from Althusser, could be called the ideological conditions for the material reproduction of the nation. But if Balibar's work consistently discourages the view that one can simply escape from the scene of interpellation or simply imagine and then choose alternate scenes, I would argue that it does suggest that *the meaning of the scene of interpellation is equivocal.* Althusser's "little theater" thus dramatizes the thesis of subjugation he sought to confirm. But it also could be argued to dramatize the opposite thesis as well.

In saying this I do not mean to suggest that Althusser was simply wrong, that interpellation does not have the repressive or oppressive character he ascribes to it as its essence. I mean rather that the scene of interpellation even as Althusser constructs it is ambiguous, that in and of itself it cannot confirm that we are always already "in" ideology and already subjugated to a system of cultural practices that support capitalism—or the nation. Only when the scene in question is viewed in terms of a closed cultural system or order of language can it be interpreted as a scene of subjection. But if such presuppositions about language are tested and found wanting, then the scene can be complicated and opened up to the possibility of other interpretations. In other words, in the terms of the scene itself (and, I might add, of the word *interpellation,* which as we have seen can have various meanings in French), there is no reason to assume that the act of interpellation is exclusively or primarily aggressive, hostile, or repressive—any more than there is any reason to assume that it is friendly or "positive." It could be either (or both), some of each in the other, open and undetermined in its ultimate effects and consequences.

This means that there is no reason to assume that the subject in question in the scene, that is, the interpellated subject, is always or originally interpellated as a subjugated subject rather than as a free subject, or vice versa. As Balibar puts it: "We do not want here to consider [the] figure of the subject as a postulate or as an indisputable ideal. We would rather like to see it as the *equivocal* noun [or name], which covers [*recouvre*] a permanent tension, an uncertain process, with two sides, one of *subjugation* or subjection and the other of *subjectification* or emancipation."[40] And I would add, in scenes of interpellation that dramatize this tension and thus a contradictory process that includes both subjectification and emancipation, the one as the limit or possibility of the other, one cannot assume that it is a masculine subject who is being interpellated. Emancipation would imply at the very least a tension between and within all gendered subjects as well.

If the subject is an equivocal name or noun, then this would suggest that the practices that produce the subject are also "equivocal," and that the various obstacles those practices present to the emergence of a critical theory and critical practices can be seen as weak points in the hegemony of the nation and, therefore, as challenges or opportunities for the elaboration of alternative critical theories and practices that do not attempt to resolve the tensions within the subject. Indeed, Balibar argues, it is not enough to evoke the ideal of cosmopolitanism as a means of overcoming the restrictions placed on democracy by the equation of citizenship and nationality. Democracy needs to be put to work on "determined matters,"[41] that is, democracy needs to be practiced and defined by practice, because ethics and judicial norms alone do not and will not suffice to overcome the hegemony of nationalism. *Citoyenneté* (that is, a citizenship that would no longer be directly linked to and determined by nationalism), Balibar argues, "is not simply a status but a practice or an ensemble of practices."[42]

What, then, are these "practices" and what are the *chantiers* or worksites where they can or are being performed? They are not to be looked for in areas other than the ones in which nationalism imposes itself, because, like the subject itself, the institutions and practices where nationalism most clearly makes its hegemony felt are also potentially "equivocal." Borders—understood both as external limits which demarcate the territory of the nation and also as limits that are internalized and therefore lived as symbolically determining—define the nation and condition its hegemony. But this means that borders are also the sites where resistance to the hegemony of nationalism "must" and "should" be mounted. They are also, it could be argued, sites where such resistance is already apparent. The fact that in the nation it is above all "the symbolic difference between

'ourselves' and 'foreigners' which wins out and which is lived as irreducible"[43] means, Balibar claims, that the frontier or the border, both
real and imaginary, that separates the nation from what and who is
foreign is also a privileged site for the practice of citizenship: "The
rights of immigrant workers, their protection against overexploita-
tion and discrimination, the organization of their access to citizenship by naturalization or dual citizenship, or, even more fundamentally, by a development of social and political rights, . . . in a
word, the abolition of the condition of subjection or of minority constitutes a privileged indicator of the degree of force of citizenship
and of its dynamic, even if they do not exhaust them."[44]

The defense of immigrants' rights can thus be identified as a key
component in critical cultural practice, but it is important to state
clearly why and in what sense this is so. The point is not to replace
the "hatred" of the immigrant (expressed in France, for example, by
the Front National) with "love," because both "hate" and "love" ob-
jectify the immigrant and absolutize his "difference" with the native
citizen. Balibar proposes that the immigrant be taken rather as a
model, at least in certain respects, for the so-called native citizen,
whose "belonging" to the nation is in principle no less problematic
than that of the immigrant. Indeed, the idea of instituting more
democratic borders, he claims, "goes far beyond the theme of 'welcoming the Foreigner,' . . . since *everyone* including the 'natives,' must
at least symbolically put their already acquired civic identity, inherited from the past, up for grabs and *reconstruct it in the present* along
with everyone else. . . . This does not mean that the past no longer
exists, or that it is irrelevant, but it does mean that it is not an inheri-
tance or a birth right. . . . that there are no 'first occupants' as concerns the civic territory."[45] The "belonging" of the national subject to
the nation must thus be continually negotiated and renegotiated,
not only because the reality of the exclusion of the immigrant can always be mirrored by the equally real interior exclusion of the national or of certain nationals, but also because ultimately every
subject is implicated in the scene of interpellation in the same (complex) way, as an equivocal name or noun that designates a permanent tension between a "subjugation" on the one hand and a
"subjectification" or potential emancipation on the other.[46]

Something similar could be said about schools or universities as
worksites of critical cultural practice. Schools constitute one of the
preeminent institutions for the creation of the sense of national be-

longing, not only because national ideals and cultural practices are inculcated through education but also because the school "is the principal institution which produces ethnicity as linguistic community."[47] But it is therefore also in the school that the concept of language as a closed totality, the expression of a community equally closed in on itself, must and should be put into question in both theory and practice. It could even be argued that it *is* being put into question, not only when Romantic or structuralist ideas of language are explicitly challenged but also by the necessary implementation of practices of translation that are becoming increasingly central to social life but whose need was arguably first felt both at particular worksites and in the schools, which in this respect do not so much mirror the dynamic of the larger society as anticipate it.

It is with respect to the closely related subjects of language and immigration that it could be argued that new, critical cultural practices which could lead to greater inclusiveness (but not simply to greater homogeneity) not only are possible but already exist. Europe can serve as one example of this state of affairs, even if it is only one among many others, because the question of language has become central to the debates and discussions concerning the future of Europe as a supernational or transnational entity. The question of the language of Europe is also taken up by Balibar in *Nous, citoyens d'Europe?*, where he asks what the language of Europe will be as the European union becomes increasingly formed and integrated. To those who have argued that it will, inevitably, be English, his answer is that it cannot and will not be, because English is already much more (than a European language) and at the same time therefore less (than the language of Europe). The "language of Europe" is not a "code but a system of hybrid usages [*usages croisés*] in constant transformation." In other words, the language of Europe is, he writes, "*translation*" (my emphasis).[48]

But in order to entertain the proposition that translation will be and even already is the language of Europe, one must have first put into question the concept of language in general and the fiction of the national language as a totality closed in upon itself in particular.[49] In other words, the language of Europe is not only a language that will be added to the different national languages spoken and written in Europe today but a language already "within" those languages in the form of their possible and actual translation. The "exclusion" of the possibility and reality of translation could thus be seen as one of many instances of what Balibar calls "interior exclusion," that is, of an exclusion not only of different languages and different communities but also of and within the "same" language and the "same" community to the extent that translation inhabits and is integral to the construction of every language and every community. In other words, translation should not be conceived merely as a (meta)language capable of including in some way the national languages that are exterior to it; rather it "includes" what is "interior" in the sense that translation itself is always already "within" the so-called national language.

Thus with regard to the problem of language, laws or legislation alone cannot dictate that "translation" will one day become the language of Europe, but neither can legislation or laws prevent it from becoming its language. If translation does become the language of Europe, it will not be the result of laws or of laws alone but rather because it has become a matter of cultural practice. As Balibar argues, translation is today "unequally developed,"[50] but it is significant that it is a practice not confined to a single group or to several closely related social or political groups. Instead, it is concentrated in two extremely diverse groups, one of which is comprised of "intellectuals formed by advanced scientific humanistic studies" and "writers of uprootedness and exile," and the other made up of "anonymous immigrants who in general occupy inferior positions in the division of labor and employment."[51] The existence of the first group is perhaps not so surprising—as Balibar himself points out, the practice of writing/translation within exile communities of intellectuals goes back at least a century and probably further, and is associated with such well-known figures as Heine, Canetti, Joyce, and Conrad. But the practice of translation by the other group is arguably a defining characteristic of a different era—our own—and gives translation and writing very different practical cultural and political implications.

The "writers" of today, that is, the modern heirs of Heine, Canetti, Joyce, and Conrad, are found not only in formal and informal academies of letters but also in factories, restaurants, and the lowest level of civil services. Or, to put it another way, the cultural vanguard as concerns the practice of translation is to be found among the most protected and supported but also among the most disadvantaged groups within the different nations of Europe and all other modern nations. Thus it is always too late, in a sense, to expel "illegal aliens" (the *sans-papiers*), because they have not only already assumed the status of members of a given society through their work and their many other ties to the countries to which they have emigrated, but also because their practice of translation puts them in the cultural vanguard of those societies and of a greater, European society as well. Not only could immigrants be seen as being in the process of integrating themselves into the life of the European nations and of Europe as a whole; they could also be seen in Balibar's terms as "Europeans par excellence,"[52] that is, as practitioners par excellence of "translation," understood as the "concrete metalanguage made up of all the equivalences and all the attempts to overcome the 'untranslatable' that separates particular idioms."[53] In other words, the scene of interpellation in Europe today could be thought of in terms of a very different type of theater, one in which different scenes of translation are performed, in which subjects are not only "hailed" as national subjects but as transnational subjects, who have always already been defined not exclusively or even predominantly by a mother tongue but who are defining themselves otherwise by the process of translation itself.

Althusser and Balibar thus each in his own way warns us against what could be called the illusion of the outside, that is, the illusion that we can escape from the "little theater" of interpellation, that we can occupy a position that has not always already been decisively shaped by ideology and language. But in the light of Balibar's work, I would say that the problem is not only to guard against this particular illusion. It is also to guard against the symmetrical illusion that we are totally "within" ideology and language and therefore totally determined by them. Balibar's work thus confirms the importance of Althusser's view of the centrality of language (and culture in general) to the functioning of ideology and at the same time provides the means of questioning the model of language (and culture) Althusser proposed or assumed, a model based on a principle of closure, or, in other words, on the idea that language can be defined in terms of its internal functions, as an "inside" closed off from all "outsides"—that is, from all other closed language systems and all non-language systems. Moreover, to the extent that the model of language as a closed totality is also the model assumed or postulated by the ideology of nationalism, Balibar could be argued to have broken decisively with the hegemony of nationalism and the theories of language and "race" that support it.

My point, once again, is not however to argue that Althusser's scene of interpellation is either true or false, positive or negative, good or bad. It is rather to emphasize the ambiguity of that scene and to acknowledge that there are no unassailable, indisputable principles that can be referred to in order to determine its ultimate meaning, not only with respect to the work of the two philosophers who have concerned me here but also in relation to the broader context of contemporary debates on nationalism, immigration, internationalism, and transnationalism. These debates themselves, however, cannot help but take the form of multiple scenes of interpellation, in which "subjects" call out to or address each other—and even themselves. Intervening critically in these debates necessitates that the status of the subject not be taken as given once and for all, that the "equivocal" character of the subject be recognized and critically analyzed. It also suggests that we need to find ways to respond to the transformations currently taking place on the "borders" of all culture and nations, where language itself is "equivocal." Where what is "outside" of (a given national) language becomes the "inside" and where the "inside" is projected "outside." Where interpellation could become—or, perhaps it would be better to say, has always already become—translation.

NOTES

1. Louis Althusser, "Ideology and Ideological State Apparatuses (Notes Towards an Investigation)," in *Essays on Ideology* (London: Verso, 1984), 1–60.

2. That work includes two books not yet translated into English: *Droit de cité, culture et politique en démocratie* (Paris: De l'Aube, 1998) and *Nous, citoyens d'Europe?* (Paris: La Découverte, 2001). All translations from these texts appearing in this essay are my own.

3. These and other paradoxes of the postcolonial era are discussed in an article by Balibar in *Droit de cité*, "Algérie, France, une ou deux nations?" [Algeria, France: One or Two Nations?]: the title is meant to be anything but rhetorical.

4. The second example or set of examples of interpellation provided by Althusser involves a friend or friends. Althusser writes: "When we recognize somebody of our (previous) acquaintance . . . in the street, we show him that we have recognized him (and have recognized that he has recognized us) by saying to him, 'Hello, my friend,' and shaking his hand" ("Ideology and Ideological State Apparatuses," 46).

5. Judith Butler rejects Althusser's contention that "guilt" cannot account for the spontaneous reaction of the interpellated ("Ideology and Ideological State Ap-

paratuses," 48) and emphasizes the essentially religious character of "the call," arguing that Althusser's scene of interpellation thus makes "guilt" the condition of interpellation and subjection. See her article, " 'Conscience Doth Make Subjects of Us All,' " in *Depositions: Althusser, Balibar, Macherey, and the Labor of Reading*, ed. Jacques Lezra, *Yale French Studies* 88 (1995): 6–26.

6. Althusser, "Ideology and Ideological State Apparatuses," 48.

7. Ibid., 48, 46.

8. Ibid., 49.

9. Warren Montag, " 'The Soul is the Prison of the Body': Althusser and Foucault, 1970–1975," in *Depositions: Althusser, Balibar, Macherey, and the Labor of Reading*, ed. Jacques Lezra, *Yale French Studies* 88 (1995): 55.

10. Michel Pêcheux provides a detailed discussion of the conception of language that Althusser borrows from Lacan and defends its critical value in illuminating the workings of ideology in his *Language, Semantics and Ideology*, trans. Harbans Nagpal (New York: St. Martin's Press, 1982), 97–109.

11. Balibar, *Nous, citoyens d'Europe?*, 317.

12. Althusser introduces the idea of interpellation by illustrating it with the words: "Hey, you there!" ("Ideology and Ideological State Apparatuses," 48). In a subsequent passage he adds another element when he writes: "verbal call or whistle, the one hailed always recognizes that it is really him who is being hailed" (48). The "whistle" raises the question of whether Althusser is defining interpellation in terms of language or in terms of something other than language, which would be represented by the "whistle." I think it could be easily shown that in Althusser's terms language *is* the true medium of interpellation. In other words, even the "whistle" is a linguistic sign with different meanings in different language and cultural contexts and in that sense is discursive.

13. David Macey discusses the scene of interpellation and notes certain of these details but without himself developing their theoretical implications in his essay, "Thinking with Borrowed Concepts: Althusser and Lacan," in *Althusser: A Critical Reader*, ed. Gregory Elliott (Oxford: Blackwell, 1994), 150–51.

14. Etienne Balibar, "The Nation Form: History and Ideology," in Etienne Balibar and Immanuel Wallerstein, *Race, Nation, Class: Ambiguous Identities*, trans. Chris Turner (London: Verso, 1991), 86–106.

15. Althusser, "Ideology and Ideological State Apparatuses," 31.

16. Balibar, "The Nation Form," 102–3.

17. Ibid., 102.

18. Ibid., 89.

19. Ibid., 96.

20. Ibid., 94.

21. Ibid., 96.

22. Ibid., 99.

23. Ibid., 103.

24. Etienne Balibar, "Racism and Nationalism," in Etienne Balibar and Immanuel Wallerstein, *Race, Nation, Class: Ambiguous Identities*, trans. Chris Turner (London: Verso, 1991), 38.

25. Ibid., 54.

26. Balibar, "The Nation Form," 99. While it may be true that, as David Lloyd writes, it is the "inassimilable differences" of minority culture that "cause the anxiety of pluralists," my contention would be that the all too easy assimilation of immigrants into the linguistic community is as much a source of "anxiety" both for the pluralists referred to by Lloyd (who presumably would see these differences as nothing more than ingredients for a "melting pot" of the whole nation) and also for racists who absolutize cultural and linguistic differences, taking them to be the signs of differences of essence. See David Lloyd, "Foundations of Diversity: Thinking the University in a Time of Multiculturalism," *Culture and the Problem of the Disciplines*, ed. John Carlos Rowe (New York: Columbia University Press, 1998), 40 n. 7.

27. Balibar, "The Nation Form," 98.

28. Althusser, "Ideology and Ideological State Apparatuses," 49.

29. Balibar, "The Nation Form," 97.

30. My observations on this point concern Althusser's scene of interpellation in particular. In his essay on "Freud and Lacan" Althusser frequently writes of the entry into the Symbolic order of both the male and the female child. But even in this latter essay, Althusser at times adopts a focus that foregrounds the experience of the boy alone, as when he writes of "the Order, of the Law, lying in wait . . . for the little man [*le petit homme*] to be born" ("Freud and Lacan," *Writings on Psychoanalysis*, ed. Olivier Corpet and François Matheron, trans. Jeffrey Mehlman [New York: Columbia University Press, 1996], 26. Translation modified.)

31. Balibar, "The Nation Form," 94.

32. Ibid., 102.

33. Balibar, *Nous, citoyens d'Europe?* 24.

34. The old French word *cité* is derived from the Latin *civitas*, and like it can be regarded as a translation of the Greek *polis*.

35. Balibar, *Nous, citoyens d'Europe?*, 116.

36. Ibid., 246.

37. "By definition there is no 'citizenship' unless there is a '*cité*,' that is a place where citizens as a group are clearly distinguished from 'foreigners' in terms of rights and obligations" (Balibar, *Nous, citoyens d'Europe?*, 246).

38. Ibid., 116.

39. Ibid., 187.

40. Ibid., 57–58.

41. Ibid., 311.

42. Ibid., 209.

43. Balibar, "The Nation Form," 94.

44. Balibar, *Nous, citoyens d'Europe?*, 80–81.

45. Ibid., 212.

46. Ibid., 57–58. In a recent essay, Pheng Cheah has criticized what he calls "hybridity theory," exemplified for him by the work of James Clifford and Homi Bhabha, arguing that it amounts to a celebration of the "migrant 'minority' subject, who subverts *metropolitan* national space" at the expense of a recognition and analysis of the plight of a majority of subjects in the formerly colonized world, "who remain in peripheral space by choice or by necessity." (Pheng Cheah, "Given Culture," in *Cosmopolitics: Thinking and Feeling beyond the Nation*, ed. Pheng Cheah

and Bruce Robbins, [Minneapolis: University of Minnesota Press: 1998], 300, 314). Cheah is certainly right to suggest that "hybridity" should not be fetishized or treated in all instances as a necessarily positive phenomenon. But it is also a mistake, I would argue, to dismiss the phenomenon of "hybridity" on the grounds that it concerns only the metropolitan space, while national citizen/subjects in the formerly colonized countries exist in a nonhybrid environment and therefore need the nation and nationalism to defend their interests. Some of the most glaring examples of the exclusions wrought by nationalism are provided by the contemporary history of what Cheah calls "peripheral spaces" or formerly colonized nations, where ethnic and linguistic minorities are frequently the objects of exclusion and repression. In other words, "borders," as Balibar puts it, and "hybridity," as Clifford and Bhabha might say, are everywhere. For a further discussion of this issue, see James Clifford, "Mixed Feelings," in *Cosmopolitics*, 364–66.

47. Balibar, "The Nation Form," 98.
48. Balibar, *Nous, citoyens d'Europe?*, 318.
49. Ibid., 317.
50. Ibid., 318.
51. Ibid., 318–19.
52. Balibar, *Droit de cité*, 52.
53. Balibar, *Nous, citoyens d'Europe?*, 318.

Essentially Ambiguous:
On the Nature of Language,
the Epistemology of Modern Science,
and the Relationship Between
the "Two Cultures"

Arkady Plotnitsky

I WOULD LIKE TO BEGIN BY EXPLAINING THE "ESSENTIAL AMBIGUITY" of my title or, I should say, the phrase *essentially ambiguous* of my title. The ambiguity between the phrase and the possibly ambiguous character of my title, along with other ambiguities possibly involved (such ambiguities tend to accumulate quickly and uncontrollably) are worthy of a paper of their own. For the moment, however, I shall restrict myself to the phrase *essentially ambiguous* and to the question of why it is essential, unambiguously essential, for understanding the nature of the three phenomena of my subtitle: language, modern science, and the relationships between the "two cultures," (as C. P. Snow proverbially defined them in the 1950s)—the humanities and the sciences.

The term *science* will be understood here to include (beyond natural sciences, such as physics, chemistry, or biology), first of all mathematics and secondly certain social sciences, most especially post-Saussurean linguistics, a large part of which may also be assigned a kind of logico-mathematical character (akin to that found in analytic philosophy). From this viewpoint linguistics would, along with most of modern economics (which is expressly mathematical in its character) belong to the science side of the two cultures. At the same time, however, certain key conceptual features of Saussurean and post-

Saussurean linguistics have had a shaping role in the development of a radical form of epistemology, the epistemology that deals with and indeed entails that which is essentially ambiguous, and theories defined by and defining this epistemology. I shall here call both this epistemology and these theories nonclassical. I shall explain classical epistemology and theory presently, merely noting for the moment that as one of its features it aims to reduce the essentially ambiguous, at least in principle if not in practice. Nonclassically, it would not be possible to do so, not only in practice but also and most crucially in principle.

Saussure's own work in linguistics had a decisive impact on the nonclassical theories in the humanities to be addressed here, such as those of Jacques Derrida and Paul de Man. While less predictable and less explicit than the questions of difference or arbitrariness most commonly associated with Saussure and especially with Derrida and de Man, the question of ambiguity is crucial for their work and the epistemology emerging from it. Accordingly, linguistics and certain key aspects of its *language* as a science, the science *of* language, is one of my points of departure here.

Quantum theory is the other, for the following reason. Since the 1930s the concept and the very phrase *essential ambiguity* have proven to be essential, unambiguously essential even for physics, the paradigmatic modern science and inescapably one of Saussure's models in his project of linguistics. Indeed, it may be argued that Saussure's linguistics was modeled (directly and through mediation) on classical, Newtonian physics, the science intended to be essentially unambiguous in its description of its objects, such as falling bodies or planets moving around the sun. (These are essentially the same type of phenomena, resulting from the force of gravity acting upon either type of object.) On the other hand, Saussure's linguistics was born at the moment when an essential ambiguity of any such reference (and, hence, of the language used) by physics to the ultimate physical objects physics considered—the ultimate constituents of nature, their properties and behavior—was about to become essential, unambiguously essential, in relativity and in quantum mechanics (both introduced around 1900). The phrase *essentially ambiguous* arrives courtesy of Niels Bohr and his radical—ineluctably noncausal and nonrealist—epistemology of quantum mechanics, known as complementarity.[1] The phrase occurs in Bohr's analysis of Einstein's argument questioning the adequacy of quantum theory as the final description of nature at the ultimate level of its constitution, and, it might be added, doing so on strictly epistemological grounds.[2] Einstein accepted the practical utility and effectiveness of quantum theory. I shall first explain how this *essential ambiguity* comes about in physics and then consider the significance and implications of this concept for nonclassical epistemology and theories in linguistics and elsewhere in the humanities.

First, according to Bohr's interpretation, quantum mechanics (unlike classical physics) is defined by the "*impossibility of any sharp separation between the behavior of its objects and the interaction with the measuring instruments which serve to define the conditions under which the phenomena appear*" (Bohr's emphasis).[3] In other words, in contrast to classical physics (when we speak of, say, the moon moving around the earth), in quantum physics it is never possible to refer to such objects apart from their interactions with measuring instruments and their manifest effects upon certain parts of those instruments. Nothing beyond such effects could be observed in quantum physics. Secondly, however—and here Bohr makes his truly radical but impeccably logical step—"*under these circumstances an essential element of ambiguity is [always] involved in ascribing conventional physical attributes to atomic [quantum] objects*" (emphasis added).[4]

It is crucial—and this point defines the radical nature of Bohr's argument—that such a reference is impossible even if one talks of a single such attribute, say, the position or momentum of a particle. We never know where a particle really is or was and when, but only where we find (or statistically predict where we can find) a trace of its collision with an instrument, which is never sufficient to establish where the particle has ever been in space or time. It is always, in Lucretius's remarkable phrase, *incerto tempore—incertisque loci* [in an uncertain time, in an uncertain space].[5] This is what Heisenberg's famous uncertainty relations rigorously mean. Admittedly, this (namely as disallowing one to know or to attribute both position and momentum or time and energy to a given quantum object at the same time) is not how they are usually explained. In other words, the corresponding precise measurements (within the capacity of the instruments involved) are mutually exclusive or, in Bohr's terms, complementary. The ultimate physical meaning of uncertainty relations, however, at least in Bohr's interpretation (which is at least as complete and consistent as any available) lies in the impossibility of ever attributing any physical properties to quantum objects themselves or their behavior:

not even single properties, such as a position or a momentum of a quantum object, an "elementary particle." Indeed, we cannot attribute to quantum objects anything, neither position nor momentum, nor time nor energy, not even such terms as *particle*, or *wave*, or *object* in whatever sense, nor anything else. These and all conceivable concepts are metaphors or, as de Man would see them, allegories, ultimately inapplicable to quantum entities.[6] Such allegories, allegories of classical physics, are useful as shorthand. They are also essential in considering the effects of quantum objects on measuring instruments, which are described by means of classical physics and to which such concepts and other conventional physical properties can and indeed must unambiguously apply in order for quantum physics to function as a scientific discipline. The possibility or, conversely, impossibility of this application is the epistemological difference between classical and quantum objects, and the two different types of physics such objects require, according to this view.

However it is not physics that is most essential for me here, but Bohr's formulation as such in stating that, to paraphrase Bohr slightly by way of generalization, *in certain theoretical circumstances an essential element of ambiguity is [always] involved in ascribing conventional (physical or other) attributes to the ultimate objects the theory in question considers.* This formulation can thus be generalized so as to define a certain form of epistemology which I call nonclassical, and correlatively certain conditions under which scientific practice must take place.[7] This type of science, when possible, would *in some respects and at a certain level* still involve classical science (defined by analogy with classical physics) and its epistemology, which I shall, accordingly, call classical epistemology. One of the reasons for this necessary usage is to avoid ambiguity in the definition of scientific concepts and the communication of scientific findings (including those concerning ambiguities). Unambiguousness appears to be necessary for the disciplinary practice of science, at least given the way science is currently constituted and functions. This is also true and is insisted upon by Bohr in the case of quantum mechanics.[8] A nonclassical science must however relate to its ultimate objects (in linguistics, those pertaining to the ultimate nature of language and signification) in epistemologically nonclassical ways—that is, without the possibility of speaking rigorously or unambiguously of these objects or their attributes, including, ultimately, as "objects" in any conceivable sense.

Such a nonclassical science is, then, possible in the case of quantum physics (for instance, relativity may ultimately be nonclassical in its character as well by allowing or even entailing a nonclassical interpretation). Accordingly, it could be used as a model for scientific practice in other cases where phenomena entailing nonclassical epistemology appear, just as classical physics has been used as a model for classical sciences elsewhere; and, as I said, nonclassical science necessarily and even irreducibly involves some classical science.[9] Now, I would argue that nonclassical epistemology defines the problem of Saussure's and post-Saussurean linguistics and its applications elsewhere (specifically in philosophy and literary theory), as the work of Derrida on writing, de Man on allegory, and other related investigations (such as Jacques Lacan's analysis of what he calls "the Real") tell us.

Such work also indicates how nonclassical epistemology might be done in linguistics, without, once again, undermining its disciplinary practice as a science. In other words, work like Derrida's, de Man's, or Lacan's suggests the necessary epistemology (analogous to Bohr's epistemology of quantum mechanics) and a workable set of generalized concepts (such as Derrida's "writing" and its satellites [*différance*, dissemination, trace, etc.; this list is, by definition, interminable] or de Man's "linguistic materiality"), in part intimated in Saussure's key concepts, such as those of difference, the sign, the arbitrariness of the sign, and so forth. This work, however, does not provide or even significantly contribute (at least so far) to the apparatus of disciplinary linguistics in the way Heisenberg's work has done in quantum mechanics. (Heisenberg discovered quantum theory and its nonclassical epistemology first in 1925 by no longer making quantum theory deal with the physical behavior of quantum objects but only with the effects of those objects upon measuring instruments involved.) Accordingly, it might be said that having had its Newton in Saussure, linguistics now needs its Heisenberg. Perhaps Saussure has already pointed the way to such a new, nonclassical science of language, although linguistics has so far only used the more classical part of his work. It could be shown how this argument is conditioned and motivated historically, in particular by extending it to both C. S. Peirce's theory of the sign and Louis Hjelmslev's linguistics, thus epistemologically bringing together two great Copenhagen schools of this century, Bohr's in quantum physics and Hjelmslev's in linguistics. Here, however, I must restrict myself to sketching my epistemological argument alone, which may well be ultimately more essential. I shall primarily elaborate the concepts of classical and nonclassical science and only indicate (it is difficult to do more within my limits here) how linguistic considerations and the question of language fit into the scheme. This analysis is bound to stop far short of what Bohr sometimes invokes (although never in print) as "the dream of great interconnections." Indeed it is not clear how far beyond "dreaming" one can pursue this dream, given the current state of the relationships between the two cultures or between different fields or, again, cultures within each. I would like, however, to stress with Bohr that "we are not dealing here with more or less vague analogies, but with an investigation of the conditions for the proper use of our conceptual means of expression. Such considerations not only aim at making us familiar with the novel situation in physical science, but might . . . be helpful in clarifying the conditions for description in wider fields."[10]

Classical sciences consider all of their objects as, at least in principle (it may not be possible in practice), available to conceptualization and often to direct representation in terms of or relating to particular properties of these objects, their behavior, and the relationships between them. Thus, classical mechanics, the part of classical physics that deals with the motion of individual physical objects or systems composed of such objects, is or at least may be interpreted as such a theory. It fully accounts, at least in principle, for its objects and their behavior on the basis of physical concepts and abstracted or idealized measurable quantities of material objects corresponding to them, such as the "position" and "momentum" of material bodies. The equations of classical mechanics allow us to know the past state and to predict the future state of the system under investigation at any point once we know it at a given point. Classical physics is thus by definition, realist and usually causal. As such, within its proper scope it offers both excellent *descriptions* of the natural objects it considers (or constructs) and excellent *predictions* of the outcome of experiments it performs upon natural objects. By contrast, quantum mechanics, at least in a nonclassical interpretation, allows only for *predictions* concerning the outcomes of experiments, but not for a *description* of its ultimate objects or their behavior; indeed, it rigorously disallows such a *description*, which is the most crucial point here. For nonclassical theories do *not describe* their ultimate objects but only *predict* and describe certain *effects* that such indescribable and ultimately inconceivable objects could produce and through which their existence could and must be inferred. Indeed, these effects themselves are described by means of classical theories that nonclassical theories employ, as they must for these purposes, even though classical theories cannot account either for the emergence of such effects individually or for the sum of these effects collectively.

In contrast to classical theories, the *ultimate* "objects" of nonclassical theories are irreducibly, in practice, and in principle (this defines the difference between classical and nonclassical thinking), inaccessible, unrepresentable, inconceivable, and so forth by any means that are or ever will be available to us, including as objects in any conceivable sense. Hence they cannot be assigned any conceivable attributes, such as those introduced by analogy with those of objects of classical theories. Thus, as I said, it is not possible to assign the standard attributes of the objects and motions of classical physics to those of quantum physics. Some of these complexities transpire already in Einstein's special relativity of 1905, which deals with the propagation of light in a vacuum. According to this theory, this speed (in a vacuum) is always constant—the famous *c*—regardless of the state of motion of the source, which cannot be accelerated so as to change the speed of the emitted light relative to it. It follows from the latter fact that in the case of light itself such classical properties as time dilation or space region cannot apply. Were it possible (it is not) to install a clock on a photon and associate a reference frame with it, according to relativity the time shown by this clock would stand still. By the same token, in the photon's own frame of reference it is simultaneously at all points through which it travels: clearly at variance with physical assumptions which we view as basic. Thus, in relativity and quantum theory alike, it may no longer even be possible to speak of objects or motions, or any physical properties describing their spatial-temporal behavior, nor at the nonclassical limit can the term "quantum" or "objects," or any conceivable term or concept apply. All these are classical physical attributes, defined as a refinement of everyday experience and language, which makes classical physics possible and which appears no longer applicable at the level of the ultimate constitution of matter. It is indeed not clear why it should be, as Nietzsche was perhaps first to realize. On the other hand, how else can we even conceive of such attributes, except by means of classical theories? For in this understanding, only classical theories or thinking, and only they, could allow us such an attribution. Thus, the ultimate objects of nonclassical theories are not their objects insofar as one means by the objects of a theory anything that can actually be described by the theory. The impact of such objects on what the theory can account for is crucial, however, and the efficacity of this impact cannot be described classically, which is what makes a nonclassical description necessary in such cases. I use the term "efficacity" in its dictionary sense of power and agency producing effects, but, in this case, without the possibility of ascribing to this agency causality, similarly to the way Derrida's *différance* or Foucault's "power" work.[11]

The key features of both the classical and, then, the nonclassical situation in physics can be generalized to classical and nonclassical theories elsewhere, for example, to linguistics as a *science* of language—where most, if not all, standard conceptions and practices have so far been classical—or to philosophy, where understanding of such concepts as thinking (or conception) may require a nonclassical regime, as Kant was perhaps first to anticipate to some degree. It may indeed be shown that especially within Saussure's scheme the question of thinking, and hence nonclassical thinking, is inevitable in linguistics. Classical physics may itself be seen as derived from classical theories elsewhere and as a refinement of everyday experience and language (no longer applicable to physical objects at the quantum level), a point often made by both Bohr and Heisenberg. Both also thought these classical aspects of everyday language and specifically the possibility of unambiguous definition and communication necessary in both classical and quantum physics, but sufficient only for classical physics. I would argue, however, that a rigorous analysis suggests that the practice—even the everyday practice of language (to which most disciplinary linguistics restricts itself) or of thought—cannot be contained classically and requires nonclassical theory.

Derrida's analysis of Saussure and others, such as Rousseau and Hegel, shows precisely this, in part—and this is crucial—by investigating (deconstructively) the critical or nonclassical resources of classical thought.[12] The epistemology of Derrida's conceptuality (specifically that related to the problematic of language or, inescapably for Derrida, writing) is nonclassical, as is most of Derrida's own philosophical practice—in contrast to, it appears, most disciplinary practices of linguistics. Once signification and language are essentially arbitrary (which is not the same as capricious or random),

Derrida's writing (whether written or spoken) or de Man's allegory is rigorously inevitable.[13] In other words, *the essential arbitrariness of the sign, defining Saussure's linguistics, entails an essential ambiguity as concerns any reference to the properties of the ultimate possible referent or origin of any given sign.* It follows of course that one cannot rigorously speak of an ultimate possible referent under these conditions. Rigorously speaking, the same machinery takes places already at the level of the signifier and the signified, and of their irreducible entanglement, which is what makes the arbitrariness of the sign inevitable.

Both Peirce and Hjelmslev (in glossematics), and already Saussure himself advance quite far toward this type of understanding and help, among others, Derrida and de Man to travel this path to its ultimate epistemological limits. A number of Derrida's early (more linguistically oriented) works and ideas, as well as those of Lacan, or earlier Nietzsche (speaking here only of those thinkers whose work is more closely linked to the question of language) could be brought up to support this argument. I would like, however, to invoke de Man's conception of allegory as given in his extraordinary essay on Pascal, which could be linked to the present discussion in many ways. De Man writes: "The difficulty of allegory is rather that this emphatic clarity of representation does not stand in the service of something that can be represented."[14] This clarity may be said to stand in the service of that which cannot be represented by any means, is intolerant of attribution of any properties or ontological predicates, and is ultimately beyond any conception or phenomenalization.

That "something" can enter and split the representational clarity at any point so as to give us no choice except to engage one irreducibly unrepresentable by means of another irreducibly unrepresentable, even if (it would not be possible otherwise) by means of some representations. In other words, within Saussure's or, with due qualifications, Nietzsche's, Lacan's, Derrida's and de Man's schemes of signification, we are sometimes and ultimately always dealing with the irreducible inconceivability of a *signifier, not* the *signified* (in Saussure, roughly, the conceptualization "mediating" the relationships between the signifier and the referent within signification). Its signified and its referent may sometimes be seen as even more "remote" and "inaccessible" or inconceivable. In any event one needs to think here in terms of the ultimately inaccessible nature (which is not to say identity in terms of their functioning) of all three—the signifier, the signified, and the referent. This is why the irreducible inaccessible or inconceivable is represented in terms of something that is it-self irreducibly inaccessible or inconceivable, if one still wants to think of the latter as an object in any way, and this is accordingly why, as I said, the nonclassical regimes of thought and philosophy are al-ways involved here as well. It would be more rigorous to think in terms of representative (phenomenal) effects or properties that are *associated* more directly (although still ultimately as effects) with such an object rather than to attribute them to this object as such. It fol-lows that one can further split this situation into a potentially infinite chain, similarly to and radicalizing both Peirce's and Hjelmslev's views of signification, both of which are, along with Saussure's semi-otics, among Lacan's, Derrida's, and de Man's sources.[15] Although I can only indicate this point here without considering it in detail, this splitting is at the core, even if also against the grain, of Saussure's conceptuality, beginning with the introduction of the concept of the sign and the possibility of its unambiguous definition, Saussure's manifest concern.[16] This is of course not to say that what is referred to by such negative terms does not exist, quite the contrary. While dif-ferent in other respects, Derrida's and de Man's conceptions of ma-teriality are related to and even defined in terms of this irreducible inaccessibility.

By the same token, this concept or "nonconcept" of the irre-ducibly inaccessible materiality allows one to maintain a rigorous analogy with quantum mechanics, and perhaps to do more than only this. For one might argue that in contrast to the linguistic process just sketched in quantum mechanics, we deal with certain ultimately material entities of physical nature. This is true. The question, how-ever, is the nature of this materiality, and I would argue that one might and indeed should apply this, as de Man in fact calls it, "lin-guistic understanding," to quantum mechanics, rather than merely use the latter as a model for linguistics. As I have indicated, quantum epistemology was in part developed by Heisenberg and Bohr through thinking about the nature of language and the way it can or cannot function in classical and quantum physics. This thinking also proceeded through certain trajectories in common with the work of Derrida and de Man, and one can mention, among others, Nietzsche, Freud, Heidegger, Wittgenstein, Lacan, and possibly Saussure.

In any event, this is what the materiality of the quantum objects, "elementary particles," is: the irreducibly inaccessible materiality of nonclassical epistemology, such as that found in Derrida and de Man. There are no elementary particles, "there is no *quantum world*"—as Bohr (reportedly) said, not coincidentally in considering the question of language in quantum physics and physics in general, or indeed beyond.[17] One must, to begin with, exercise caution in considering such reported statements. It would, however, be very difficult to conclude, on the basis of Bohr's works, that he denies the existence of something in nature to which the phrase "the quantum world" would refer. More rigorously, one could speak of the existence of something in nature on the basis of which (or, again, of certain effects of that "something" in our interactions with nature) "quantum objects" are, nonclassically, idealized in Bohr's interpretation of quantum mechanics, that is, idealized as that to which no such attributes as "quantum," "world," "nature," or any other attributes could be assigned. The statement may instead be read, especially given the context (the question of whether quantum mechanics actually represents the quantum world or whether our language could in principle do so), by putting the emphasis on *quantum*, without in any way indicating the nonexistence of the material efficacity of the effects in question, or, more accurately, efficaci*ties*. For, while each time irreducibly unknowable, such efficacities are always plural as their effects, and are each time reciprocal with these effects. Accordingly, Bohr's statement indicates the inapplicability of conventional "quantum" attributes to "quantum objects" as they are understood in Bohr's interpretation of quantum mechanics. Among such attributes are discontinuity (of radiation), indivisibility (of quanta themselves), and so forth, or any other physical attributes, even "objects," "constituents," and so forth, or indeed anything our language and thought are in principle capable of expressing, now or ever. Beyond this level (of Bohr's idealization), even this latter claim may, as I said, be inapplicable. There are only "clicks" in detectors or other traces (such as those on photographic plates or in cloud chambers) properly correlated by means of quantum theory. They are heard or seen—*written* in Derrida's sense—and leave their traces (including in Derrida's nonclassical sense) in our measuring instruments, but are produced by something material which no instruments can measure or observe except in terms of such clicks, and no thought can think and no language can approach, at least no thought or language available to us (could there be others?), now or ever. "We are suspended in language in such a way that we cannot say what is up and what is down," Bohr famously, if again reportedly, said.[18] But we must use this language (we have, again, no other) to relate to what it cannot even possibly describe, or, again, what thought cannot possibly think. But then, language itself, as a possible object of linguistics, may not only be no less beyond language (the language of "beyond" included) but may also require no less from linguistics than quantum objects require from quantum theory.

In Bohr's (nonclassical) interpretation, the possibility of quantum-mechanical predictions (there is, again, no description) is seen as enabled by the interactions between quantum objects and measuring instruments, which instruments themselves are described in terms of classical physics and classical epistemology. As a result, the role of technology becomes irreducible and constitutive—irreducibly constitutive—in quantum mechanics (and, by implication and giving the term "technology" its broader meaning, in nonclassical theories elsewhere), while it may be seen as merely auxiliary and ultimately dispensable in classical physics, but by the same token it makes any reference to quantum objects themselves essentially ambiguous. In other words, the irreducibly technological, at one end, and the irreducibly inconceivable, at another, are mutually defining. One could thus also define nonclassical theories through the irreducible role of technology in them and, conversely, classical theories by the auxiliary and ultimately dispensable functioning of technology there. This is why Derrida's writing, which is associated with *tekhnē* and through which all technology must be properly reconceptualized, is irreducibly nonclassical. This is also why Derrida's work may be more useful and even necessary to linguistics than most linguists are willing to think.

Obviously classical theories also involve things that are, at least at certain moments, unknowable and inconceivable to them, while nonclassical theories enable new knowledge, indeed often knowledge that would be impossible without the intervention of nonclassical theories. Nonclassical theories change the nature of the unknowable and of the relationships between the knowable and the unknowable. What we can know and conceive of is different in nonclassical theories. The *ultimate* knowledge concerning the objects of nonclassical theories becomes no longer possible, while their existence and impact upon what we can know is indispensable. *Ultimate* however, is, in turn, a crucial qualifier here and throughout this study, where it features prominently (and it is of course subject to the same *ultimate* inapplicability at the *ultimate* level of description). First of all, classical theories or ways of thinking in general are often extraordinarily effective and sometimes indispensable across a broad spectrum of theoretical thinking and other human endeavors, or indeed in everyday life. Secondly, indeed as a corollary of the definitions of the classical and the nonclassical given here, classical theories are equally indispensable in nonclassical theories, since they serve as a pathway, indeed the only pathway, to establishing the existence of and the connections to the unknowable. Or, more accurately, classical theories allow us to handle the classically manifest *effects* of the unknowable in question in nonclassical theories, which unknowable cannot be inferred or treated otherwise. How would we *know* about the unknowable were the latter not manifest in something that we can know? By the same token, however, some among such knowable effects, specifically certain configurations of such effects, cannot be properly explained by means of classical theories and require nonclassical theories. The latter are able to use them, while leaving the ultimate nature of the *efficacities* of these effects unknowable and inconceivable, even at the level of idealization, and indeed requiring this character of these efficacities in order to account for the effects in question. Naturally, the term *efficacity* or *effect* is as provisional as any term here deployed at the level of the nonclassical unknowable.

Although traceable elsewhere in the works mentioned here, the epistemology of knowable effects of the irreducibly unknowable efficacity/ies is especially indebted to the work of Georges Bataille, one of the most significant and influential nonclassical thinkers, and specifically to his concept of "unknowledge" [*nonsavoir*].[19] This concept, as (helped by it) Lacan's Real and Derrida's *différance*, extends and radicalizes Freud's concept of the unconscious. It is worth noting that, in Lacan's and Derrida's cases, this extension is also enabled by coupling Freud's psychoanalysis with Saussure's linguistics, including, specifically, their thinking of the dynamics in question in terms of effects. According to Bataille, "it would be impossible to speak of unknowledge [ultimately even as unknowledge] as such, while we can speak of its effects." Reciprocally, "it would not be possible to seriously speak of unknowledge independently of its effects," that is, the existence of unknowledge is a rigorous consequence of a particular architecture of certain manifest, classical configurations, effects, the efficacities of which cannot be explained classically. The situation is rigorously analogous to that of quantum mechanics (quantum epistemology having itself significantly influenced Bataille's work). Conversely the language of effects (naturally, the terms are in turn provisional) is found and is analogously used throughout Bohr's and Derrida's writings. Indeed the idiom of "effects" is analogously deployed by Saussure, specifically in describing the effects of language [*langue*] within speech [*parole*], as well as, it is worth noting, in Freud's contemporary writings (concerning the effects of the unconscious). Both these types of effects, Saussurean and Freudian, the effects of language and the effects of the unconscious, are brought together, via Bataille, in a more fully nonclassical way in Lacan and then in Derrida. In quantum mechanics, the existence of quantum objects, specifically as irreducibly unavailable to any theory, classical or quantum, is a rigorous consequence of certain peculiar characteristics of the experimental data, resulting from the effects of the interaction between quantum objects and measuring instruments upon the latter. The situation led Bohr directly to speak of "the necessity of a final renunciation of the classical ideal of causality and a radical revision of our attitude towards the problem of physical reality," and ultimately of a final renunciation of the ideal or even idea of reality at the level of the ultimate constitution of nature.[20]

Thus, any science of that type (Bataille refers to such sciences as "general economies," in contrast to restricted economies, which are more or less the same as classical theories in the present definition) would only describe, in a classical and specifically realist manner, certain configurations of effects. But it will not only not describe the efficacities of such effects but will rigorously suspend the possibility of so doing. On the other hand, in part by virtue of this rigorous suspension, it does account for the fact of the conditions of the possibility of such effects, which classical theories fail to do, even though, I stress, it cannot account for the actual dynamics—that is, the efficacities—of this emergence anymore than classical theories can. Accordingly, under certain circumstances the nonclassicality, far from making science as a rigorous theoretical endeavor impossible or even inhibiting its practice, becomes the condition of the possibility of this practice and its enabling resource, including as concerns unambiguous definition and communication. In other words, the essential ambiguity of reference at the ultimate level of description, that is, indescribability, is the condition of possibility of unambiguous definition and communication at the level of the disciplinary language of articulation and communication. That, naturally, includes those concerning all our ambiguities, even though and, again, because the latter are irreducibly at the ultimate level. Indeed, Bohr argued that in quantum mechanics the essential ambiguity involved in any reference to the ultimate objects of the theory "provides room for new physical laws, the coexistence of which might at first sight appear irreconcilable with the basic principles of science."[21] It also enables the discovery of such laws, which has been the fundamental task of physics since, at least, Galileo or perhaps Aristotle. Quantum mechanics is the science of effects not only without classical causes but also (but this is perhaps the same) without the possibility of now or ever theorizing the ultimate efficacities of such effects, the ultimate nature of processes through which they emerge. To cite Bohr's statement: "In quantum mechanics we are not dealing with an arbitrary renunciation of a more detailed analysis of atomic phenomena, but with a recognition that such an analysis is *in principle* excluded" (Bohr's emphasis).[22]

However, by thus realizing that such an analysis is, in principle, excluded beyond a certain point, quantum physics was and continues to be able to achieve extraordinary theoretical and practical results, including its application to our technologies, specifically the new technologies of writing, computers, and copying machines among them. It is fitting (and perhaps not altogether coincidental) that it is a nonclassical physical theory that ultimately grounds the phenomenon, that of writing, that is irreducibly nonclassical, by virtue of the essentially arbitrary and, as I have argued here, essentially ambiguous nature of all signification. The latter was discovered by Saussure, coincidentally or perhaps not altogether coincidentally, in the same year, 1900, when Max Planck discovered the quantum nature of light. I would argue that the discipline of linguistics has not, so far, capitalized on Saussure's discovery as much as physics managed to do much faster on Planck's. But then it did not happen overnight in physics either; indeed it is far from clear how far physics as yet has to go on this road. There is still time for linguistics to catch up with physics and philosophy, at least some philosophy, such as that invoked in this essay, or even get ahead to help physics, since physics, too, is a refinement of language, and the practice of reading and writing. Its materiality, what the Greeks called *physis*, in physics and philosophy, requires "linguistic understanding."

This remains a crucial project, for linguistics itself, other disciplines in the humanities and science (again, not inconceivably, physics and other sciences, for example and in particular modern biology and genetics), or culture at large, including our two cultures, or always, irreducibly more than two and perhaps less than one. As Derrida said in 1967, thus opening the problematic (found across the horizon of our culture, sciences included) leading him and, according to him indeed entailing his concept or "neither term nor concept" of writing, arguably to the most comprehensive conception of writing and perhaps of language itself:

> However the topic is considered, the *problem of language* has never been one problem among others. But never as much as at present has it invaded, *as such*, the global horizon of the most diverse researches and the most heterogeneous discourses, diverse and heterogeneous in their intentions, method, and ideology. . . . This inflation of the sign "language" is the inflation of the sign itself, absolute inflation, inflation itself. Yes, by one of its aspects or shadows, it is itself still a sign: this crisis is also a symptom. It indicates, as if in spite of itself, that a historico-metaphysical epoch *must* finally determine as language the totality of its problematic horizon. [Derrida's emphasis—translation slightly modified.][23]

This assessment is still true; this is still our historico-metaphysical epoch. In some respects this assessment is even more true now than in 1967, notwithstanding many significant transformations and developments that have reshaped our many horizons—intellectual, disciplinary (or interdisciplinary), cultural, and political, our geopolitical horizons (or sometimes lack thereof) included. Naturally, these transformations and developments include those, indeed especially those (Derrida's work among them) that have changed and continue to change our view of language. This assessment also remains true, all the more true, in spite of and because some of these transformations and developments might have shifted our main concerns to historical and political, and specifically geopolitical, dimensions of our many cultures, assuming that such dimensions could ever be dissociated from the *problem of language*. They cannot be, as this statement and Derrida's analysis indeed makes clear—even though and, again, because they reciprocally shape this problem and our language, the many languages of our many cultures (in either C. P. Snow's sense or in general). It is not possible within my limits here to address the considerable political aspects and implications of this statement, including for Derrida's own analysis, either in his subsequent writing, for example, in *Specters of Marx* (1993), or, contrary to common misconceptions, in his earlier writing, specifically *Of Grammatology* (1967).[24] My main point is that we may well need a new understanding of language, by now quite possibly beyond Derrida's "writing," and a new linguistics and transformations of other disciplines dealing with language, to address these politics and these cultures: always, irreducibly politics and cultures that are more than two and less than one. Linguistics' complex and perhaps essentially ambiguous position between the "two cultures," the humanities and the sciences, may well be determined by this broader cultural dynamic, heterogeneous and interactive—interactively heterogeneous and heterogeneously interactive—including as concerns the very interplay of the ambiguous and the unambiguous found in this dynamic and often defining it. To return to Bohr's statement, "we are suspended in language and do not know which way is up and which down," or perhaps always, and ultimately always essentially ambiguously, both at once. Perhaps, in the end, there is always an essential ambiguity of the relationships between the ambiguous and the unambiguous themselves, a kind of "uncertainty principle" between the ambiguous and the unambiguous, once our knowledge involves the irreducibly unknowable—and, it appears, that all our knowledge ultimately does. In closing his "Discussion with Einstein on Epistemological Problems in Atomic Physics," his arguably most comprehensive and refined exposition of his view, Bohr writes:

> We used, when in trouble, often to comfort ourselves with jokes, among them the old saying of the two kinds of truth. To the one kind belong statements so simple and clear that the opposite assertion obviously could not be defended. The other kind, the so-called "deep truths," are statements in which the opposite also contains deep truth. Now, the development in a new field will usually pass through stages in which chaos becomes gradually replaced by order; but it is not least in the intermediate stage where deep truth prevails that the work is really exciting and inspires the imagination to search for a firmer hold.[25]

It is at that stage that we are, perhaps especially but not exclusively by our engagement with quantum mechanics, "so forcefully reminded" of and indeed where we enact "the old truth"—a deep truth?—"that we are both actors and spectators in the great drama of existence" (translation slightly modified).[26]

In the twentieth and by now the twenty-first century we have moved into extraordinarily complex territories of both knowledge and the unknowable in mathematics and science. A similar progression (one may even speak of progress here, if only against some recent critics) can be traced in the humanities, and in the interactions among these fields or between them and mathematics and science, and hence in the relationship between the two cultures. The confrontation between them apparently refuses to go away, or continues to return (or, as Nietzsche would have it, eternally returns), even though and perhaps also because there are more than two cultures involved in these interactions and confrontations, more than two and less than one. The "two cultures" still appear to one another as ghostly strangers and confront each other in the way Levinas and Blanchot describe the nature of ethical relationships. In Blanchot's words: "The Stranger comes from elsewhere and is always somewhere other than we are, not belonging to our horizon and not inscribing himself upon any representable horizon whatsoever, so that his 'place' would be invisible."[27] It is not so easy for the two cultures, or for all of us, to hear in this expression what Blanchot wants us to hear, since he would only accept this description provided that at stake here is that invisible "which turns away from everything visible and everything invisible," that unknown that turns away from everything knowable and everything unknowable.[28] To hear this we may indeed need a very different sense and usage of language. Instead, we tend to prefer more convenient and more comfortable forms of blindness, often under an illusion of sight, or even of insight, especially when we approach the strangeness of, and strangers from, other fields, or strangers from far afield. It is not that we can ever completely avoid blindness or illusion here, or elsewhere. The significance of Blanchot's insight could not be more profoundly misunderstood. The question is which illusions we offer to others, both to our fellow countrymen, or to our fellow culture-men, and to strangers from other countries and cultures. Perhaps, the ultimate ethics or (since the ultimate ethics may not be possible, classically, in practice—and be possible, nonclassically, in principle) at least a good ethics of intellectual inquiry or of cultural interaction is the following. Being strangers ourselves, to offer other strangers, strangers in our own or in other cultures, those ideas that bring our own culture—say, science, on one side, and the humanities, on the other—to the limits of both what is known and unknown, or unknowable, to them. Naturally, we can never be fully certain how our offerings will be received, not even within our own culture, since we are often strangers there, too. Nor can we be fully certain as to what we know and what we do not know. On that score, the nonclassical unknowable, the irreducibly, essentially unknowable in the heart of our best knowledge leaves us only an essential ambiguity. By doing so, however, it also gives us a chance for the ambiguity of a deep truth and a stage (in either sense) when "the work is really exciting and inspires the imagination to search for a firmer hold."

NOTES

1. The term *complementarity* itself owes much to Bohr's view that certain types of phenomena (such as, most famously, the wave-like and the particle-like) involved in quantum mechanics are always mutually exclusive and thus can never apply simultaneously, even though they are both necessary for an overall comprehensive quantum-theoretical description. This statement is indeed his actual definition of complementary features of the quantum-mechanical description. This aspect of Bohr's argument will be somewhat less important than the more general epistemology to which it eventually led Bohr. The term *complementarity* itself came to designate this overall epistemology of quantum physics in Bohr's writings. For an extended discussion of Bohr's overall argument, including in the context of nonclassical theory and the "two cultures," I permit myself to refer the reader to my recent study *The Knowable and the Unknowable: Modern Science, Nonclassical Thought, and the "Two Cultures"* (Ann Arbor: University of Michigan Press, 2002) and further references there.

2. Niels Bohr, "Can Quantum-Mechanical Description of Physical Reality be Considered Complete?" in *Quantum Theory and Measurement*, ed. John A. Wheeler and Wojciech H. Zurek (Princeton: Princeton University Press, 1983), 146 .

3. Niels Bohr, *The Philosophical Writings of Niels Bohr*, 3 vols. (Woodbridge, Conn.: Ox Bow Press, 1988), 2:39–50.

4. Ibid., 2:40.

5. On this point I am indebted to Carlo Rovelli's article, " 'Incerto Tempore, Incertisque Loci': Can We Compute the Exact Time at Which a Quantum Measurement Happens?", *Foundations of Physics* 28, no. 7 (1998): 1031–43.

6. I shall comment on De Man's concept of allegory below. It is difficult to speak of "metaphor" in situations, such as this, where there is strictly speaking no second object of comparison to which a metaphor would refer.

7. This generalization allows me to bypass or mention only in passing the well-known features and complexities of quantum physics, such as wave-like and particle-like phenomena, indeterminism, nonrealism, and so forth, on which again I refer

the reader to my extended discussion in *The Knowable and the Unknowable* and further literature cited there.

8. The mutually exclusive character of complementary arrangements, such as those dealing with, respectively, position or momentum measurements, or with wave-like and particle-like observational effects, allow Bohr to achieve precisely this type of unambiguous reference and a possibility of unambiguous communication.

9. This type of case has been argued by Jean-François Lyotard in *The Postmodern Condition: A Report on Knowledge*, trans. Geoff Bennington and Brian Massumi (Minneapolis: University of Minnesota Press, 1984).

10. Bohr, *The Philosophical Writings of Niels Bohr*, 2:1–2.

11. I refer to Derrida's well-known earlier works, most specifically "Différance" in *Margins of Philosophy*, trans. Alan Bass (Chicago: University of Chicago Press, 1982), 1–27, and Michel Foucault, *The History of Sexuality: An Introduction, Vol. 1*, trans. Robert Hurley (New York: Vintage, 1990).

12. See especially Derrida's analysis in *Of Grammatology*, trans. Gayatri Chakravorty Spivak (Baltimore: Johns Hopkins University Press, 1974), and also his "The Pit and the Pyramid: Introduction to Hegel's Semiology," and "The Linguistic Circle of Geneva," in *Margins of Philosophy*, 69–108 and 137–53.

13. On these questions, see especially Derrida's discussion in "Linguistics and Grammatology," in *Of Grammatology* (27–73), and other essays cited above.

14. Paul de Man, *Aesthetic Ideology* (Minneapolis: University of Minnesota Press, 1996), 51. I have discussed de Man's work in this context in detail in "Algebra and Allegory: Nonclassical Epistemology, Quantum Theory, and the Work of Paul de Man," in *Material Events: Paul de Man and the Afterlife of Theory*, ed. Barbara Cohen, et al. (Minneapolis: University of Minnesota Press, 2000), 49–92.

15. See Derrida, "Linguistics and Grammatology," 48–50, 57–58.

16. Ferdinand de Saussure, *Course in General Linguistics*, trans. Wade Baskin (New York: McGraw-Hill, 1966), 67 ff.

17. The statement is reported in Aage Petersen, "The Philosophy of Niels Bohr," in *Niels Bohr: A Centenary Volume*, ed. A. P. French and P. J. Kennedy (Cambridge: Harvard University Press, 1985), 305; emphasis added.

18. Cited in Aage Petersen, *Quantum Physics and the Philosophical Tradition* (Cambridge: MIT Press, 1968), 188.

19. See Jacques Derrida, "From Restricted to General Economy: A Hegelianism Without Reserve," *Writing and Difference*, trans. Alan Bass (London: Routledge, 1978), 263, 269.

20. Bohr, "Can Quantum-Mechanical Description of Physical Reality be Considered Complete?", 146.

21. Ibid., 148.

22. Bohr, *The Philosophical Writings of Niels Bohr*, 2:62.

23. Derrida, *Of Grammatology*, 6.

24. Jacques Derrida, *Specters of Marx: The State of Debt, the Work of Mourning, and the New International*, trans. Peggy Kamuf (New York: Routledge, 1993).

25. Bohr, *The Philosophical Writings of Niels Bohr*, 2:66. It should be noted that Bohr's primary reference here is to complementarity, that is, in his terms, a mutual exclusivity of certain statements of truth concerning quantum-mechanical experi-

ments (such as those linked to uncertainty relations or wave-like vs. particle-like phenomena), rather than the essential ambiguity of reference to quantum objects—although, as I have argued here, these two issues are deeply related. For a further discussion, see my *The Knowable and the Unknowable.*

26. Bohr, *The Philosophical Writings of Niels Bohr,* 1:191 and also 2:263.

27. Maurice Blanchot, *The Infinite Conversation,* trans. Susan Hanson (Minneapolis: University of Minnesota Press, 1993), 52.

28. Ibid., 52.

Extroduction
The Irresistibility of the Posthuman:
Questioning "New Cultural Theory"

Ivan Callus and
Stefan Herbrechter

THE FOREGOING ESSAYS SUGGEST THAT AFTER THE REVISITING OF roads not taken by theory or retaken with a difference, there remains to consider the (ir)resistibility of post-theory. That which succeeds theory must, by definition, be irresistible. Yet the aura of inevitability collecting around that irresistibility might not be sufficient to prevent what succeeds upon theory from being, in fact, resistible. It is at least thinkable that the appeal of post-theory, if this ever were to materialize in the most straightforward of ways—in a form superseding theory—might after all not be very beguiling, both to theorists themselves but also to anti-theorists who, on the face of it, would not be expected to mourn the passing of theory. To explore this paradox further we have chosen to speak of one form of post-theory the momentum of which appears to be irresistible, and yet one whose rationale has been viewed with some consternation by both theorists and anti-theorists. We have chosen to speak of the posthuman, and shall be presenting its (ir)resistibility as exemplary not only of the (ir)resistibility of post-theory, but also as a warning that the readiness of theory to find reasons for not thinking its own passing is to be guarded against. The reasons why theory should bring to consciousness what it represses, together with the implications for its disciplinary status and practice once it does, are what will concern us.

Thesis

It is always tempting to think post-theory in terms of *anti*-theory, which Frank Kermode once famously characterized as "a genre in its own right."[1] It was within that genre that George Steiner once digressed from an attack on deconstruction to lament that "at the heart of futurity lies the byte and the number."[2] The remark captures the tone of commentaries fearful that the encroachment of digitalism, together with the appeal of the natural and applied sciences, will abet the contraction of the humanities' constituency. Steiner writes that "modern biology, genetics, physics, chemistry, modern engineering and cosmological conjectures can no longer be put forward or debated in non-mathematical language." He bemoans the fact that they are "accessible not to the literate, but only to the numerate."[3] This is at the root of widespread apprehension that the *lettered* disciplines are about to face a crisis. To quote Steiner again, there is at work a "numerization" that is leading to "the new clerisy, a clerisy of the young and the very young who are, flexibly, pre- or counter-literate."[4]

Steiner's words are expressive of what has been termed the posthuman, or at least one form of it: the simplifying view that an age is at an end, that another is about to start, that catalyzing change is digital technology, and that technoscience will proceed to alter the present and the very nature of the human more radically and more completely than anything previously experienced in history, culture, or epistemology. Underpinning such scenarios is the apparent indisputability of the assumption critiqued by Martin Heidegger: "Technology is the fate of our age, where "fate" means the inevitableness of an unalterable course."[5] In the context of general acceptance of that fate, the Lyotardian effort to combat the glibness with which "the [prefix] 'post-' indicates something like a conversion: a new direction from the previous one," has its work cut out. Lyotard's mistrust of the notion that "it is both possible and necessary to break with tradition and institute absolutely new ways of living and thinking"[6] is ignored by the kind of approach to the posthuman which takes as a truism the statement in Robert Pepperell's *The Post-Human Manifesto* (1995) that "all technological progress of Human society is geared towards the redundancy of the Human species as we currently know it."[7] This is plainly not the kind of attitude to the "post-" that theory would endorse. To a theorist, Pepperell's statement is unbelievably jejune: almost as unbelievable as his statement that "Post-Humans never get bogged down in arguments about language. The scholars and humanists will always try to restrict debate to the battleground of language because they know no one can win."[8]

Pepperell's brand of posthumanism embodies an unattunedness to theory that is likely to find all of the following positions very resistible: the concern with the tropological dimension of language, seen by Paul de Man as precipitating "the indeterminate residue" that finds its most mysterious instantiation within literariness; the Derridean idea that literary language is unable "to be abiding" [*être à demeure*]; the Heideggerian conviction that "language is the house of Being. In its home man dwells. Those who think and those who create with words are the guardians of this home."[9] Pepperell's posthumanism would scoff at such positions, which are founded in what our introduction viewed as theory's capacity for "letter-al mindedness." Indeed most posthumanist positions, while recognising that "philosophy is hounded by the fear that it loses prestige and validity if it is not a science," would not set about exorcising that fear with the "effort to return thinking to its element": an element that for Heidegger is approachable only in the conviction that "Language still denies us its essence: that it is the house of the truth of Being."[10] Consequently it will not want to follow through the Heideggerian exploration of the question "*Comment redonner un sens au mot 'Humanisme?'*": an exploration that ends up with the conclusion that "what is needed in the present world is less philosophy, but more attentiveness in thinking; less literature, but more cultivation of the letter."[11] Posthumanism, because it is a numerized thought, is not minded to the letter-al. Posthumanism is in fact this also, and perhaps above all: the utter unattunedness to a thinking of the difference between literature and the letter. It is an unattunedness that comes about once language "falls into the service of expediting communication along routes where objectification—the uniform accessibility of everything to everyone—branches out and disregards all limits,"[12] a fall which as will be seen below privileges what can be "operationalized."

To an intellectual temper given to operationalization, language must be allowed to be transparent—which is not far from saying that it should be resistible as an object of investigation in its own right. As intimated by Plotnitsky in his essay in this volume, a *science* of language—a linguistics—is comprehensible to that temper; anything other is however inapprehensible. This is why the thought that finds within language an unaccountable alterity palls upon that which operationalizes—suggesting that if de Man is right to say that the resistance to theory is the resistance to language about language, then theory (particularly a *literary* theory) might well be posthumanism's antithesis. Whereupon it is timely to recall what Lyotard says in "A Gloss on Resistance," namely that the "desire for [language] to be able to say something other than what it already knows how to say" is what allays a Newspeak, because "literary writing, artistic writing . . . cannot cooperate with a project of domination or total transparency, even involuntarily."[13]

Of course, posthumanism does not lead ineluctably to Orwellian nightmares, and the time of the lettered may not be utterly "over," as some accounts would have us believe. Yet it is as well to recall Jean Baudrillard's view that "today language is confronted by the hegemonic fantasy of a global and perpetual communication—the New Order, the new cyberspace of language—where the ultrasimplification of digital languages prevails over the figural complexity of natural languages."[14] Theory, committed to "figural complexity," then finds itself ranged against an "ultrasimplification" that is anathema to it. Meanwhile, as the unsuitedness of theoretical discourse to a "project" of "transparency" and "ultrasimplification" deepens, positions like Pepperell's acquire the topicality of a not implausible futurology because there is abroad, to borrow a phrase from Kermode again, "a sense of an ending." It is a sense that Pepperell-like "manifestoese" plausibly positions in terms of a receptivity to a posthumanism that might come to exceed not only humanism but the human itself—as anybody familiar with the pronouncements of the Extropian Society on "transhumanism" will know.[15] It could indeed be argued that the posthuman, in its most fundamental form, is nothing if not this experience of the palpability of terminality.

Theory has typically responded to that palpability by questioning the nature of the apocaplyptic and problematizing it. It does so in line with the Heideggerian insistence on not thinking the finite (or the technological, as that which could precipitate the finiteness of the human) straightforwardly. All of de Man's, Lyotard's, and Derrida's resistance to the idea of post-theory being conceived of according to a logic of successiveness builds on this suspicion of supersedence.

One consequence of all the palaver (theoretical and not) about post-history, post-industrialism, (post-)post-modernity, post-art, post-capitalism, post-philosophy, (post-)post-structuralism, post-gender, post-race—indeed post-everything, including notions of super-sedence itself—is that theoretical inquiry needs to assay a trenchant diagnosis for our times. Rather than referring to theory's well-known but perhaps tired attempts at this, we would like to work from the intuition of Robert Musil, author of *The Man Without Qualities* (1930–42), that "since 1914, humanity has revealed itself as a mass that is astonishingly more malleable than we had been accustomed to assume."[16] Less than a century later, radically deconstituting change in the astonishingly malleable human has become eminently thinkable, as shown by the fact that researchers in Artificial Intelligence, Artificial Life and the sciences of cognition are becoming almost blasé about scenarios like those conceived by Hans Moravec in *Mind Children: The Future of Robot and Human Intelligence* (1988), when he declared that "it will soon be possible to download human consciousness into a computer."[17] As N. Katherine Hayles reports in her book *How We Became Posthuman*, Moravec

> invents a fantasy scenario in which a robot surgeon purees the human brain in a kind of cranial liposuction, . . . transferring the information into a computer. At the end of the operation, the cranial cavity is empty, and the patient, now inhabiting the metallic body of the computer, wakens to find his consciousness exactly the same as it was before.[18]

Hayles admits to consternation at this idea. She records, however, that she was "shocked into awareness" that Moravec was "far from alone" in his suppositions,[19] and proceeds to install Moravec within a genealogy of the posthuman. She traces "the unfolding story of how a historically specific construction called *the human is giving way to a different construction called the posthuman*" (Hayles's emphasis).[20]

Talk of supersedence has already been identified above as intrinsic to posthumanism, whose acquisition of a genealogy (through Hayles's and others' pioneering work) is the inevitable first step to the acquisition of disciplinarity. That such talk is not shunned in *How We Became Posthuman* (the very title makes this obvious) confirms that even as theoretically aware a posthumanist as Hayles finds it difficult to accommodate the problematization of straightforward successiveness that is a fixture of poststructuralist and postmodernist thought. This may or may not be indicative of an impending and wider repositioning of the orthodoxies of theory as it comes to terms with a rivaling coming to disciplinarity. Leverage—to return to the Archimedean scene of our introduction and all that is inaugurated in Derrida's essay "Mochlos"[21]—would thereby be exerted upon theory, which may need to shift in a displacement that, though it is unlikely to precede outright replacement, cannot help accommodating what supervenes.

The accommodating will in that case proceed from theory, since what supervenes always has one disposition above all: that of inducing the accommodating disposition of what it supervenes upon. In this respect, it is symptomatic that Hayles (who is scarcely unfamiliar with theory's positions) does not raise the issue of the differences between the posthumanist apprehension of time and the time of theory. Posthumanists tend not to modulate the idea of one paradigm displacing another with Lyotardian conceptualization of the event, Derridean reflections on the *arrivant*, or Heideggerian questionings of time and technology, and they are unlikely to go along with Nicholas Royle's pronouncement that "If post-theory has a time, it would be the time of this phrase [*déjà vu*]."[22] The understanding of temporality according to the "paradox of the future anterior" and the operations of *Nachträglichkeit* is an understanding incongruous with posthumanist perceptions. Instead, in an age when physicists like Stephen Hawking have shown us how time is multidimensional, the posthuman keeps its timescapes very strategically linear and irreversible. Within that form of resistance to theory, if post-theory has a time at all it is the time that linearly renders theory *passé* and very resistible to the irresistibility of the posthuman.

The teleology implied by that linearity will not disturb the clerisy Steiner spoke of, which will be unfazed by the thought that not only futurity, but the human itself, might become "byte and number." Meanwhile, the evidence on whether theory is at all disturbed is ambivalent. Occasionally, as will be seen below, theory appears to engage with the posthuman by taking on prostheses to what it was doing already, accepting adjuncts to its repertoire rather than substantively engaging with scenarios like those imagined by Moravec and with the implications they carry for the (re)conceptualization of "theoremes" like subjectivity, cognition, the unconscious, language, and death. Whether this amounts to maturation or capitulation is a moot point. The one thing that is certain, as the title of Hayles's book—*How We Became Posthuman*—suggests, is that the posthuman is not mere potentiality. It is, rather, the "structure of feeling" of a supposedly futuristic time that is already experienced in the present.

It has become a platitude to say that this "already present" futurity acquires tangibility through the encounter with technology. There is now a generalized experience of technology's ongoing prosthesization of the human. It therefore seems intuitive that technology carries the human to a beyond of the human, as Hayles makes clear in her foundational formulation of the posthuman:

> First, the posthuman view privileges informational pattern over material instantiation, so that embodiment in a biological substrate is seen as an accident of history rather than an inevitability of life. Second, the posthuman view considers consciousness . . . as an evolutionary upstart trying to claim that it is the whole show when in actuality it is only a minor sideshow. Third, the posthuman view thinks of the body as the original prosthesis we all learn to manipulate, so that extending or replacing the body with other prostheses becomes a continuation of a process that began before we were born. Fourth, and most important, by these and other means, the posthuman view configures human being so that it can be seamlessly articulated with intelligent machines. In the posthuman, there are no essential differences or absolute demarcations between bodily existence and computer simulation, cybernetic mechanism and biological organism, robot teleology and human goals.[23]

This is a more restrained expression of the idea behind the Moravec thought experiment, but the implications are just as momentous. Hayles's portrayal raises at every point questions that could hardly be more intrinsically amenable to theoretical investigation. After all, within its various denominations theory has assiduously thought through questions relating to being and alterity, prosthesization and supplementarity, bodies and consciousnesses. Yet the posthuman as it plays itself out at present in its manifestoes rarely modulates itself with awareness of that amenability. In illustration, consider the answer that posthumanists might give to the question "Who Comes After the Subject?"[24] Short and simple, it has the rare distinction of travestying both Pontius Pilate and Friedrich Nietzsche: "Ecce Robot."

Not surprisingly, this "soundbite" approach to posthuman issues has the advantage of making good copy. Indeed, the posthuman thrives on and speaks to the popular imagination. That "popular" touch contrasts with theory's resistance to contemplating its own demise straightforwardly, with the ability of theory to lend cogency to the counterintuitive and to thinking "otherwise," with the insistence that the "*post-*" be approached according to the paradox of the future anterior, and with critiques of the "depthless" cultural logic of late capitalism (a logic that cradles the posthuman). Theory might be able to "think very hard": to common experience and good copy, though, it does not do so apprehensibly. Its irresistibility is a construction of its own making, born from its rhetoric about itself. What is popular will find such rhetoric resistible by finding it easy to pass over.

Theory might respond that its counterintuitive temporalities are never as necessary as when they appear to be out of phase; consequently, this being "out of phase" of theory, which can be dangerously close to a "phasing out," could defeat anachronism if theory were to bring to bear a sense of its own timeliness upon drifts that would render it *passé*. That comforting notion is however unsettled by the feeling that there exists a fundamental incommensurability between the posthuman and theory. To resolve this by seeking to explain the irreconcilability in terms of a differend, of rival discourses which cannot be referred to an authority that might be *super partes*,[25] would be to retreat into the refuges provided by theory's "otherwise." Indeed, there arises the intuition that the posthuman might disarm philosophical and theoretical discourse, even dispense with it. This is because the posthuman renders philosophical and theoretical readings of its characteristics formally *indecorous*, in the sense that this word was used within neoclassical literary theory. In other words, the posthuman suspends the theoretical or the philosophical. They are superfluous to it.

That is a large claim to be making. But it is hardly new, and indeed merely restates Steiner's view. Any time spent resisting the claim is better devoted to studying the implications of a choice like that of Manuel Castells, whose comments on the impact on the self in "the networked society" very noticeably downplay any kind of reference to the very diverse explorations of subjectivity within theory or philosophy.[26] In this respect the following remark by Castells is typical: "I certainly consider Lyotard a most insightful philosopher, and a brilliant intellectual. But I do not know what to do with his theory, and I am not sure that I fully understand it." Baudrillard, on the other hand, "is different," because "he is not truly a sociologist, he is indeed a philosopher, but he is a useful, and usable philosopher, for social scientists."[27] This, it is important to note, is *not* extraordinary. It captures, precisely, the temper of the posthuman. It is not extraordinary at all for the age of the matrix to put a premium on "usability." The posthuman investment in what is instrumental can have little time for the almost pathological self-awareness of much theoretical and philosophical discourse. This can be linked to the fact that the "possibility of a Perfect Crime against language, an aphanisis of the symbolic function," can be imputed to the "ultrasimplification of digital languages" that goes on within the posthuman.[28] Rather than retaining any significant reverence for "ancestral" discourses, such an age is likely to see greater sense in the scenario conceived by Jean-Luc Nancy, namely that "nowadays, [*philosophy*] would rather mean: different ways of thinking about philosophy itself . . . and even ways of understanding that the thing it names is gone, or finished."[29] It could hardly be different when, "by shifting to a virtual world, we go beyond alienation, into a state of radical deprivation of the Other," where "everything that exists only as idea, dream, fantasy, utopia will be eradicated, because it will immediately be realized, *operationalized*" (emphasis added).[30]

The idea that philosophy or theory, in either their ideality or their institutional form, can be "finished" because of an all-encroaching movement of operationalization may appear risible to anyone faintly familiar with the trials each has weathered. In any case, their own discourse provides the security of aloof retreat from the prospect of their apocalypse. The post-theoretical, the (ir)resistible arguments of theory might run, can never happen. The posthuman is characterizable as a form of messianism, too unaware of philosophy's and theory's more complex thinking of the questions it raises to deserve more than the disdain for that which does not think very hard. The posthuman is badly conceived, philosophically raw, and theoretically unelaborated. Yet while theory mounts that defense, ear will be lent outside its seminar rooms to contrasting perceptions—like the view that the humanities are merely "ancestor disciplines," and that their insistence on pronouncing themselves interdisciplinarily risks "cluttering the research agenda" of something like cognitive science.[31]

Robert Musil, whose literary inspiration was often embedded in the scientific, foresaw long ago that something like this might be on the cards. He wrote that "solutions to perennial metaphysical problems are now being hinted at from the firm ground of the exact sciences."[32] If Ulrich, in the second chapter of *The Man Without Qualities*, is to be found emblematically measuring traffic with a stopwatch in hand,[33] it is almost in advance illustration of the fact that Heidegger's intuition in "The End of Philosophy and the Task of Thinking" would be fundamentally sound. "The development of the sciences," Heidegger says in that essay, "is at the same time their separation from philosophy and the establishment of their independence. This process belongs to the completion of philosophy," a completion that has philosophy turning into "the empirical science of man," so that "no prophecy is necessary to recognize that the sciences . . . will soon be determined and regulated by the new fundamental science that is called cybernetics"—the very cybernetics that finds a potent symbol in the traffic measured by "the man without qualities," Ulrich.[34] As, for Heidegger, "philosophy is metaphysics,"[35] and as "every humanism remains metaphysical,"[36] any posthumanism must be deeply involved with the overcoming of the metaphysical, and the passing of the philosophical. Indeed, for Heidegger "the development of the sciences" is not "the mere dissolution of philosophy," but "in truth precisely its completion," a move toward "the end of philosophy" as "that place in which the whole of philosophy's history is gathered in its utmost possibility."[37] In the present context, the most important questions that Heidegger asks are then those which structure "The End of Philosophy and the Task of Thinking." "To what extent has philosophy in the present age entered into its end?" "What task is reserved for thinking at the end of philosophy?"[38]

The posthuman will find Heidegger's response to the questions he himself poses eminently resistible, for a paradigm that perceives technology as it does will neither give much consideration to the view that "the question concerning technology is the question concerning the constellation in which revealing and concealing, in which the essential unfolding of truth propriates,"[39] nor find any affinity with the insistence on the somewhat arcane faith in *Lichtung* and *aletheia* that marks the conclusion of "The End of Philosophy and the Task of Thinking."[40] Instead, the "task of thinking" will for the posthumanist paradigm inhere in calculative thinking and "the intoxicating quality of cybernetics."[41] It is a thinking that will necessarily marginalize the theoretical, the discourse whose language is "the language of self-resistance." Perhaps this is why theory repositions itself to disciplinarily take in the posthuman (as demonstrated below). Even so, it is unlikely thus to delegate to itself the kind of task of thinking envisaged by Heidegger: a task attuned to "the primally granted revealing that could bring the saving power into its first shining-forth in the midst of the danger that in the technological age rather conceals than shows itself."[42]

Plainly, that task is not proceeding within the institution. For the posthuman it is utterly uncompelling, and theory has embraced it fitfully if at all. The thinking of the technological and its relation with *poesis*, "that revealing which holds complete sway in all the fine arts, in poetry,"[43] is only marginally a concern for the disciplinarity of theory. At most it becomes, as in R. L. Rutsky's *High Technē* (1999) and indeed in this very essay, an obligatory point of reference for discussions of the posthuman, something to argue (away) from.[44] So since the task envisaged by Heidegger is not undertaken *as such* within the institution and if at all only very skimmingly within theory, what *is* happening at the disciplinary interface between theory and the posthuman? How is the former taking on the latter, prosthetically, in order to prolong for itself ("a better quality of") life within the university? How, then, is theory coming to terms with the fact that it no longer "just is," and that its appointment to critical practice—whether this devolves upon literature, politics, or itself—becomes underwritten, like much else, by pedagogically sound and "practical" (and therefore very un-Heideggerian) answers to the question concerning technology?

PROSTHESIS

Answers to these questions are more possible if it is recognized that Hayles's *How We Became Posthuman* is just one of several studies abetting the coming to disciplinarity of the posthuman. It is a coming announced by the pedagogic timeliness of a collection like Neil Badmington's *Posthumanism* (2000). Though it may be premature to talk of a new paradigm or episteme, the legitimation within the university of the study of "the posthuman condition" suggests that this coming is irreversible. Posthumanism or "new cultural theory" as it has also been called, can no longer be ignored.

New cultural theory is a label that acquired prominence after it was employed in the subtitle of a special issue of the journal *Angelaki*. The issue, edited by John Armitage, was called *Machinic Modulations:*

New Cultural Theory and Technopolitics. For theory, the last term in the label seems to suggest a reassuring continuity, but everything else brings to the fore the question of repositioning. The question arises in the wake of the realization that, in the collection, theory does far more self-modulating than modulating. This is because theory is there seen reconciling itself to "seismisms" and accepting the importance of possibly having to be "new," rather than "post."[45] It quietly acknowledges the factualness of rupture, rather than the option of a Lyotardian perlaboration of the logic behind that rupture's recognition; it is disposed to be *cultural,* rather than literary (after de Man), or critique-al (after Zavarzadeh and Morton);[46] it devolves some of the singularity of its appointedness to practice upon a *techno*politics. Therefore the question concerning theory's (re)positioning is rhetorical, because it knows in advance that any answer will probably acknowledge that which imposes itself in the place of a repositioned theory: "Are cultural and postmodern cultural theories yielding to new "hypermodern" and "recombinant" cultural theories of technology?"[47] If the answer is indeed "yes," then something has shifted, making way for a post-theory that, grown pragmatic, takes on aspects that neither a post-theory possibly "after" de Man nor one possibly "after" Zavarzadeh and Morton would have countenanced.[48]

To put it another way: it might seem that a "new cultural theory"—predicated on work like that by George Landow on hypertextuality and digital texts, by Sadie Plant on the genderedness of the digital, by Paul Virilio on dromology, by Arthur and Marilouise Kroker on digital delirium, by Donna Haraway or Chris Hables Gray on cyborgs, by Scott Bukatman on virtual subjectivity—amounts to an abdication of theory as it might have literarily or radically been.[49] Indeed, "new cultural theory" seems to extend theory's disciplinarity and extend it to the posthuman. Theory thereby behaves like one of those discourses identified by Zavarzadeh and Morton that co-opt what might have been adversarial (as seen in the introduction, above). This scarcely suggests radical practice, and may indeed be ranged against it. That is because "technopolitics" may be nothing more than a politics of theory that is, strategically, immersed in a digitalism very different to that envisaged by Zavarzadeh and Morton:

> "Digitalism," in our analysis . . . is not used as the "cause" of changes (it is not a new "mode of information" that displaces "the mode of production") in contemporary capitalism and the labor force. It is

deployed here, rather, as a mediating concept that points to the shift in the superstructural discourses and practices that, in response to material changes, are involved in constructing (post)modern subjectivities and the "consciousness skills" needed for the rising labor force of late capitalism."[50]

Zavarzadeh and Morton's is cultural theory which is not "new," even if it takes the term *digitalism* and redefines it in order not to allow it to be too uncritically given over to its more generally accepted (and ironically "older") meaning. Theory has always played this game of relexicalization, for instance with the words *writing, post(-), resistance,* and *theory* itself. It is a game which exemplifies how important it is for theory to work through counterintuitiveness and against the popular understanding of a term, even if it cannot realistically hope to displace what is otherwise understood generally by that term. But now that a new *digital writing* has come to be—a writing (into being) of the digital—there occurs a redimensionalization of the *resistance* of theory to thinking its own *post* as otherwise as it always has. In the midst of the posthuman, theory therefore has to face up to the possibility of its own passability, and to be ready to think the "*post-*" in terms of the most literal meaning of this fateful word. It will find that difficult, as it is a procedure that moves against all of its instincts concerning the past and the "*post-*," the present and the unpresentable, the intuitive and the counterintuitive: instincts that risk making theory mannered. What is needed, then, is a less "instinctual" engagement with the posthuman on the part of theory.

It is in this context that we should like to pay *Machinic Modulations* the compliment of saying not only that it is "required reading" for anybody interested in the posthuman, but that it avoids any "mannered" theorese. *Machinic Modulations* suggests that the posthuman can distance itself from the kind of approach exemplified by Pepperell's writing. To emphasize this, we should like to draw attention to Armitage's introduction to the special number of *Angelaki*: an introduction that is a solid and reliable guide to "the rising interest in the theoretical humanities and the social sciences in new cultural and theoretical debates over technology and politics."[51] The introduction builds on the remark that "modern and postmodern cultural thinkers all gravitate toward aesthetic, experiential, moral, practical, and political questions concerning the essence, interpretation, actuality, rhythm, and riddle of technology."[52] This sets the tone for the whole collection, in which many of the essays deploy "theo-remes" in an inquiry into "new" culture. It is to their credit that this exercise in recontextualization of "the theoretical humanities" arouses no sense of incongruity when it articulates, for instance, a reading of Maurice Blanchot's *The Writing of the Disaster* (1980) with David Cronenberg's *Crash* (1996).[53] Indeed, such articulations serve as an instructive exercise in the renegotiation of critical and cultural theory, even if this renegotiation may marginalize a great deal that is important. What is certain is that such articulations exemplify Armitage's view that "in the age of the recombinant world-picture, foraging among the fragments of cultural doctrines and debates is an extremely important activity."[54] *Foraging* is a key term here. It expresses the need for a salvaging that is also a scavenging: a going over of the (dead) body of theory in order to recover the scraps that might help to constitute what Arthur and Marilouise Kroker call the "data body" more studiedly.[55] And indeed, the scavenging metaphor appears irresistibly temptable:

> The Krokers' efforts to characterise technology as a constituent part of the contemporary emergence of recombinant cultural theory— surely a phenomenon that catches the technological mood of our times—comes close to capturing what I shall call *new cultural theory*. New cultural theorists, therefore, demand a recombinant approach to technology—a perspective that is based on their contemporary cultural experience of everyday life. To be sure, it is for this reason that new cultural theorists are currently acknowledging the importance of Marxism, post-situationism, post-structuralism, cyberfeminism, and postmodernism. In short, a growing number of new cultural theorists are taking to *scavenging among the remnants of modernism and postmodernism to construct hypermodern and recombinant cultural theories of technology* [our emphasis].[56]

Theory, then, cannot remain integrally itself in the face of "the technological mood of our times." To this mood, the best theory is a scavenged theory, its remnants taken over to construct—no doubt very usably—a rethinking of the theoretical that, in being "new" and "cultural," can by definition not be "literary" and may well not be "critical" in the sense of "radical." Whereupon it becomes diplomatic to insist that the theory, of body and a certain spirit that breathe through it, will remain intact: "Fashioning such an image of technology does not necessarily involve the complete abandonment of mod-

ernism, postmodernism, modernity, history, and radical conceptions
of culture derived from Marx."[57] "Not necessarily," perhaps, but quite
foreseeably, especially because although "it is important [and doubtless political] to state that hypermodern conceptions of technology
are neither a defence nor an attack on the theory of artistic, philosophical, and scientific modernism"—that is, on the "modern cultural tradition" that "has been developed in the twentieth century
through a general commitment to phenomenology, psychoanalysis,
existentialism, critical theory, poststructuralism, feminism, and postmodernism"[58]—it is difficult to see how "new cultural theory" will not
end up making the body of theory unrecognizable as it mutilates it.
At best, then, theory itself becomes prosthetic. It provides certain
conceptual supports to the thinking of the technological and the
networked, lest this proceed too limpingly in the wake of that which
it sets out to keep up with.

    This redefined role of theory is not allowed much scope for the
letter-al "option" reviewed in our introduction. Indeed, few if any of
the essays in *Machininc Modulations* raise the question of the literary.
When they do so it is exemplifyingly, as in Armitage's reference to
"The Book of Machines" in Samuel Butler's *Erewhon* (1872),[59] and
definitely not with any intent to ask what literariness might mutate
into in the age of technology. However, new cultural theory may at
least seem to have some claim to the "radical" option envisaged by
Zavarzadeh and Morton. That is because of its interest in "technopolitics." In paragraphs which construct a curriculum vitae of technopolitics, Armitage lists issues that engage "technopolitical commentators," among them the Internet, autonomist Marxism, and the
Zapatista rebellion in southern Mexico; "high-tech" capitalism and
the changing class struggle; conceptions of technology that take in
"ontological anarchy"; virtual communities and the post-geographi-
cal; the impact of "the city of bits," the "motorization of art" and the
coming of non-humans"; the changing role of the state and questions of democratic access; and the praxis of collectives like the Critical Art Ensemble and other exponents of the post-avant-garde.[60]
Underwriting all this is the notion that "technopolitics eschews the
idea that technology can, in any meaningful sense, be separated
from politics."[61]

    Whether this eschewing suffices to answer to Zavarzadeh and
Morton's understanding of digitalism is another matter. In this respect, the most significant analysis of technopolitics in the collection

is that supplied by Armitage himself, in his reading of Hakim Bey whose radical writings on the role of (post-)anarchy might seem to institute a new space for the critique-al. Armitage shows, however, that Bey's "poetic [and cyber] terrorists" instead, either "dance alone in the micro-spaces of globalitarian finance capital but commit acts of art sabotage in the name of nothing but an inner dialogue with themselves," or else participate in an "anarcho-syndicalism"—in both cases refusing "to recognise that the overwhelming force of presence or solidarity really does arise from the reality of class." Technopolitics, it seems, is not as radical as it would like to think.[62]

New cultural theory, then, is going to be tenuously if at all after de Man, and very probably not after Zavarzadeh and Morton. The fact remains, however, that it yields a credible coming of the posthuman not only to disciplinarity, but also to theory itself. What *Machinic Modulations* does admirably is to show that theory, apart from being about the literary, the critical, the cultural and the radical, can now also be about the digital. That is a significant development, opening up new concepts, vocabularies, and agendas for the theory of curricula and for the process of its disciplinarity. It is—and this is not to hint at cynicism and mercenariness—a good move toward diversification: an identification of a new niche and a move onto it. This may seem opportunistic, but it is an effect of disciplinarity, and theory can now no more resist this attribute about itself than it can resist wondering whether its commitment to the tropological dimension of language represents a flourishing or a fall. Is it surprising that theorists, who as the editors of *Post-Theory* remind us "also have mortgages,"[63] are anxious to peg its continued flourishing to the new curricular presence on the academic block?

That presence is worth characterizing, if only to reject the thought that posthumanism might yet be ill defined within academic departments and academic publishing. We should therefore like to identify six "types" of the posthuman. These types do not set out to present "a poetics of the posthuman." They are far too schematic for that. They may, however, help in the recognition of the comprehensiveness of the posthuman's repertoire, and its potential. The first "type" is, fittingly, a self-announcing posthumanism. It is a posthumanism that works hard to establish a complex and multifaceted identity for itself, and in fact ranges from defiant calls to attention (as in Pepperell's manifesto) to tracts that attempt a founding history of the posthuman (as with Hayles's book). It also comprises outlooks which do not doubt the topicality of the posthuman but are judiciously dissenting and critiquing (as exemplified by Neil Badmington's unease at Hayles's title and at the posthuman's countenancing of the "straightforward, present, instantly graspable").[64]

The second type of the posthuman is more unalloyedly critical. It acknowledges the unignorability of the effect on the theoretical humanities of the new technologies, but laments it, as occurs in Robert Markley's *Virtual Realities and their Discontents* (1996). The third posthumanism is to be found in work like that of Elaine L. Graham,[65] and inscribes the posthuman within a genealogy of its prefigurations. Thus, for instance, the third book of Jonathan Swift's *Gulliver's Travels* (1726), in which the hero encounters the strange academicians of the imaginary city of Lagado and their efforts at mechanization and formalization of the arts and sciences, provides fictive and debunked prototypes for Charles Babbage's Difference and Analytical Engines, today's microprocessors, and indeed the apparently overreaching designs of the posthumanist vision. One might also mention the Pygmalion myth or Mary Shelley's *Frankenstein* (1818) as Ur-texts for contemporary posthumanism, together with the identification of the automaton Hadaly in Villiers de L'Isle Adam's *L'Eve future* (1880–81) as a fictional precursor of the creatures abounding in such founding narratives for the posthuman as *Bladerunner* (1982), *Lawnmower Man* (1992), or Richard Powers's novel *Galatea 2.2* (1995).

From these founding narratives arises a fourth, more "cultish" posthumanism. The cultish is central to the posthuman, and indeed a number of posthumanists tend to like their manga, their androids and their tales from the techno-crypt as much as the next techno-head. They see no reason why those narratives should not receive the respect reserved for more conventional masterpieces. This is the posthuman most amenable to scenarios like those conceived by Moravec and to the transhumanist declarations of a body like the Extropian Society. George Steiner's fears about the pre- or counterliterateness of the young might thereby appear justified, especially in view of the indications emanating from a film like *The Matrix* (1999) being approached as reverentially as *Macbeth*, or the installing of William Gibson's *Neuromancer* (1984) as posthumanism's answer to the niche afforded in a humanist culture to William Shakespeare's *Hamlet*. A very "new" form of cultural studies might emerge from this, hence the scope for a label like "new cultural theory" that designates a discipline and a practice that may already be with us. Whatever one's thoughts on this, the profile of Gibson's novel confirms that science fiction is the genre of choice in posthumanist criticism of narrative. That is the corollary to the perception that science and technology might be the last "metanarrative" in the "meatworld," and self-evidently the only viable one in the digital "mentalverse." The rise of "Science Studies" as a subdiscipline within theory attempts to challenge this,[66] as does the work undertaken by Arkady Plotnitsky in his contribution to this volume and in his work on complementarity between poststructuralism and theoretical physics more generally. These developments attest to a subtle reordering of the priorities for theoretical debate.

The fifth type of posthumanism is more philosophical and theoretical in orientation, and indeed seeks to bring to the posthuman the protocols of readings conducted in the theoretical humanities. It is represented by texts like the essays in *Machinic Modulations* or by Rutsky's excellent *High Tekhnē*, which remains the most complete and rigorous book-length study of the affinities that posthumanism has with philosophy and theory. What such texts attempt is a move away from "the wearisome sameness" of "debates over technology and techno-culture"[67] to the discovery within the posthuman of an amenability to appropriation by "philosophemes" and "theoremes." On this basis, Rutsky reads Heidegger's "The Question Concerning Technology" and Freud's "The Uncanny," assesses the parallels between "the machine aesthetic" and theories of the avant-garde, and inscribes the posthuman as "always already" within the work of figures like Walter Benjamin and Fredric Jameson, "always already" within modernism and postmodernism. This type of philosophically-cum-theoretically elaborated posthumanism, present also in significant essays on cybernetics by figures like Geoffrey Winthrop-Young and Andrew Pickering,[68] provides the kind of academic respectability essential to posthumanism's accrual of a disciplinarity that is not merely bandwagon-servicing or opportunistic, but a genuinely rigorous engagement with what is very arguably an emergent paradigm.

There is a lot that could potentially exist on the interface between philosophy, theory, and that paradigm. Indeed there can be no doubt of the relevance, for instance, to post-phenomenological philosophical inquiry of posthumanist explorations of subjectivity, or of the notion of "distributed cognition" to post-Lacanian interrogations of divided selves and subjects. Similarly, talk by commentators like Milan Kundera about the "death of the novel" could do worse than look

at the creations of researchers in Artificial Life and Artificial Intelligence. As Hayles suggests in her analysis of the Santa Fe Tierra program in Artificial Intelligence, the self-replicating narratives produced there offer scope for a redimensionalization of the concept of
fictional and possible worlds.[69] Because of such possibilities, it is re-
grettable that the nemesis of theory so often continues to be conceived in terms of anti-theory rather than post-theory. Indeed, it is
ironic that Steiner's words on the insuperability of byte and number
and the threat to the lettered should have embedded themselves di-
gressively and almost unnoticeably in an anti-theoretical polemic.
Real Presences is remembered as anti-deconstructionist, while it should
have been clear, even in 1989, that the greater urgency lay in engaging more deeply with the implications of the numerate and the digital for the lettered: in critiquing the belief that the days of the theoretical and even the anti-theoretical are, in more ways than one,
numbered. It sometimes seems that while certain areas within theory
have been engrossed in vexatious polemics with each other—disagree-
ing about the resistance to theory and theory as resistance, most notably in terms of poststructuralism's beyond[70]—posthumanism, as
one manifestation of that beyond, has come up irresistibly on all
their blindsides, illustrating in the process the resistibility of theory.

It is for this reason that it is so crucial to draw attention to the
sixth type of posthumanism. It is the posthumanism that is already
contained within theory. Is it not surprising, for instance, that
posthumanism largely overlooks Lyotard's essay "Can Thought go on
without a Body?" This title can be glossed in terms of "thought di-
vested of the body, that is, the body which binds and bounds the consciousness from which thought springs" but also as "thought outside
a body," which marks one state of the posthuman. It is perhaps a
measure of current thinking within the posthuman that these possibilities are stifled by the brouhaha over Moravecian scenarios. The
downloading of a mind is now part of the *episteme* of the posthuman,
in concept if not in fact. Since such scenarios appear to downplay reference to the Cartesian "body in a vat" or the Lyotardian "thought
without a body," a philosophical and theoretical substratum to
posthumanism's thinking of the dispensability of the "biological sub-
strate" of thought is optional and in practice dispensable, not constitutive. This is all of a piece with the glaring fact that a work like
Pepperell's *The Post-Human Condition* opts to make no reference to
Hannah Arendt's *The Human Condition* (1958).

The omission in such texts of any reference to Lyotard is arguably, however, a more serious oversight. Lyotard's opening essay in *The Inhuman* evades the unproblematized scientism of a certain kind of posthumanism, all sold on cyborgia and postapocalyptic survival narratives, to place at the centre of the posthuman the issue of consciousness. Notoriously, the essay remarks that "after the sun's death there won't be a thought to know that its death took place."[71] Lyotard's essay speaks of this as "the sole serious question to face humanity today."[72] When the essay disingenuously refers to the importance of providing "software with a hardware that is independent of the conditions of life on earth,"[73] the congruence with the posthuman appears confirmed. That is where the similarities end, however. Lyotard writes: "It isn't enough for these machines to simulate the results of vision or of writing fairly well. It's a matter (to use the attractively appropriate locution) of 'giving body' to the artificial thought of which they are capable. And it's that body, both 'natural' and artificial, that will have to be carried far from earth before its destruction if we want the thought that survives the solar explosion to be something more than a poor binarized ghost of what it was beforehand."[74] Most importantly, he later warns that "the pilot at the helm of the spaceship *Exodus* will still be entropy" unless it is realized that "thought is inseparable from the phenomenological body."[75] So, no postphenomenology then, which would, as Lyotard's collection in itself suggests, be more *in*human than *post*human.

Such approaches might make it possible for the posthuman to read and be read by the theoretical. There is much within theory that has already broached this, and it may be time to acknowledge those texts of theory that can with hindsight be shown to have been always already concerned with the posthuman: David Wills's remarkable *Prosthesis* (1995); Avital Ronell's *The Telephone Book* (1989); all the deliberations by Blanchot and others about the end of the Book and its coextensiveness with the finiteness of the human; Derrida's remarks on the finiteness of memory and on the consequent *technē* of archivization; all the work on subjectivity and postsubjectivity, for which the landmark *Who Comes After the Subject?* (1991) provides an unignorable sample; inescapably, Gilles Deleuze and Félix Guattari's *Thousand Plateaus* (1980).[76]

There are, however, dangers in this attempt to prospect within the body of theory's texts for an attunedness to the posthuman *avant le nombre*, as it were. We should like to point to two of these. The first is

to think that dissenting explorations are sufficient in theory's encounter with the posthuman. The idea that there exists already a theoretical critique of the posthuman could conceivably lead to
complacency, to the view that the critique need not be extended or
deepened, and consequently to both theory and the posthuman remaining integral to their respective clerisies. It leaves theory and the
posthuman concerned only tokenistically with the other. Theory, it
has to be said, has already had a number of nonencounters,[77] and it is
doubtful whether it can afford another one where posthumanism is
concerned.

The second danger lies in the temptation to reduce the posthuman to those aspects of it already contained within the repertoire of
theory, so that its specificity as an object of investigation is obscured.
An analogy from philosophy can make this clear. Attempts in the
philosophy of, say, Hilary Putnam to cultivate an adaptability to the
posthuman can create the impression that philosophy is trying to
reappropriate what it might consider to be properly its own. Thus,
for instance, when Putnam appears to give time to the view that "a
human being is just a computer that happens to be made of flesh
and blood" and to speak of "Probabilistic Automata,"[78] it is as if he is
undertaking a more sober reworking of the Artificial Life scientist
Edward Fredkin's view that "reality is a program run on a cosmic
computer."[79] Putnam can thereby proceed towards the conclusion
that such ideas "mistake a piece of science fiction for an outline of a
scientific theory."[80] His position may be philosophically sounder, but
it underestimates an important aspect of the posthuman: its capacity
to dispense with the kind of self-searching that can become pathological within philosophy or theory. Unlike feminism, which has
been characterized as being "beside itself," and literature, which
Peggy Kamuf sees as divided from itself,[81] posthumanist discourse is
unassailed by the tortured exploration of its own essentialities or protocols. Consequently, the kind of anguished self-scrutiny of philosophical and theoretical language which marks the work of, for
instance, Emmanuel Levinas or Maurice Blanchot is incomprehensi-
ble and embarrassing to the posthuman. For the opposite to have occurred, the posthuman would have required a work of theorization
that immediately accompanied its expression when it was being articulated as such. But that accompaniment, where it has occurred already, has occurred under the alias of theory. Although there is a
theory which among other things is also posthumanist, there is com-

paratively little posthumanism that among other things is also theoretical. The sixth type of the posthuman, in other words, is much more replete than the fifth.

This suggests that in the posthuman time of mutability, it is theory which is the more likely to take on the appurtenances of the posthuman rather than the other way round. Theory affects the posthuman as prosthesis. The posthuman becomes another aspect of the disciplinarity and curricula of theory. The posthuman, concerned with supplementarity to the human, itself becomes a supplement to another discourse, feeding off the latter's disciplinarity even while it acquires some itself. Theory, as a result, becomes posthuman, growing into it even as it allows posthumanism to grow upon it. It is a mutation which arguably deconstitutes theory in forcing it to a renegotiation, or rearticulation—definitely a (post-)theoretical (self-)repositioning—that would be more far-reaching than any reconsideration of a radical melding between the critical and the cultural. Undoubtedly, an *inter*disciplinary posthumanism, ready to be theoretical *as well*, gives theory a renewed end at the time of its supposed end. The reactions to this can be philosophical: "It cannot be helped, it is pragmatic, it is what had to happen once theory acquired disciplinarity, it actually is quite all right (theory is healthier and leaner and meaner and more 'with it' as a result)." No melodrama or overdramatization then: to borrow the words of Belsey at the close of her essay in this volume, "we only have to carry on," with the posthumanist and the theoretical together. But there is always, instead, the possibility of regret, of nostaglia, and perhaps even of mourning for a "being theoretical" whose status becomes increasingly precarious. If prosthesization and rearticulation are so urgent, what positions might (post-)theory strike?

EPILOGUE

Is there really a need to reposition theory? Could it really be possible that there might occur a synchronization between post-theory and a moment of rupture called "the posthuman," to the mortification of all of the orthodoxies of theory on the *post-*? Is this, after all of theory's angst about alterity and the difference between messianism and messianicity, what the *post-* of theory comes down to: the posthuman as *arrivant*? And if it really were to be believed that this might come

to pass, that the posthuman is the glibbest but also the most believ-
able herald of theory's "displacement by replacement," where does
that leave theory? What levers will need to be pulled in theory's repositioning, "before" the posthuman?

Undeniably, the posthuman remains the clearest expression of a
form of post-theory which, with no use for the temporalities of uncanny returns and future anterior re-cognitions, might straightforwardly leave theory "behind." In opposition to that, theory cannot
merely seek comfort in the possibility that "post-theory" may represent nothing more cataclysmic than a gentle riding of the "next"
wave. Something *is* happening, palpably. It may not be something
very sublime, but then again it may be something that redefines the
sublime itself, as Rutsky intimates in his suggestion that technology
(with which posthumanism is concerned above all) becomes "a figure of the sublime."[82] If the latter is the case then theory is right to
"be about" the posthuman, in all the senses of that phrase. Theory,
then, cannot but rethink its ends, as it always has done when it has
most flourishingly resisted itself. "Before" the posthuman, and
against its nature, it has to recognize that those ends are conceivable
both as objectives *and* obsolescence. Indeed, the reconsidered ends
(as objectives) of theory may never have been more vital than when
it finds itself "before" that which forces contemplation of its end (as
obsolescence). In the midst of the posthuman, those ends are modulated to inquire how theory, in the university and through its disciplinarity, is supposed to react to what has become incumbent upon
it: namely to think the imponderables of immanent impermanence,
which technology has instituted within the fabric of dailiness and in
the very definition of the human. And with that immanent impermanence resulting, potentially, in the posthuman transformation
(not to say transference) of consciousness, how is the loss of the theoretical mind to be prevented? How should theory, then, keep the
posthuman in mind in order to ensure that the posthuman can itself
be minded to the theoretical? And how can it do so irresistibly, to the
posthuman as well as to itself?

There are no ready answers to these most theoretical of questions.
Nor is there consolation to be had in Lyotard's view that unanswer-
ability is the calling of the philosophical.[83] For theory, which attempted once the "Answer to the Question: What is the Postmodern?" any answer to the posthuman seems to compel a forgetting of
the answer to the preceding question: "*Postmodern* would be un-

derstood according to the paradox of the future (post) anterior (modo)."[84] The posthuman, this later answer might run, is to be understood according to the intuitiveness of the investment in the flight of time's arrow of the simple rather than the complex tenses. To follow, then, the counterintuitive with the intuitive, to follow the "thinking very hard" with the "ultrasimplistic" and what theory might consider too banal for words: this is itself the resistance confronting theory "before" the posthuman, a resistance that it must learn to put up against what comes most naturally to it. It is a resistance sustained by the thought that unless theory problematizes what comes most instinctively to it, it will not be resisting itself, or its orthodoxies. And if it does not do so it will be only possible to say, in the simplest and most valedictory way imaginable, "From theory, post-theory."

That is because the instinct of theory to problematize its demise in terms of supplementarity, of the future anterior, of its capacity for self-resistance, risks becoming mannered, and hence expected, insipid, evident. It brings to mind the Gadamer-Derrida encounter in Paris in 1981, in which Derrida referred with some affectation of weariness to that which is "extremely evident."[85] It would be tragic were theory itself to start becoming evident to itself, to start becoming what at its best it guards against: correct, an attribute that de Man taught us to be wary of. De Man's instincts on the proper of any discipline were surely right. What theory finds boring it must not confront with what is "correct" to itself: a course which always risks being "boring [in turn], monotonous, predictable and unpleasant," and which might also lull it into a false sense of its own irrefutability. For theory, it has become correct—and therefore seemingly and delusively irrefutable—that theory's "post" is not to be thought in the facile terms of the simple past; that it needs to be thought "otherwise." Yet, following de Man's equivalences, this "technically correct" gambit becomes "teachable, generalizable and highly responsive to systematization,"[86] at least to theory's own audience. In other words, within theory it has become orthodox. Such correctness and orthodoxy become (too) practiced; take them further, persistently, and a dangerous tediousness looms.

That eventuality needs to be evaded. The evasion may require theory to "think otherwise" otherwise. One way of doing this is for theory to do the unexpected by going along with the expected. Paradoxically, it might be able to allay correctness by giving some thought to the banal. To be specific: it might actually have become less insipid for theory now to (re)think through the simple past, rather than to reelaborate the relevance to its conceptualities, and to its own demise, of the future anterior. Otherwise, theory's alibi of not thinking its own apocalypse because it was elsewhere, importantly thinking otherwise the nature and relevance of the *post-*, of ends and of the apocalyptic, may start to wear a bit thin.

It therefore all comes down, in the end, to the importance of avoiding correctness, or the resistible. Theory must address what is ordinarily insipid to it: the "ultrasimplistic" notion that the digital may prefigure—without figuration—its passing. This challenge is all the harder because if the posthuman is truly a time and a paradigm confirmed in depthlessness, in its unattunedness to the lettered, in the operations of successivness, it divests itself of any real amenability to the theoretical. One suspects that all the strategies of the fifth and sixth types of the posthuman, which attempt articulation and renegotiation at both epistemological and disciplinary levels, might then become a fudge. They mark an uneasy alliance that theory enters into while barely concealing its distaste. Theory continues to hanker, secretly or perhaps transparently, after "qualities" that did not need to be redefined as a result of the encounter with the culture of the posthuman. Those qualities have much to do with the kind of critical practice that sustains the position of theory as the true radical among the theoretical humanities (after Zavarzadeh and Morton, as seen in the introduction to this volume), or, alternatively, with a "pure" focus on literature as the discourse most steeped in an unaccountable, nonulterior alterity (after de Man). Posthumanism, however, resists those qualities. Its consequent insipidity to theory makes it pertinent to adapt the title of Robert Musil's novel, *The Man Without Qualities*, and start to contemplate a *posthuman without qualities*. Indeed, it becomes vital to inquire whether Ulrich, the man without qualities who struggles against all-pervasive boredom, might herald the posthuman. His deliberate divestiture of that within him which is distinguishing seems almost like an honorable abdication of the humanist from the posthumanist order stealing upon Kakania. Whatever one thinks of the analogy which positions Ulrich as a crypto-(post)humanist, a (*post-*) *homme* very deliberately *moyen sensuel*, it becomes important to come to terms with the fact that the posthuman that desists from living on the borderlines of theory and philosophy is now firmly part of the culture that theory defines as its object. If it really wants to be about culture, it must be about that as well.

What hope, then, for a very resolutely lettered theory, and for a "radical" critical practice? How is theory to negotiate the posthuman, given that its would-be "otherwise" holds out for the mass only the prospect of boredom, in turn, with the letteredly fogeyish, and with a "radicality" that might only prompt (and this, ironically, from those most immersed in the "virtual" and the "hyperreal") the retort "Get real!" To answer that, we should like to return to Catherine Belsey's essay at the start of this volume, and its intuition that theory must now be about a Cultural Criticism that, ambitiously, takes the whole of culture for its purview, and not just literature or "English." Theory cannot be above all and most purely about literature, as de Man might have wished. Neither can it be radical, forever resisting its disciplinary definition, as Zavarzadeh and Morton might wish. To continue to hope that it might be so is to a very large extent noble, but it is also childish. It is childish because it resists entering into the processes of negotiation and renegotiation that are so much part of the adult world. It would be more grown up for theory to accept the process of its own disciplinarity: to accept that disciplinarity *is* its practice. Of course, this disciplinarity prevents theory from being what it might have been if there had been no need for a (re)negotiation of its practice: if it could have continued to childishly and unrestrainedly be itself, whether that self is seen as essentially literary or essentially and un-disciplined-ly radical. And the point about theory as a discipline, now, is that it has no option but to give up the rhetoric of what Zavarzadeh and Morton call "disparticipation" and participate in its own disciplining.[87] In other words, and discomfiting as it might appear, what theory must live up to most of all now is nothing if not the commitment it undertook, once it entered the university, to discipline its instinct to be unrestrainedly itself—to teach instead. Very arguably, what it should teach most of all is the Cultural Criticism that, as Belsey argues, should take the whole of culture as its purview.

True: that can be neither very literary nor very radical. True, also, that as posthumanism is now so inextricably part of the contemporary experience of culture, theory will have to teach the posthuman as well. The editors of *Post-Theory* made no bones about this. Teaching, as the most obvious manifestation of disciplinarity, is now the point of theory, and "the point is not just that [teaching] is Theory's day job, but also that it is its destination."[88] If teaching is what theory must consider as its day job, as that which keeps most of its mortgaged practitioners in clover while its more privileged "disparticipants" conduct literarity's and radicalism's more exhilarating work of resistance, then so be it. Famously, even T. S. Eliot (whose attempt to exclusively delimit culture is studied in Belsey's essay in this volume) had a day job, and even Musil's Ulrich found it hard to resist one when it was offered by the very worldly Arnheim.

Theory, then, has to dare to teach the culture of the posthuman, to "account for" it in the sense used by Simon Morgan Wortham in his essay within these pages, to contribute more to all the types of posthumanism. Teaching, that most solid and stolid of pursuits, is what it becomes incumbent upon theory not to resist: a course of action, this, that moves against all of the instincts of theory to resist the "teachable," the "generalizable," and what is "highly responsive to systematization." Yet for theory to teach would be for it to speak "the language of self-resistance," for theory will no doubt have to resist itself almost unnaturally if it is to speak in the classroom about what it might find resistible conceptually but irresistible pragmatically. In doing so its flourishing becomes very much like a fall, its fall the condition of its flourishing. De Man would no doubt have hated it, but it is worth remembering that even he ended up hailed as a teacher, his "lesson" a supreme instrument in theory's disciplinarity.[89] And this, at least, can be confidently predicted: there will be no more valuable and intriguing contribution to the study of the posthuman than theory's—were theory indeed to undertake, in the manner of the de Manian "Lesson," a demonstration of the insights available to a critical reading of posthumanism's blindness to certain very exemplary "philosophemes" or "theorems." If it can accept this disciplinary call, theory's seminar rooms might yet modulate (rather than simply be modulated by) and induce a repositioning of (rather than unilaterally suffer a repositioning by) the posthuman "ultrasimplification" and insipidity elsewhere, of which (as Eliot and Musil foresaw, and as theory senses all too well) there is already quite enough. And that, whether it happens under the name of theory or post-theory, cultural criticism or new cultural theory, humanism or posthumanism, would be truly irresistible.

NOTES

1. Frank Kermode, *An Appetite for Poetry: Essays in Literary Interpretation* (London: Collins, 1989), 6.

2. George Steiner, *Real Presences: Is There Anything in What We Say?* (London: Faber and Faber, 1989), 115.

3. Ibid., 114.

4. Ibid., 115.

5. Martin Heidegger, "The Question Concerning Technology," in *Basic Writings*, ed. David Farrell Krell, rev. ed. (1954; London: Routledge, 1993), 330.

6. Jean-François Lyotard, "Note on the Meaning of 'post,' " in *The Postmodern Explained to Children: Correspondence 1982–1985* (1985; London: Turnaround, 1992), 90.

7. Robert Pepperell, *The Post-Human Condition*, 2d ed. (Exeter: Intellect, 1997), 180.

8. Ibid., 183.

9. Martin Heidegger, "Letter on Humanism," in *Basic Writings*, ed. David Farrell Krell, rev. ed. (1947; London: Routledge, 1993), 217. For a consideration of the positions of de Man and Derrida that are referred to here, see the introduction in this volume.

10. Ibid., 219, 223.

11. Ibid., 219, 265.

12. Heidegger, "Letter on Humanism," 221.

13. Jean-François Lyotard, "A Gloss on Resistance," in *The Postmodern Explained to Children: Correspondence 1982–1985*, ed. Julian Pefanis and Morgan Thomas (1985; London: Turnaround, 1992), 105, 103.

14. Jean Baudrillard, *The Vital Illusion*, ed. Julia Witwer (New York: Columbia University Press, 2000), 69.

15. The following pronouncement encapsulates Extropian beliefs: "Extropianism is a transhumanist philosophy. The Extropian Principles define a specific version or 'brand' of transhumanist thinking. Like humanists, transhumanists favor reason, progress, and values centered on our well being rather than on an external religious authority. Transhumanists take humanism further by challenging human limits by means of science and technology combined with critical and creative thinking. We challenge the inevitability of aging and death, and we seek continuing enhancements to our intellectual abilities, our physical capacities, and our emotional development. We see humanity as a transitory stage in the evolutionary development of intelligence. We advocate using science to accelerate our move from human to a transhuman or posthuman condition. As physicist Freeman Dyson has said: 'Humanity looks to me like a magnificent beginning but not the final word.' " —Max More, "Extropian Principles 3.0: A Transhumanist Declaration," 2002 [online]. Available at: <http://www.extropy.org/ideas/principles.html>.

16. Robert Musil, "Helpless Europe: A Digressive Journey," trans. Philip Beard, in *Precision and Soul: Essays and Addresses*, ed. Burton Pike and David S. Luft (1922; Chicago: University of Chicago Press, 1990), 120.

17. Hans Moravec, *Mind Children: The Future of Robot and Human Intelligence* (Cambridge: Harvard University Press, 1988), 109–10.

18. N. Katherine Hayles, *How We Became Posthuman: Virtual Bodies in Cybernetics, Literature, and Informatics* (Chicago: University of Chicago Press, 1999), 1.

19. Ibid., 1.

21. See Jacques Derrida, "Mochlos," in *Logomachia: The Conflict of the Faculties*, ed. Richard Rand (Lincoln: University of Nebraska Press, 1992), 1–34.

22. Nicholas Royle, "*Déjà vu*," in *Post-Theory: New Directions in Criticism*, ed. Martin McQuillan et al. (Edinburgh: Edinburgh University Press, 1999), 5.

23. Hayles, *How We Became Posthuman*, 2–3.

24. This was of course a question asked in theory's own imagining of the (post)human subject: see Eduardo Cadava, Peter Connor, Jean-Luc Nancy, eds., *Who Comes after the Subject?* (London: Routledge, 1991).

25. See Jean-François Lyotard, *The Differend: Phrases in Dispute*, trans. Georges van der Abbeele (1983; Minneapolis: University of Minnesota Press, 1988).

26. Manuel Castells, *The Information Age: Economics, Society and Culture*, 3 vols. (Oxford: Oxford University Press, 1996–98), 1: prologue.

27. Joanne Roberts, "Theory, Technology and Cultural Power: An Interview with Manuel Castells," *Angelaki* 4, no. 2 (1999), 34.

28. On this point, and the Perfect Crime's ultimate imperfection, see Baudrillard, *The Vital Illusion*, 69.

29. Jean-Luc Nancy, introduction to *Who Comes after the Subject?* ed. Eduardo Cadava, Peter Connor, and Jean-Luc Nancy (London: Routledge, 1991), 1.

30. Baudrillard, *The Vital Illusion*, 66.

31. Don Ross, "Is Cognitive Science a Discipline?," in *The Future of the Cognitive Revolution*, ed. David Martel Johnson and Christina E. Erneling (Oxford: Oxford University Press), 103, 107.

32. Musil, "Helpless Europe," 125.

33. See Robert Musil, *The Man without Qualities*, trans. Sophie Wilkins and Burton Pike (London: Picador, 1997), 6.

34. Martin Heidegger, "The End of Philosophy and the Task of Thinking," in *Basic Writings*, ed. David Farrell Krell, rev. ed. (1966; London: Routledge, 1993), 433–34.

35. Ibid., 432.

36. Heidegger, "Letter on Humanism," 226.

37. Heidegger, "The End of Philosophy and the Task of Thinking," 433.

38. Ibid., 431.

39. Heidegger, "The Question Concerning Technology," 338.

40. Heidegger, "The End of Philosophy and the Task of Thinking," 441–49.

41. Ibid., 449.

42. Heidegger, "The Question Concerning Technology," 339.

43. Ibid., 339.

44. See R. L. Rutsky, *High Technē : Art and Technology from the Machine Aesthetic to the Posthuman* (Minneapolis: University of Minnesota Press, 1999).

45. See Jacques Derrida, "Some Statements and Truisms about Neologisms, Newisms, Postisms, Parasitisms, and other small Seismisms," in *The States of Theory*, ed. David Carroll (New York: Columbia University Press, 1989), 63–94.

46. Refer to the introduction in this volume for an exploration of de Man's and Zavarzadeh and Morton's respective positions.

47. John Armitage, "Machinic Modulations: New Cultural Theory and Technopolitics," *Angelaki* 4, no. 2 (1999): 1.

48. For a review of these alternative "options" of (post-)theory, see our introduction to this volume.

49. See George P. Landow, *Hypertextuality 2.0: The Convergence of Contemporary Critical Theory and Technology* (Baltimore: Johns Hopkins University Press, 1997); Sadie Plant, *Zeroes and Ones: Digital Women and the New Technoculture* (London: Fourth Estate, 1997); Paul Virilio, *Speed and Politics: An Essay on Dromology*, trans. Mark Polizzotti (1977; New York: Semiotext(e), 1986); Arthur and Marilouise Kroker, *Digital Delirium* (Montreal: New World Perspectives, 1997); Donna Haraway, "A Manifesto for Cyborgs: Science, Technology and Socialist Feminism in the 1980s," *Socialist Review* 180, no. 2 (1985): 65–108; Chris Hables Gray and others, ed., *The Cyborg Handbook* (New York: Routledge, 1995) and *Cyborg Citizen: Politics in the Posthuman Age* (New York: Routledge, 2001); Scott Bukatman, *Terminal Identity: The Virtual Subject in Postmodern Science Fiction* (Durham: Duke University Press, 1993).

50. Mas'ud Zavarzadeh and Donald Morton, *Theory as Resistance: Politics and Culture after (Post)structuralism* (New York: Guilford, 1994), 139.

51. Armitage, "Machinic Modulations," 1.

52. Ibid., 2.

53. See Roy Boyne, "Crash Theory: The Ubiquity of the Fetish at the End of Time," *Angelaki* 4, no. 2 (1999): 41–52.

54. Armitage, "Machinic Modulations," 3.

55. John Armitage, "Dissecting the Data Body: An Interview with Arthur and Marilouise Kroker," *Angelaki* 4, no. 2 (1999): 69–74.

56. Armitage, "Machinic Modulations," 3.

57. Ibid., 3.

58. Ibid., 2, 1.

59. Ibid., 12.

60. Ibid., 3–4.

61. Ibid., 4.

62. John Armitage, "Ontological Anarchy, the Temporary Autonomous Zone, and the Politics of Cyberculture: a Critique of Hakim Bey," *Angelaki* 4, no. 2 (1999): 122, 124. See also Hakim Bey, *T.A.Z: The Temporary Autonomous Zone, Ontological Anarchy, Poetic Terrorism* (New York: Semiotext(e), 1991).

63. Martin McQuillan, Graeme MacDonald, Robin Purves and Stephen Thomson, "The Joy of Theory," in *Post-Theory*, ed. Martin McQuillan and others (Edinburgh: Edinburgh University Press, 1995), xi.

64. See Rutsky, *High Technē*; Neil Badmington, "Pod almighty!; or, Humanism, Posthumanism, and the Strange Case of *The Invasion of the Body Snatchers*," *Textual Practice* 15, no. 1 (2001): 13.

65. See Elaine L. Graham, *The Representation of the Post/Human: Monsters, Aliens and Others in Popular Culture* (Manchester: Manchester University Press, 2002) and Judith Halberstam and Ira Livingston, *Posthuman Bodies* (Bloomington: Indiana University Press, 1995).

66. See Mario Biagioli, ed., *The Science Studies Reader* (New York: Routledge, 1999).

67. Rutsky, *High Technē*, 1.

68. Geoffrey Winthrop-Young, "Silicon Sociology; or, Two Kings on Hegel's Throne? Kittler, Luhmann, and the Posthuman Merger of German Media Theory," *Yale Journal of Criticism* 13 (2000): 391–420; Andrew Pickering, *The Mangle of Practice: Time, Agency and Science* (Chicago: University of Chicago Press, 1995).

69. See Milan Kundera, *L'Art du roman* (Paris: Gallimard, 1986).

70. See Wendell V. Harris, ed., *Beyond Poststructuralism: The Speculations of Theory and the Experience of Reading* (Pennsylvania: Pennsylvania State University Press, 1996).

71. Jean-François Lyotard, "Can Thought Go On without a Body?" in *The Inhuman: Reflections on Time*, trans. Bruce Boone and Lee Hildreth (1988; Stanford: Stanford University Press, 1991), 9.

72. Ibid., 9.

73. Ibid., 13.

74. Ibid., 17.

75. Ibid., 23.

76. See David Wills, *Prosthesis* (Stanford: Stanford University Press, 1995); Avital Ronell, *The Telephone Book: Technology, Schizophrenia, Electric Speech* (Lincoln: University of Nebraska Press, 1989); Maurice Blanchot, *The Writing of the Disaster*, trans. Ann Smock (Lincoln: University of Nebraska Press, 1985) and *Le livre à venir* (1959; Paris: Gallimard, 1971); Jacques Derrida, *Archive Fever: A Freudian Impression*, trans. Eric Prenowitz (Chicago: University of Chicago Press, 1995); Gilles Deleuze and Felix Guattari, *A Thousand Plateaus: Capitalism and Schizophrenia*, trans. Brian Massumi (Minneapolis: University of Minnesota Press, 1987).

77. On this issue, see Diane Michelfelder and Richard E. Palmer, introduction to *Dialogue and Deconstruction: The Gadamer-Derrida Encounter*, ed. Diane P. Michelfelder and Richard E. Palmer (New York: State University of New York Press, 1989).

78. Hilary Putnam, "Functionalism: Cognitive Science or Science Fiction?," in *The Future of the Cognitive Revolution*, ed. David Martel Johnson and Christina E. Erneling (Oxford: Oxford University Press), 32–33.

79. Quoted in Hayles, *How We Became Posthuman*, 11.

80. Putnam, "Functionalism," 37.

81. Diane Elam and Robyn Wiegman, eds., *Feminism Beside Itself* (New York: Routledge, 1995); Peggy Kamuf, *The Division of Literature; or, The University in Deconstruction* (Chicago: University of Chicago Press, 1997).

82. Rutsky, *High Technē*, 146.

83. Lyotard, "Can Thought Go On without a Body?," 8.

84. Jean-François Lyotard, "Answer to the Question: What is the Postmodern?," in *The Postmodern Explained to Children: Correspondence 1982–1985*, ed. Julian Pefanis and Morgan Thomas (1982; London: Turnaround, 1992), 24.

85. See Jacques Derrida, "Three Questions to Hans-Georg Gadamer," trans. Diane Michelfelder and Richard E. Palmer, in *Dialogue and Deconstruction: The Gadamer-Derrida Encounter*, ed. Diane P. Michelfelder and Richard E. Palmer (New York: State University of New York Press, 1989), 52.

86. Paul de Man, "The Resistance to Theory," in *The Resistance to Theory* (Minneapolis: University of Minnesota Press, 1986), 19.

87. On disparticipation, see Zavarzadeh and Morton, *Theory as Resistance*, 150, and our own brief references to the idea in the introduction, above.

88. McQuillan, "The Joy of Theory," xiii.

89. On this issue, see *The Lesson of Paul de Man*, *Yale French Studies* 69 (1985).

Contributors

CATHERINE BELSEY chairs the Centre for Critical and Cultural Theory at Cardiff University. Her books include *Critical Practice* (1980), *Desire: Love Stories in Western Culture* (1994) and *Shakespeare and the Loss of Eden: The Construction of Family Values in Early Modern Culture* (1999).

IVAN CALLUS is Lecturer in English at the University of Malta, where he teaches courses in literary theory and postmodern fiction. His current research interests focus on the anagram notebooks of Ferdinand de Saussure and also on the issue of cultural memory in the Mediterranean.

SUZANNE GEARHART is Professor of French at the University of California, Irvine. She is the author of *The Open Boundary of History and Fiction: a Critical Approach to the French Enlightenment* (1984) and *The Interrupted Dialectic: Philosophy, Psychoanalysis, and Their Tragic Other* (1992).

SUSAN HEGEMAN is an Associate Professor at the University of Florida, where she teaches American literature and cultural studies. She is the author of *Patterns For America: Modernism and the Concept of Culture* (1999), and of articles in the fields of modernist literature, Native American studies, museum studies, and the history and theory of American anthropology. She is currently working on a book on modernism and women's labor at the turn of the century.

STEFAN HERBRECHTER is Senior Lecturer in Cultural Analysis at Trinity and All Saints, University of Leeds, where he teaches critical and cultural theory. He is the author of *Lawrence Durrell, Postmodernism and the Ethics of Alterity* (1999) and the editor of *Cultural Studies: Translation and Interdisciplinarity* (2002)

260 DISCIPLINE AND PRACTICE

JEAN-JACQUES LECERCLE is professor of English Linguistics at the University of Nanterre (Paris X). His main publications are: *The Violence of Language* (1990), *Philosophy of Nonsense* (1994), *Interpretation as Pragmatics* (1999), *Deleuze and Language* and, with Richard Shusterman, *L'Empire des Signes* (2002).

LAURENT MILESI is a Lecturer in English/American literature and Critical Theory at the University of Wales, Cardiff, and a member of the ITEM Research Group on Joyce's manuscripts in the C.N.R.S. (France). He previously held a Research Fellowship in Corpus Christi College, Cambridge (1988-1991), taught as a Lecturer in the Department of English at Swansea University (1991–1995) and was a Visiting Professor at the University of Pisa (1994). His essays are mainly on Joyce and related aspects of modernism, nineteenth- and twentieth-century (American) poetry (Whitman, Eliot, Pound, Olson, Duncan, Ashbery), postmodernism/postcolonialism (Pynchon, Nabokov, Fowles, Barnes, Rushdie) and poststructuralism (Barthes, Lacan, and Derrida). He is currently completing *Post/ Effects: Literature, Criticism and the Future Perfect* and a book of essays on Jacques Derrida in French. He is also editing a collection of essays on *Joyce and Language: Critical Intersections* for Cambridge University Press.

SIMON MORGAN WORTHAM is Senior Lecturer in English Literature at the University of Portsmouth. He is the author of *Rethinking the University: Leverage and Deconstruction* (1999). Other recent publications include "Multiple Submissions and Little Scrolls of Parchment' (1997), "Surviving Theory 'as if I[t] were Dead,' " (1998) and " 'To Come Walking': Reinterpreting the Institution and the Work of Samuel Weber," (2001). He jointly edited *Angelaki* (1996): "Authorising Culture" and also the second edition of the electronic journal *Culture Machine* (2000): 'The University Culture Machine," writing articles for both these projects. He is currently editing a collection of essays on the work of Samuel Weber.

ARKADY PLOTNITSKY is a Professor of English and a University Faculty Scholar at Purdue University, where he is also Director of the Theory and Cultural Studies Program. He has written extensively on critical and cultural theory, continental philosophy, British and European Romanticism, and the relationships among literature, philosophy, and science. His books include *Reconfigurations: Critical Theory and General Economy; In the Shadow of Hegel* (1993); and *Complementarity: Anti-Epistemology After Bohr and Derrida* (1994). He has also coedited (with B. H. Smith) a volume entitled *Mathematics, Science, and Postclassical Theory,* published in 1997. His most recent book is *The Knowable and the Unknowable: Modern Science and Nonclassical Thought; Essays on Bohr, Heisenberg, Lacan, Derrida, and "The Two Cultures"* (2002). He is currently at work on two books: *Minute Particulars: Romanticism and Epistemology* and *Niels Bohr: Physics, Philosophy, and the Practice of Reading.*

LAWRENCE VENUTI is the author of *Our Halcyon Dayes: English Prerevolutionary Texts and Postmodern Culture* (1989), *The Translator's Invisibility: A History of Translation* (1995) and *The Scandals of Translation: Towards an Ethics of Difference* (1998). He is the editor of *Rethinking Translation: Discourse, Subjectivity, Ideology* (1992), *Translation and Minority* (St. Jerome, 1998), and *The Translation Studies Reader* (2000). His translations of Italian prose and poetry have included the work of such authors as Dino Buzzati (1983 and 1984), Milo De Angelis (1995), Aldo Rossi (1981), and I. U. Tarchetti (1992 and 1994). His latest translations are Juan Rodolfo Wilcock's *The Temple of Iconoclasts* (2000) and his selection of Antonia Pozzi's writing, *Breath: Poems and Letters* (2002). He is currently Professor of English at Temple University.

Index

263

Palmer, Richard E. *See* Michelfelder, Diane and Richard E. Palmer
Parsons, Elsie Clews, 15, 160–62, 167, 176
Pascal, Blaise, 213
Patterson, Thomas C., 177
Pêcheux, Michel, 202
Pefanis, Julian and Morgan Thomas 44, 253, 256
Peirce, C. S., 209, 213–14
Penley, Constance, 25
Pepperell, Robert, 227–29, 238, 241, 244, 253
Perkin, Harold, 176
Peterson, Aage, 224
Picard, Raymond, 117
Pickering, Andrew, 243, 256
Pike Burton. *See* Wilkins, Sophie and Burton Pike.
Pike, Burton and David S. Luft, 253
Pilate, Pontius, 232
Planck, Max, 219
Plant, Sadie, 237, 255
Plato, 65, 76
Plotnitsky, Arkady, 15–16, 18, 205–25, 228, 243, 260–61
Poe, Edgar Allan, 116, 121–22
Polizzotti, Mark, 255
Ponge, Francis, 36
Pound, Ezra, 260
Powers, Richard, 242
Pozzi, Antonia , 261
Prenowitz, Eric, 256
Propp, Vladimir, 115
Proust, Marcel , 156
Putnam, Hilary, 246, 256
Pynchon, Thomas, 260

Rabaté, Jean-Michel, 43
Rabbi Jacob, 69
Racine, Jean, 117
Rafael, Vicente L., 87, 105
Rampersad, Arnold, 176
Rand, Richard, 44, 153, 254
Rapaport, Herman, 30, 43
Readings, Bill, 14, 127–30, 132, 145, 148, 151–52
Renoir, Jean, 157
Resnais, Alain, 177

Rey, Alain, 122
Richards, I. A., 111
Richardson, William J. *See* Muller, John P. and William J. Richardson
Richart, Mabel , 151
Riesman, David, 158
Riffaterre, Michael, 111
Rilke, Rainer Maria, 157
Rimbaud, Arthur, 112
Robbins, Bruce, 176, 204
Roberts, Joanne, 254
Robey, David. *See* Jefferson, Ann and David Robey
Ronell, Avital, 245, 256
Roosevelt, Theodore, 165
Rorty, Richard , 25, 76
Rosenberg, Harold, 158, 176
Ross, Andrew, 25
Ross, Don, 254
Rossi, Aldo, 261
Roszak, Theodore, 177
Rothberg, Michael, 177
Rottenberg, Elizabeth, 43
Roudinesco, Elisabeth , 120
Rousseau, Jean-Jacques, 121, 212
Rovelli, Carlo, 223
Rowe, John Carlos, 203
Royle, Nicholas, 151, 231, 254
Rushdie, Salman, 260
Ruskin, John, 57
Rutsky, R. L., 236, 243, 248, 254–56
Ruwet, Nicolas, 111

Said, Edward, 60
Sallis, John, 153
Sarkonak, Ralph, 18
Sartre, Jean-Paul, 110
Saussure, Ferdinand de, 52, 59, 63, 68, 112–13, 115, 119, 129, 185, 205–6, 209, 212–14, 217–19, 224, 259
Schleiermacher, Friedrich, 100–101, 106
Schlesinger, Jr., Arthur, 165
Scorsese, Martin, 57
Scott-Fox, L. and J. M. Harding, 121
Screen, 59
Scrutiny, 109
Searle, John, 66
Sebeok, Thomas A., 77